FEE-FREE INVESTING

How to Buy Stocks and Bonds and Never Pay a Broker's Fee

Jeff Baryshnik

Doubleday Canada

Canadian Cataloguing in Publication Data

Baryshnik, Jeff
Fee-free investing : how to buy stocks and bonds and never pay a broker's fee

ISBN 0-385-25899-2

1. Blue-chip stocks. 2. Bonds. 3. Investments. I. Title.

HG4661.B37 1999 332.63'22 C99-931392-4

Cover design by Flex Media / Toronto
Text design by Heidy Lawrance Associates
Printed and bound in Canada

Published in Canada by
Doubleday Canada, a division of
Random House of Canada Limited
105 Bond Street
Toronto, Ontario
M5B 1Y3

TRAN 10 9 8 7 6 5 4 3 2 1

For my grandparents—
Cecil, Lillian, Morris, and Sonia

CONTENTS

ACKNOWLEDGMENTS

Fee-Free Investing was created with the help of many people. First and foremost, I would like to thank Netstock Direct Corporation (www.netstock.com) for allowing me to reproduce their database of U.S. and international Fee-Free EasyStocks. At Netstock, Keith Ranney, Nicole Cox, and Carrie Casanas were all helpful and enthusiastic about the project. I am also grateful to Dale Vanderheyden at the U.S. Treasury's Bureau of Public Debt for permission to reproduce portions of Treasury Direct's information and forms.

I had been planning to market this book on my website and through the mail; thank you to Ray Serpkenci and Sheldon Baryshnik for convincing me to pursue a publishing contract. Elliott Wahle as well as Larry, Janice, and Devra Baryshnik also deserve mention for reviewing the initial versions of the manuscript. I owe a great deal to Abe Simkin, who read my edited manuscript and suggested I submit it to Doubleday for review.

I was amazed at the speed with which this project was undertaken at Doubleday, and would like to acknowledge the help of the entire Doubleday team. In particular, John Neale, Kathryn Exner, Christine Innes, and Brad Martin have been especially helpful and skilled in reworking the manuscript into a professional form and will no doubt be successful in marketing the final product.

Finally, I would like to thank my parents, family and friends for all their support and guidance.

INTRODUCTION

Did you know that you can invest directly in blue-chip stocks, without paying any brokerage fees? You can also invest in bonds, directly with the U.S. Treasury, without paying the one- or two-percent commission that a broker normally charges.

If you are like many individual investors, you possibly own some no-load mutual funds. Or maybe you're just starting out and have given that route some thought. Either way, you are probably not thrilled about paying management fees and front-end fees as high as three percent on some mutual funds. And if you've ever bought stocks through a broker, you already know that the fees he or she charges can be high enough to prevent you from buying more shares when the price is low, a process called dollar-cost averaging.

These concerns were first brought to my attention during the Green Line Investment Challenge, a nation-wide investment competition in which I placed first nationally in both 1996–97 and 1997–98. I was approached over and over again with queries such as, "I'd like to invest in the stock market, but I don't want to pay a lot of fees. Where should I invest my money?" I began to think there must be a better and more cost-effective method to invest anywhere from $500 to $500,000 or more.

There is a better way. Fee-Free EasyStocks™, as I like to call them, are the evolution of Dividend Reinvestment Programs. Over 450 U.S. and international EasyStocks—blue-chip stocks such as General Electric, Wal-Mart, Merck, BP Amoco, and Unilever—allow investors to buy their first share and each share thereafter directly from the company, without ever paying a broker's fee and without the help of a broker. (Only some of these companies levy a small fee to cover their expenses.) In addition, over thirty Canadian EasyStocks—solid companies like BCE, Nortel Networks, and the Bank of Montreal—let you buy more shares directly from them, without any commissions, once you own your first share. Either way, you can still reinvest your dividends into more of the company's fee-free shares. You can even register online for some of these easy investment plans at www.netstockdirect.com.

In Part One, I will show you how to get started with Fee-Free EasyStocks and introduce you to ten major benefits for those who invest in them. One of the best features of this low-cost, high-return investment plan is that it allows you to invest regularly—weekly, monthly, or quarterly. (This allows you to take advantage of dollar-cost averaging, a process of buying fewer shares when the price is high and more shares when the price is low, with amounts that may be as low as ten to fifty dollars or as large as $250,000 for some companies, without ever paying any commissions.) These low minimums make Fee-Free EasyStocks a great way to get your kids saving and investing. You can even authorize a direct debit from your bank account to make monthly investments in many of these plans.

In Part Two, I will show you how easy it is to start investing directly in bonds. As I briefly mentioned, the U.S. Treasury also allows American and international investors to buy bonds directly from them, without requiring the standard one- or two-percent hidden commission charged by brokers. The TreasuryDirect™ program, which offers what I like to refer to as Fee-Free EasyBonds™, also allows you to reinvest your maturing treasury securities without paying a cent in fees.

Armed with this easy-to-follow guide, you can join thousands of investors who profit from this low-cost, high-return method for investing in American, Canadian, and international blue-chip stocks and U.S. Treasury bonds. Even if you've never bought stocks or bonds before, in Part Three you will find out how simple it is to create a winning portfolio of Fee-Free EasyStocks and Fee-Free EasyBonds. Everything comes together in this section as I suggest solid companies that could become the basis for your investment portfolio, and I offer methods for minimizing risk by investing in Fee-Free EasyBonds. I also discuss how to get your children and grandchildren interested in saving and investing, and how to create a Junior Capitalist Portfoli-Yo™ for them, complete with kid-friendly stocks such as Disney, Wal-Mart, and Mattel.

Part Four gives you easy access to information about the companies that offer their shares directly to investors. This section has been separated into U.S. and International (not including Canadian) Fee-Free EasyStocks, and Canadian Fee-Free EasyStocks. There is also a list of

Fee-Free EasyStocks classified by industry group as well as one classified by country. In this section, you will also find a list of Federal Reserve Bank servicing offices.

This guide will save you hundreds or thousands of dollars in commissions over the life of your investments. As an added bonus, you can access the Easy Investing website at http://www.easyinvesting.com for links to investment research sites and free updates on Fee-Free EasyStock plans—hundreds of new plans were created just this year.

PART ONE

Getting Started With Fee-Free EasyStocks™

How many times have you read about the phenomenal sales growth enjoyed by blue-chip companies such as Wal-Mart, GE, and Nortel Networks and wished you could participate in the company's success—without being stung by commission charges? Or have you ever thought about owning a part of your bank's mega-sized profits, but were intimidated by the quantity of shares you would have to buy to offset the brokerage fees? Fee-Free EasyStocks make it possible to do both without using a broker or paying a fee in most cases. And you don't need a large initial investment. In fact, you can invest in *some* Fee-Free EasyStocks for only fifty dollars.

In this section, you will discover the many benefits of EasyStocks, including how to:

- invest in blue-chip stocks without paying a broker's fee.
- buy some stocks for only ninety-five cents on the dollar.
- take advantage of dollar-cost averaging, by investing ten dollars or more per month, without paying any brokerage fees.
- teach your kids or grandchildren how to save and invest.

WHAT ARE EASYSTOCKS?

While compiling a list of the companies that offer their shares to investors like you and me free of commission charges, I devised a single system that would unify the various investment plans offered by each company. I chose to call this system Fee-Free EasyStocks since this truly is the easiest and most economical way to invest in stocks. With EasyStocks, you won't pay a broker's fee to buy your first share or to make additional investments. And you gain the same rights and privileges that are offered to someone who pays commissions and uses a broker. You can also choose to reinvest your dividends for more shares of the company's stock, again without paying a broker's fee. (Canadian EasyStocks require that you own one share before joining their plans.) EasyStocks make it possible to invest in approximately five hundred American, Canadian, and international blue-chip companies without a broker.

There are three different variations on the EasyStock system: Direct Stock Purchase Plans, Optional Cash Payment Plans, and Dividend Reinvestment Plans.

DIRECT STOCK PURCHASE PLANS

American and international (excluding Canadian) companies offer Direct Stock Purchase Plans or DSPs. These plans allow investors to buy their first share and every additional share directly from the company. Within this investment plan, any person can call the company's transfer agent at the 1-800 phone number provided in Part Four of this book and become a shareholder. You won't pay any brokerage fees to buy your first share or any share thereafter, and you can usually start investing with just $250. Some DSPs, however, do charge a nominal fee to cover mailings and account processing. Most DSPs also include optional cash payments and dividend reinvestment. Currently, there are more than 450 such plans, an increase of over 300% since 1997.

OPTIONAL CASH PAYMENT PLANS

Optional Cash Payments or OCPs allow investors already putting money into a public company to buy subsequent shares without paying any commissions. With Canadian EasyStocks, an investor needs to own one share of the company before he or she can participate in the company's plan. Therefore, while American and international companies allow Direct Stock Purchases and Optional Cash Payments as one plan, Canadian companies only allow OCPs. This plan also allows for the reinvestment of dividends without the assistance of a broker. (Investors who do not wish to own Canadian stocks should skip down to Dividend Reinvestment Plans.)

GETTING THE FIRST SHARE

So how do you get that first registered share in a Canadian company such as BCE, the Bank of Montreal, or Nortel Networks, to name a few? If you are already a shareholder in the company, your shares are probably in street name, meaning that the brokerage firm you used to acquire the shares is the registered owner. Ask your broker to register at least one share in your name. Once you are registered as the shareholder, you're ready to reinvest in the company without paying brokerage fees.

If you don't have a share in the company you'd like to invest in, you can acquire shares by joining the Canadian Shareowners Association (CSA), by purchasing them with the help of a discount broker, or with the assistance of a friend or family member who owns shares in the same company.

Canadian Shareowners Association

This association allows members to buy their first share, or up to $2,500 in stock, in most of the Canadian and some American plans that offer Optional Cash Payment Plans. A transaction charge of about three dollars applies and an annual membership in the association costs just over fifty dollars. To join the Canadian Shareowners Association, call (416) 595-9600 or visit their website at http://www.shareowner.ca.

Discount brokers

A discount brokerage firm, such as TD Waterhouse, Action Direct, or E*Trade, executes stock trades for fees well under fifty dollars but provides few or no recommendations. Make sure the discount broker you use to purchase your first share will execute an odd lot investment (one share in this case). You should not have to pay more than twenty-five to thirty-five dollars in one-time fees. In such a case, ask a friend who has a discount brokerage account or who already owns shares in the company you are interested in to buy the shares for you, register them in your name, and then have them mailed to you.

Friends and Family

If your rich uncle or a generous friend is already a participant in a company's Optional Cash Purchase Plan, ask him to write the transfer agent a letter requesting that one of his shares be transferred into a new account with the company in your name. (For each EasyStock you invest in, the transfer agent creates a new account under your name.) Have your friend include your full name, current address, and social insurance (or social security) number in the correspondence. This is also an excellent way to induce your children to save money, and makes a great birthday gift if you request an actual hard copy of the share, which is suitable for framing.

DIVIDEND REINVESTMENT PLANS

Dividend Reinvestment Plans or DRIPs allow anyone registered in a company's plan to reinvest their quarterly or monthly dividends into new shares of the company, at current prices. All of the companies that offer DSPs or OCPs offer DRIPs as well. However, close to six hundred U.S. companies and sixty Canadian companies that do not offer DSPs or OCPs do offer a Dividend Reinvestment Plan to their investors. For more information on DRIPs, visit the Easy Investing website at www.easyinvesting.com.

For the sake of simplicity, I will hereinafter use the term Fee-Free EasyStocks to refer to both Direct Stock Purchase Plans and Optional Cash Purchase Plans. Just remember that you can buy your first share of a U.S. or international Fee-Free EasyStock right from the company, but a Canadian Fee-Free EasyStock requires you to own one of the company's shares first.

INVESTING IN FEE-FREE EASYSTOCKS

Once you decide that you want to invest in McDonald's, the Bank of New York, BCE, Compaq or any other EasyStock, you will be astounded by how simple the whole process is. Let's follow the steps Melissa Simpson took to participate in General Electric's EasyStock plan:

STEP ONE: MAKE THE CALL AND DO YOUR RESEARCH

First and foremost, Melissa checked up on the company's financial performance. Referring to the phone number and website address provided in Part Four, she called General Electric's transfer agent to get a copy of the investment plan materials. Then, Ms. Simpson checked the General Electric website at www.ge.com to find out more about the company and its financial position, and to review recent news releases. (For more information about investment research, see Part Three.) Lastly, Melissa called the GE investor relations department for an annual report.

STEP TWO: FILL OUT THE FORM

Once Melissa confirmed her decision to invest in General Electric, she filled out the enrollment form and the W-9 Taxpayer Certification Form. (Note: Non-U.S. investors should also request a W-8 Certificate of

Foreign Status.) Since she wanted to reinvest all her dividends, Melissa checked the corresponding box on the enrollment form.

STEP THREE: CUT A CHECK

After carefully completing the forms, Melissa wrote a check payable to the Bank of New York, General Electric's transfer agent, for $250, the minimum investment required for participation in that plan. Finally, she mailed the forms and the check, in the envelope provided, to the Bank of New York. It's that easy! Note: If Melissa wanted to invest in a Canadian EasyStock, she would have referred to the previous section, Getting the First Share, and thereafter would have followed the steps above.

THE NITTY-GRITTY DETAILS

Once Melissa or any other investor purchases a Fee-Free EasyStock, a number of investment opportunities and benefits are revealed. Before I show you what some of the major benefits of EasyStocks are for the individual investor, we must first go over some of their basic characteristics. Understanding these facts will allow you to maximize the amount that you invest and enable you to take advantage of the many benefits these companies offer to EasyStock investors.

1. FRACTIONAL SHARES

Many investors who pay full commission to a broker are often upset that they can't invest all the funds they have designated into a particular stock. For example, when you contact a broker and tell him or her that you have $1,500 to invest in XYZ, which trades at $11.50 per share, you will only receive one hundred shares and your commission would likely cost anywhere from twenty-five to over one hundred dollars. The reason you would only receive one hundred shares is that your purchase is limited by commission charges and your broker's usual requirement to purchase round lots of one hundred shares.

However, if XYZ were a company with an EasyStock plan, your investment of $1,500 would afford you 130.435, shares since your investment is made in dollar terms instead of round lots ($1,500 ÷ $11.50 = 130.435). If you invested $250 in Home Depot when it was trading at

$43 per share, the proceeds to you would be 5.814 shares ($250 ÷ $43 = 5.814). EasyStocks allow you to invest the entire amount you plan to save, without having to worry about commissions and round or odd lots. Because you can own fractions of a share, all the money you commit to a certain stock will be invested.

2. EASY-TO-MANAGE ACCOUNTS

When you make an initial investment with any Fee-Free EasyStock company, their transfer agent will begin the process of maintaining your account for you. A transfer agent performs a number of functions, including updating your account and sending out account statements, paying the dividends to all shareholders on record (including EasyStock investors), and safekeeping the shares for EasyStock holders.

- Account Statements. You will receive an account statement approximately every three months, after the company pays its regular dividends. This statement will set out the amount of cash dividends paid, the number of new shares purchased, the purchase price per share, and the total number of shares held in the account. After your first investment you will usually also receive a confirmation that your account was successfully opened.
- Dividend Payments. Receiving dividends could not be easier under the Plan, since the transfer agent simply credits the dividend, in the form of new shares, to your account. For example, if the dividend was $0.14 per share and you owned 127.864 shares at the current price of $20 each, 0.895 shares would be credited to your account ($0.14 × 127.864 ÷ $20), bringing your holdings to 128.759 shares. Alternately, you can choose to receive your dividends as cash, wired directly into your bank account.
- Share Certificates. The company's transfer agent also performs safekeeping services, much the same as a mutual fund company does. If you make an initial EasyStock purchase with The Home Depot for $250, for example, a share certificate will not be mailed to you. As your dividends increase the value of your holdings, you will still not receive a share certificate. However, if you request a share certificate, as a gift for a relative or for any other reason, just write or fax the

transfer agent. Most investors, though, do not want the hassles involved in keeping share certificates in a safety deposit box and would rather have the transfer agent hold onto them.

3. PRICE OF ADDITIONAL SHARES

Each company's method for calculating the price of additional common shares may vary slightly but the two most common methods are the Weighted Average Price and the Average Market Price. The company usually calculates its stock's average price over the week before the dividends are paid, and credits additional shares to participants' accounts accordingly.

- Weighted Average Price. For some plans, the transfer agent calculates the weighted average of the high and low prices for board lots—multiples of one hundred shares—of the common shares traded on the five days before dividends are paid. Using this method, the company usually specifies that the price be calculated using prices from the stock exchange that traded the largest amount of shares. This method is no different than a regular average except that it does not incorporate trades of fewer than one hundred shares.
- Average Market Price. Making use of this method or a slight variation of it, a transfer agent will calculate the stock's average closing price for the five days leading up to a dividend payment date in which at least one board lot of 100,000 shares was traded. Again, the company's transfer agent will calculate these figures using information from the most active stock exchange, for stocks that are interlisted on more than one exchange.

4. FULL VS. PARTIAL DIVIDEND REINVESTMENT

With some EasyStocks, you are given the option to reinvest either all or part of your dividends as additional shares in the company. There are hundreds of international stocks and U.S. companies that provide this option as well as a handful of Canadian firms that allow partial reinvestment.

- Full Dividend Reinvestment. If you choose the full dividend reinvestment option—in some cases it's the only option available—your earnings will be credited to your account in the form of shares, based on the share prices calculated by the transfer agent, as outlined above. Should you change your mind, you can send a letter or fax to the transfer agent authorizing him or her to reinvest only a portion of your dividends, if partial reinvestment is an option.

- Partial Dividend Reinvestment. With companies that offer a partial reinvestment option, you simply check the appropriate box on the application form—25% reinvestment, 50% reinvestment, or 75% reinvestment—and the company will credit that amount to your account, in the form of new shares. The balance of the funds will be mailed to you, and in the case of some EasyStocks, may be directly deposited into your bank account through an electronic funds transfer.

5. ADDITIONAL INVESTMENTS

Among the vast majority of companies, you may make additional optional investments over and above your initial minimum investment, so long as they comply with the individual company's requirement. Some companies, such as General Electric, allow investors to submit optional investments well under fifty dollars. Others, such as Mattel, require investors to submit at least one hundred dollars for additional purchases.

Regardless of the company's requirements, there are two basic ways to acquire additional shares—by check or money order or by automatic withdrawal from your bank account.

- Check or Money Order. You can make an additional investment in an EasyStock by sending a check or money order payable to the company's transfer agent, not the company itself. To facilitate additional investments, you should use the stub located on the bottom of your most recent account statement. Mail your check with the stub to the transfer agent, allowing plenty of time for it to arrive before the next reinvestment period designated by the company, as indicated on your account statements.

- Automatic Withdrawal. If you wish to make regular weekly, monthly, or quarterly purchases, you can authorize an automatic withdrawal from your bank account. This feature eliminates the need to write a check every month and is a great way to ensure you are saving regularly. To date, most U.S. and international companies recognize the value of having investors contributing a small amount each month, but no Canadian companies offer this option just yet.

6. VOTING YOUR SHARES

The transfer agent will mail you materials detailing forthcoming stockholders' meetings, including a proxy card detailing the amount of shares in your account, both full and fractional. You are entitled to the same voting benefits as other common shareholders (those who purchased stock through a broker). If you wish, you may attend the annual meeting to vote in person, or simply mail the proxy card to the transfer agent.

7. RIGHTS OFFERINGS

As a participant in a Fee-Free EasyStock plan, you are also entitled to participate in any rights offerings the company makes available to existing shareholders. For example, if the company offers shareholders of record additional common shares or other securities, rights certificates, or warrants (the option to buy more shares at a fixed rate) to be exercised at a specified price, you will also receive these benefits. The agent will issue the rights to you according to the number of whole (but not fractional) shares in your account.

8. STOCK SPLITS AND SPECIAL DIVIDENDS

When a company initiates a stock split, which reduces the cost of investing in round lots of 100 shares, all shareholders receive an additional amount of shares, depending upon the terms of the split—usually the price of three shares for two shares or two shares for one share. As an Easy Investor, the new shares will be credited to your account by the transfer agent. For example, if you had 84.525 shares of Disney at fifty dollars each and they were split three-for-two, you would now have 126.788 shares of Disney (84.525 × 3 ÷ 2) at seventy-five dollars. Likewise, if the company issues a special dividend to shareholders, for example, on a one-time gain through the sale of one of the company's subsidiaries, you will receive a portion of the proceeds appropriate to your share ownership. You will also be given the option of reinvesting the funds in additional shares of the company.

9. AMENDMENT AND TERMINATION

Public companies such as Alcan or the Bank of Ireland are under no obligation to provide their shares to investors free of commission charges. As a result, they may amend or terminate their plans with sufficient notice to EasyStock investors. Fortunately, termination of a plan rarely happens since these companies recognize the value of these programs and do not want to aggravate their shareholders. In most cases, an amendment to the plan benefits the investors more than the companies. An example would be a company that modifies its plan allowing investors to take advantage of automatic withdrawals or partial dividend reinvestment, which might not have been part of their plan previously.

However, you may terminate your participation in a plan at any time by mailing or faxing a letter to the company's transfer agent. (Their fees for selling will be clearly stated before you invest in the plan, and usually amount to a few cents per share.) You may find that it is less expensive to have your shares transferred to your discount broker, if you have one, who can then sell the shares for a flat fee, usually under thirty-five dollars.

10. TAXES AND OTHER NUISANCES

Fee-Free EasyStocks are subject to the same tax rules as shares purchased through a stockbroker. Easy Investors are responsible for paying taxes on their dividends and must pay capital gains taxes when they sell their shares in the future. (The U.S. government deems that you have received a "taxable benefit" when an EasyStock subsidizes your commission costs, so you might also be on the hook for an additional small tax for the hundreds of dollars you save. It is unclear whether the Canadian government has an opinion on the matter, but it is always smart to consult an accountant at tax time or to ask the transfer agent for an update.) In all of the above cases, the company's transfer agent will send you a form each year around tax time, indicating the amount of tax that you owe.

It is important to note that not every EasyStock pays for 100% of your transaction fees. In some cases, a few dollars per year or a couple of cents per share will be charged to your account to cover postage expenses or share transfers. However, in every case, these fees—which rarely cover the cost of servicing your account— are still well below the commissions charged by the mainstream discount brokers. In the case of Canadian

EasyStocks, no fees are charged within your Easy Investment Program once you own your first share.

WHY DO PUBLIC COMPANIES PAY YOUR FEES?

Now that you know how Fee-Free EasyStocks work, you are probably wondering why EasyStocks work. Why would a rational company, looking to maximize its profits, want to pick up your investment tab, so to speak? By offering shares to the public on a monthly basis, companies create a built-in support for their shares, provided that investors keep making optional cash purchases. There are three main reasons why companies will start a Fee-Free Investment Plan: to create brand loyalty, to tap an inexpensive source of capital, and to broaden their shareholder base.

FEE-FREE EASYSTOCKS CREATE BRAND LOYALTY.

Melissa Simpson, from the previous example, is a single parent with two young children. She wants to get her children interested in saving and investing so she purchased a few shares for them in Disney, a Fee-Free EasyStock. When vacation time comes around, where do you think Melissa will want to take the kids? A trip to Disneyland® would not only be fun but would also give her a chance to show the kids how the company in which they hold some interest is being run.

Similarly, if Melissa, or any other EasyStock Investor, is interested in applying for a credit card and she owns shares in American Express, it's a good bet she won't apply for a VISA. If Melissa holds shares in Home Depot, she'll probably shop there every time she has a home repair job to complete. In cases like these, Easy Investors are part owners in companies, and are likely to be more loyal to a company's products or services than the rest of the population.

FEE-FREE EASYSTOCKS ARE AN INEXPENSIVE SOURCE OF CAPITAL.

Most often, when a public company wants to raise more capital to fund their ongoing operations or for expansion purposes, it hires an investment bank such as Goldman Sachs in the U.S. or RBC Dominion Securities in Canada. The investment bank then creates sales materials and a prospectus, and briefs its brokers on the merits of the upcoming offering of shares to the public. Meanwhile, the institutional sales staff, whose job is to sell to mutual funds and public pension plans, is busy trying to sell large portion of this new stock offering. All this costs the company large amounts of money. The investment bankers take their cut once the deal is signed, the retail brokers take their cut upon selling shares to the public, and the institutional salespeople take their cut when they sell chunks of stock to fund managers. When all is said and done, for every dollar that the public company raised, they may only keep ninety-four cents or less. While a 6 or 7% fee seems reasonable for such a large amount of work, it could easily amount to tens of million of dollars in fees.

In contrast, when a public company has a consistent base of Easy Investors who buy more shares each month, the firm benefits from this steady and inexpensive inflow of capital that can be used to fund continuing operations. The cost of the program to the company is likely no more than fifteen to twenty dollars per investor per year.

EASYSTOCKS BROADEN THE SHAREHOLDER BASE.

Many public companies are making the conversion to Fee-Free EasyStocks since it is a simple and effective way to broaden the shareholder base. When a public company is controlled by a small number of investors or mutual funds, these groups could wield significant control over the firm and its operational strategy. Individual investors like Melissa are more likely to hold their shares for the long term, creating greater stability for the company, whereas many mutual funds have a turnover rate (the number of times they buy and sell shares) of over 100% annually, according to recent studies.

Individual investors, from the company's point of view, are less likely to pressure the management into making major reforms. However, with the rise of Internet use, many individual investors are banding together to cast their votes at shareholders' meetings, so look for this reason to be less of an incentive for companies to offer EasyStocks. As they should, investors today have become more informed concerning a company's performance.

Now that we have examined why companies want to pay your fees, let's look at some of the benefits you will receive by investing.

TEN BENEFITS FOR EASY INVESTORS

Investing in Fee-Free EasyStocks is the easiest and most cost effective way to own a piece of blue-chip American, Canadian, and international companies, period. Here are some of the major benefits to this investment approach that haven't been mentioned in detail and will be expanded on further:

1. Fee-Free EasyStocks can provide investors with a greater return than mutual funds.
2. You can start investing with as little as fifty dollars.
3. By adding EasyStocks, you can create a properly diversified portfolio.
4. Some of the bluest of blue-chip companies offer Easy Investing plans.
5. Fee-Free EasyStocks enable you to invest for retirement.
6. By investing small amounts on a monthly or quarterly basis, you can take advantage of dollar-cost averaging with Fee-Free EasyStocks.
7. A broker will never pressure you to invest in any EasyStock plan.
8. EasyStocks are like supercharged no-load mutual funds.
9. By investing in some Fee-Free EasyStocks, you will get exclusive benefits not offered to shareholders who purchased their shares through a broker.
10. You can teach your kids how to save and invest with Fee-Free EasyStocks.

1. FEE-FREE EASYSTOCKS CAN OFFER INVESTORS A GREATER RETURN THAN MUTUAL FUNDS.

You will *make more money* investing in a diversified portfolio of EasyStocks than you can with mutual funds made up of the same stocks, since you pay no fees to invest in EasyStocks. To illustrate this point, let's say that Adam Smyth owns a few units of a no-load mutual fund that invests in large, solid companies. (Mutual funds pool investors' money to buy a diverse group of stocks; no-load funds do not levy a fee to open or close your account but do charge an annual management fee.) Stocks in this fund might include McDonald's, Gillette, Lucent, General Electric, Nortel Networks, Home Depot, Wal-Mart, Morgan Stanley, Bank of New York and IBM, among others.

After discovering that his no-load mutual fund charged 2.25% annually in management fees, Smyth became so fed up that he started buying those same stocks through a traditional broker. However, he was forced to pay a minimum commission of eighty dollars each time he wanted to buy more shares, so he stopped making monthly investments. Months later, Adam realized that over 450 blue-chip companies offer their shares without commission charges, directly to investors. He discovered that anyone can invest in EasyStocks without a broker. And he made a lot more money than with the same stocks he had held in a mutual fund or purchased through a broker.

THE FEE-FREE EASYSTOCKS ADVANTAGE

How much more money can you expect to make with EasyStocks than with no-load mutual funds? Assume the following in our comparison between mutual funds and Fee-Free EasyStocks:

- Today, $10,000 will be invested into mutual funds and another $10,000 will be invested into EasyStocks.
- The investment will compound at the annual rate of 10%.
- All dividends will be reinvested.
- The portfolio will be held for thirty years.
- Fee-Free EasyStocks will not charge any commissions, while the mutual fund will charge a 2.25% fee per year (calculated at the end of the year for simplicity).

How much difference do you think 2.25% in management fees makes, if it is taken out of a mutual fund account each year? You're probably thinking, "It's just 2.25%. No big deal." Actually, it is a big deal. At the 10% growth rate, Mr. Smyth's $10,000 investment in mutual funds would be worth $88,162 after compounding for thirty years, less 2.25% in fees each year. (See chart on page 18.) Not so bad, but not so good either, when you compare it to the phenomenal growth of the Fee-Free EasyStocks portfolio, compounding at the same ten-percent rate. The same $10,000 invested into a Fee-Free EasyStocks portfolio will be worth $174,494 thirty years later, (see chart on page 19), 198% more money than what the mutual funds would be worth! The amazing part is that

Adam Smyth held the same stocks with the same risk as the mutual fund but earned an extra $86,332 on his $10,000 investment in Fee-Free EasyStocks.

But how can that be? A rate of 2.25% may not seem like a lot of money if you pay that sum out once. But if you're only earning a 10% return on your mutual funds (the rate at which your funds compound in value), then 2.25% in fees reduces your 10% return to only 7.75% before inflation (10% return – 2.25% in fees = 7.75% return after fees). So if your $10,000 investment grew to $11,000 after one year, a mutual fund investor would end up with only $10,752.50, forfeiting $247.50 to the mutual fund company. While that fee represents only 2.25% of the total investment, it is equal to well over 20% of that year's gains ($247.50 fee ÷ $1,000 investment gain = 24.75% of year's gains paid as fees).

In fact, after thirty years of 10% compounded annual returns, a mutual fund with annual fees of 2.25%, will have charged $25,708 in fees on an initial investment of only $10,000. (To see how much a particular mutual fund will cost you in fees and foregone earnings, download the U.S. Securities and Exchange Commission's Mutual Fund Cost Calculator at http://www.sec.gov/mfcc/mfcc-int.htm.) All these factors contribute to make investing in EasyStocks a very attractive prospect, compared to investing in mutual funds. As you can see from the graph above, the Fee-Free EasyStocks' compounded returns keep increasing substantially over the longer term, while no-load mutual fund gains minus fees are not as impressive.

From the graph, you can see that investors are much better off with EasyStocks rather than mutual funds, assuming that their performance equals or surpasses the mutual fund's pre-fee performance. The charts on the following pages compare the returns of mutual funds and Fee-Free EasyStocks, growing at the same annual rate, over thirty years.

Recall from our example that each year a 2.25% annual expense fee diminishes the mutual fund investor's gains, lowering the amount of money available for reinvesting the following year and each year thereafter. Over the thirty years, this investor's $10,000 portfolio became $88,162 and generated $25,708 in fees that were paid to the mutual fund company. This enormous cost to the investor is dwarfed by the foregone earnings of $60,624 that the investor never had the opportunity to reinvest into more units of the mutual fund.

$10,000 GROWING AT 10% ANNUALLY OVER 30 YEARS

A) Invested in Mutual Funds (2.25% in Annual Fees)

Year	Start ($)	Gains ($)	Fees ($)	Finish ($)
1	10,000	1,000	248	10,753
2	10,753	1,075	266	11,562
3	11,562	1,156	286	12,432
4	12,432	1,243	308	13,367
5	13,367	1,337	331	14,373
6	14,373	1,437	356	15,455
7	15,455	1,545	383	16,618
8	16,618	1,662	411	17,868
9	17,868	1,787	442	19,213
10	19,213	1,921	476	20,658
11	20,658	2,066	511	22,213
12	22,213	2,221	550	23,884
13	23,884	2,388	591	25,682
14	25,682	2,568	636	27,614
15	27,614	2,761	683	29,692
16	29,692	2,969	735	31,926
17	31,926	3,139	790	34,329
18	34,329	3,433	850	36,912
19	36,912	3,691	914	39,690
20	39,690	3,969	982	42,677
21	42,677	4,268	1,056	45,888
22	45,888	4,589	1,136	49,341
23	49,341	4,934	1,221	53,054
24	53,054	5,305	1,313	57,046
25	57,046	5,705	1,412	61,339
26	61,339	6,134	1,518	65,955
27	65,955	6,595	1,632	70,918
28	70,918	7,092	1,755	76,254
29	76,254	7,625	1,887	81,992
30	81,992	8,199	2,029	88,162

B) Invested In Fee-Free EasyStocks

Year	Start ($)	Gains ($)	Fees ($)	Finish ($)
1	10,000	1,000	-	11,000
2	11,000	1,100	-	12,100
3	12,100	1,210	-	13,310
4	13,310	1,331	-	14,641
5	14,641	1,464	-	16,105
6	16,105	1,611	-	17,716
7	17,716	1,772	-	19,487
8	19,487	1,949	-	21,436
9	21,436	2,144	-	23,579
10	23,579	2,358	-	25,937
11	25,937	2,594	-	28,531
12	28,531	2,853	-	31,384
13	31,384	3,138	-	34,523
14	34,523	3,452	-	37,975
15	37,975	3,797	-	41,772
16	41,772	4,177	-	45,950
17	45,950	4,595	-	50,545
18	50,545	5,054	-	55,599
19	55,599	5,560	-	61,159
20	61,159	6,116	-	67,275
21	67,275	6,727	-	74,002
22	74,002	7,400	-	81,403
23	81,403	8,140	-	89,543
24	89,543	8,954	-	98,497
25	98,497	9,850	-	108,347
26	108,347	10,835	-	119,182
27	119,182	11,918	-	131,100
28	131,100	13,110	-	144,210
29	144,210	14,421	-	158,631
30	158,631	15,863	-	174,494

On the other hand, the Easy Investor never pays a management fee to the company that administers the EasyStock plan, although a few companies do charge a nominal safekeeping fee. This fee is rather insignificant—a couple of dollars per year, a few cents per share, or a couple of dollars per transaction—and is levied only by some companies (the amounts are minute and not levied by all companies, so they are not included in the previous graph). Since no broker's commissions are taken out of the account, the full amount of money each year is reinvested, compounding for thirty years. This investor's EasyStocks portfolio would be worth $174,494 after thirty years—almost twice what the mutual fund portfolio would be worth.

THE FORCE OF COMPOUNDING

Why does the 2.25% annual mutual fund fee make such a huge difference over time? The extra gains that Easy Investors make are due, in part, to the wonders of compounding. Any earnings you receive on your initial investment at the end of the year that do not have to be paid as fees to a mutual fund company can be reinvested and will grow at the same rate as your other investments. Furthermore, the next year and every year thereafter, you essentially make gains on your principal and on the accumulation that would normally have been paid as fees! This concept is very similar to compound interest; saving a seemingly small 2.25% annual fee by investing in Fee-Free EasyStocks will make you exponentially wealthier in the future.

In the case of Adam Smyth, compounding without fees increased his portfolio from a possible $88,162 to $174,494 just by investing directly in Fee-Free EasyStocks instead of no-load mutual funds that held the same stocks in which he directly invested. Overall, the clear message is to start investing in EasyStocks and start growing your money without the fees associated with mutual funds.

2. START INVESTING WITH AS LITTLE AS $50.

The major frustration frequently related by investors is that saving money is too expensive. What they mean is that the minimum amounts needed to start investing and maintaining a plan are often beyond their reach. Stockbrokers often require minimum account balances in the thousands of dollars to start, though mutual fund companies will often waive their minimum investment amounts if you commit to investing regularly. However, with American and international EasyStocks, you can become a shareholder with a minimum investment of $50 to $250.

There are exceptions to this rule. You can invest in the shares of Johnson Controls, Walgreens, and forty other companies for under one hundred dollars initially; however, Disney and McDonald's require a $1,000 initial cash outlay. Overall, there are approximately 330 Fee-Free EasyStocks that allow an initial investment of $250 or less. Canadian EasyStocks, which work a bit differently, require you to own at least one share (or one unit in the case of unincorporated real estate investment trusts), before you can participate in their Easy Investment Programs.

Start investing with $50 or less in the following companies:

Banco Popular Inc.
Bob Evans Farms Inc.
Carolina Power & Light Co.
Central Maine Power Co.
Duke Energy Corp.
Green Mountain Power Corp.
Idaho Power Corp.
IES Industries
Interstate Power Co.
Johnson Controls Inc.
Madison Gas & Electric Co.
New Jersey Resources Corp.
Northwestern Public Service
Pinnacle West Capital Corp.
Public Service Company of New Mexico
Puget Sound Energy Inc.
Sierra Pacific Resources
Union Electric Co.
United Water Resources Inc.
Walgreens

Start investing with $51 to $100 in the following companies:

American Water Works Co.
Ascent Entertainment Group
Chock Full O' Nuts Corp.
Connecticut Water Service
Consolidated Freightways
Crown American Realty Trust
Delta National Gas Co.
DQE Inc.
DTE Energy Co.
Emcee Broadcast Products
Florida Progress Corp.
Frontier Insurance Group Inc.
Harveys Casino Resorts
Hawaiian Electric Industries
IWC Resources Corp.
Montana Power Co.
Newport Corp.
Northern States Power Co.
Oneok Inc.
Owens-Corning
Sonoma Valley Bank
Southwest Gas Corp.
TNP Enterprises Inc.
WPS Resources Corp.
XXsys Technologies Inc.

Start investing with one share in these Canadian companies:

Alberta Energy Company Ltd.
Alcan Aluminum Ltd.
Amtelecom Group Inc.
Bank of Montreal
Bank of Nova Scotia
BCE Inc.
BC Gas Inc.
BC Telecom Inc.
Bruncor Inc.
Canadian General Investments Ltd.
Canadian Imperial Bank of Commerce (CIBC)
Canadian Pacific Ltd.
Dofasco Inc.
Enbridge Inc.
EnerMark Income Fund
EnerPlus Resources Fund
Fortis Trust Corp.
Imperial Oil Ltd.
Inco Ltd.
Island Telephone Company Ltd.
MacMillan Bloedel Ltd.
Maritime Telephone & Telegraph Ltd.
Molson Companies Inc.
Moore Corporation Ltd.
National Bank of Canada
NewTel Enterprises Ltd.
Nortel Networks Inc.
Nova Corp.
Nova Scotia Power Inc.
Pengrowth Energy Trust
RioCan REIT
Suncor Energy Inc.
Telus Corp.
TransAlta Corp.
TransCanada PipeLines Ltd.
Westcoast Energy Inc.

3. CREATE A PROPERLY DIVERSIFIED PORTFOLIO.

Without a diversified portfolio, you cannot achieve superior returns over the long term. For instance, an investor who owns shares in Exxon, Morgan Stanley, Disney, and Merck would be well-served by diversifying his or her portfolio into other industries, by investing in General Electric and Nortel Networks, for example; and internationally by purchasing shares in AXA-UAP or INC Groep. With EasyStocks, you can easily invest in American and Canadian companies in every sector of the economy.

You can also participate in the growth of market leaders around the globe, simply by investing in their American Depository Receipts or ADRs. (American Depository Receipts are shares of international companies that are traded on American exchanges in American dollars.) This is an easy way to add international shares to your portfolio without having to trade stocks on foreign exchanges at 2 a.m. in a currency that you cannot pronounce. For a complete list of Fee-Free EasyStocks listed by industry group, refer to Part Four.

4. INVEST IN THE BLUEST OF THE BLUE CHIPS.

Companies that offer their shares directly to investors are generally on solid financial ground and are often leaders in their industries. When a company decides to start an EasyStock plan, the management does so with the understanding that it is a long-term commitment that will require substantial cash outlays at the outset. If the company could not afford to pay for a long-term plan, they simply would not offer one. So the companies that do offer these plans are confident in their future ability to succeed.

Companies that comprise the prestigious Standard & Poor's 500 Index derive almost a quarter of their revenue from overseas sources. (The S&P 500 is an index of 500 large U.S. stocks that are taken as a proxy for the stock market.) As a result, by investing in some American blue chips, you are also adding international exposure to your portfolio.

EasyStocks in the S&P 500 Index:

Aetna Inc.
Air Products & Chemicals Inc.
AirTouch Communications
Alcan Aluminum
American Electric Power
American Express
Ameritech
Amoco
Bank of New York
Becton, Dickinson
Carolina Power & Light
Central & South West
Chevron
Chrysler
Coastal
Compaq Computer
Dayton Hudson
Dow Jones & Company
Duke Energy
Eastman Kodak
Enron
Entergy
Exxon
Fannie Mae
Ford Motor
General Electric
Gillette Company
Goodyear Tire & Rubber
Guidant
John H. Harland
Home Depot
Houston Industries
Inco Ltd.
International Business Machines (IBM)
Johnson Controls
Kerr-McGee
Eli Lilly & Company
Lucent Technologies
Mattel
McDonald's
MediaOne Group
Mellon Bank
Merck & Company

Morgan Stanley, Dean Witter & Company
Nortel Networks
J.C. Penney
Pharmacia & Upjohn
Procter & Gamble
Public Service Enterprise Group
Rockwell International
Royal Dutch Petroleum
Sears, Roebuck, & Company
Snap-On
Southern Company
Tenneco
Texaco
Unilever NV
US West Inc.
Wal-Mart Stores
Walgreen Company
Walt Disney Company
Warner-Lambert

Taking the findings about S&P 500 stocks one step further, one could conclude that many companies on the Dow Jones Industrial Average also derive a sizable portion of their earnings overseas. (Some companies on the Toronto Stock Exchange derive a significant portion of their earnings outside of Canada, such as Nortel Networks, but most are focused on the Canadian market.) Seventy-five percent of active mutual fund managers consistently underperform (do worse than) the following stock market indices. You should, therefore, probably consider owning shares in some of the EasyStocks listed below, provided they meet your investment criteria:

EasyStocks in the Dow Jones Industrial Average

American Express
Chevron
Eastman Kodak Company
Exxon
General Electric
Goodyear Tire & Rubber Co.
International Business Machines (IBM)
McDonald's
Merck & Company
Procter & Gamble
Sears, Roebuck
Wal-Mart Stores
Walt Disney Company

EasyStocks in the Dow Jones Utility Average

Duke Energy
Enron
Houston Industries
Public Service Ent. Group
Southern Company

EasyStocks in the TSE-35 (Canada) Index

Bank of Montreal
Bank of Nova Scotia
BCE Inc.
Canadian Imperial Bank of Commerce (CIBC)
Canadian Pacific
Dofasco
Moore Corporation
National Bank of Canada
Nortel Networks Corp.
Nova Corporation
TransAlta Corp.

5. INVEST FOR RETIREMENT WITH EASYSTOCKS.

As a result of a major shift in public opinion regarding retirement planning, more and more people are taking advantage of retirement accounts. The Individual Retirement Account (IRA) in the United States and the Registered Retirement Savings Plan (RRSP) in Canada offer investors a prudent way to shield their investments from capital gains until their retirement years.

Part Three of this book shows how to incorporate EasyStocks into an IRA or RRSP. American investors who haven't thought about saving and investing inside a retirement account should at least consider the following EasyStocks, which offer their own distinct IRA option:

Allstate Corp.
Ameritech Corporation
Atmos Energy Corp.
Bell Atlantic Corp.
Chrysler Corp.
Connecticut Energy Corp.
Connecticut Water Service
Exxon Corp.
Fannie Mae
Lucent Technologies Inc.
McDonald's Corp.
MCN Energy Group, Inc.
MidSouth Bancorp, Inc.
Mobil Corp.
Morton International, Inc.
Philadelphia Suburban Corp.
Sears, Roebuck and Co.
UtiliCorp United Inc.

6. TAKE ADVANTAGE OF DOLLAR-COST AVERAGING.

When investing in EasyStocks, remember the story of the tortoise and the hare. Everyone suspects that the hare holds an obvious advantage over the tortoise, making a race between the two seem unfairly matched. When it comes to investing, most people would assume that "professional" money managers—the hares—can outperform the Dow Jones Industrial Average and individual investors alike. Well, that's just not true; over the past few years, over 75% of mutual fund managers underperformed the Dow—even before management expenses are factored into the equation.

Individual investors, the victorious tortoises, can outperform the professional hares by investing modest amounts on a regular on-going basis and sticking to an investment plan. This method, familiar to many mutual fund investors, is called dollar-cost averaging, since it allows you to average your costs over time and prevents you from investing too much when prices are high. Remember, slow and steady wins the race.

To illustrate this point, let's assume that Melissa Simpson has been investing in EasyStocks since 1993, when she purchased shares in Profit Corp. (Since EasyStocks haven't been around for very long, the company is fictional.) Simpson invested an initial amount of $250 and was able to make additional investments for as little as $25 per transaction. She even took advantage of optional electronic fund transfers, which are now available for hundreds of companies, and had a set amount of money debited from her bank account each month. In doing so, she established a regular pattern of saving and investing.

Assuming the price history of Profit Corp. as shown in the graph on page 27, Melissa has been much more successful by investing directly in EasyStocks than she would have been had she invested through a broker. With a broker, she could only make additional investments maybe once or twice a year, since the commissions to invest monthly would be far too prohibitive. (The $25 investment is even lower than most commissions charged by discount brokers, and would not offer a traditional stockbroker any profit.) More importantly, by making monthly investments in her Fee-Free EasyStocks, Melissa is less susceptible to short-term swings in the stock price of Profit Corp. or any other EasyStock.

Looking at the chart, let's assume that Melissa had invested $250 at the start of 1993 when the shares traded at around $39. She arranged to continue investing $25 a month for more shares. Throughout 1993, the cost per share rose and fluctuated between $43 and $55. Each month that the shares rose, the additional investment caused her average cost per share to rise but allowed it to stay below the current price of the shares. That outcome is the direct result of investing a set dollar amount, such as $25 per month, into more shares. That way, when the shares are trading at $43, her regular $25 investment will buy more shares than when Profit Corp. is trading at $55 per share, allowing her to average down her costs as the price per share falls in the near term. In 1994, when the shares, and the stock market as a whole, lost some ground, these regular monthly investments provided Melissa with a larger number of shares per investment, and averaged down her costs while Wall Street pros ran for cover.

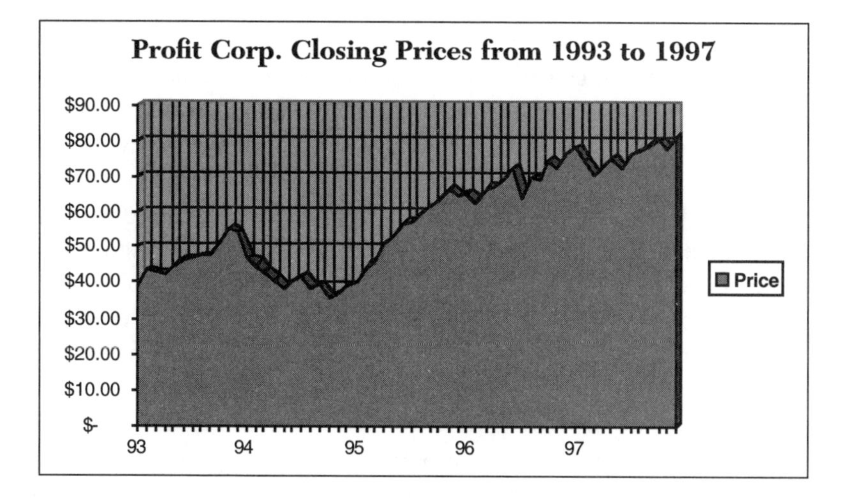

This dollar-cost averaging technique with Fee-Free EasyStocks allows any investor to buy more shares while the price is low and prevents them from buying too many shares while the price is high—assuming that, over the long run, the investment will appreciate in value. This incredible and easy-to-implement technique also prevents investors from the temptation of timing the market and guessing when the best period would be to make an additional investment. Timing the market carries significant risk since you must be right twice—first deciding when to sell, and then deciding when to re-enter the market. The best time to invest, for those of you who are wondering, is right now, next month, and every month thereafter.

The following EasyStocks are good candidates for dollar-cost averaging since they have low minimum requirements for additional investments:

There are almost one hundred EasyStocks listed in Part Four into which you may invest as little as $25 per month.

BCE Inc.
Fannie Mae
General Electric Co.
Home Depot Inc.
Inco Ltd.
Nortel Networks
RioCan REIT
TransCanada PipeLines
U.S. West Inc.
Westcoast Energy Inc.

7. NEVER FEEL PRESSURED TO TRADE.

One of the most important benefits of EasyStocks is also one that many people don't think to consider. When you invest with some brokers, you might feel pressure to trade. Most brokers are good, upstanding citizens who handle their clients' portfolios conscientiously, but the only way they make money is when you are buying and selling stocks. It doesn't matter how much your block of Berkshire Hathaway shares has gone up in the past twenty years, if you aren't buying more or selling them to buy another stock, your broker is not making a cent. That's the problem with investing through most (but not all) traditional brokers—there is often no apparent link between their compensation and the performance of your portfolio. It reminds me of an old stock market story. A very well-to-do stock broker was trying to impress a potential client on his lavish yacht in the New York Harbor. The broker pointed out the largest yachts as they left the dock, all belonging to the principals of the largest brokeage firms of the era. By this time, the client was visibly perturbed and seemed not to share the broker's ebullience. "Where are all the customers' yachts?" he demanded.

When you invest in Fee-Free EasyStocks, you never pay brokerage fees—rarely do you pay any fees—and you need not worry that someone is giving you advice just to generate commissions so they can go out and buy a yacht. In fact, every study shows that long-term investors with a buy-and-hold mentality fare better than market timers with a day-trader mentality.

8. EASYSTOCKS ARE LIKE SUPERCHARGED NO-LOAD FUNDS.

People are always impressed by how easy it is to invest in mutual funds.

All you have to do is send a voided check to the mutual fund company and specify the amount of money to be taken out of your bank account each month. Simple, right? Well, if you can invest in mutual funds, you can invest in Fee-Free EasyStocks, since the process is almost identical. Fee-Free EasyStocks are like supercharged mutual funds, since they offer you the same benefits of no-load mutual funds—stock market diversification, monthly investments, and so on—without the annual percentage management fees associated with investing in mutual funds.

As you'll recall, to start investing in EasyStocks, just send a check to the company's transfer agent, who will invest the full amount. Your quarterly dividends will be automatically reinvested into more shares and you are sometimes given the option of receiving cash instead of more shares. As with mutual funds, a transfer agent handles your account and sends you quarterly statements and confirmations when you make an investment. Annual reports and company documents arrive on time since they are sent directly from the transfer agent and not through an intermediary—a broker. Finally, your shares are held in book entry form, as they are with mutual funds. You never actually have the shares so you don't have to worry about losing them.

The main difference between the two is that with no-load mutual funds, you pay a fee as high as 2% or 3% per year to the fund manager. If you have a portfolio worth $50,000, a 3% fee can add up to $1,500 per year! Again, most EasyStocks don't charge any annual fees, but some levy a modest charge to cover mailings and other expenses. Also, unlike most mutual funds, you can vote your Fee-Free EasyStock shares in person at the company's annual meeting or by proxy through the mail.

9. BENEFITS EXCLUSIVE TO EASY INVESTORS.

Wow, have I got a deal for you. When's the last time you heard of someone paying less for a stock than the market price? Some Fee-Free EasyStocks offer investors a discount, usually between 3% and 5%, on the purchase of additional shares or the reinvestment of dividends. This may sound too good to be true, but it's for real.

The corporations that offer these discounts are content to broaden their shareholder base and, if they are a consumer products company or electric utility, are encouraging more potential customers to buy their products or make use of their services. The following EasyStocks offer investors a discount on the reinvestment of dividends and/or the purchase of additional shares:

Canadian Imperial Bank of Commerce (CIBC)
Capstead Mortgage Corp.
CRIIMI MAE
Duke Realty Investments Inc.
Entergy Corp.
Equity Residential Properties
First Commercial Corp.
Green Mountain Power Corp.
Home Properties of New York
IPL Energy
IWC Resources Corp.
Liberty Property Trust
MDS Inc.
National Bank of Canada
Oneok Inc.
Piedmont Natural Gas Co.
Public Service Company of North Carolina Inc.
Redwood Trust Inc.
Telus Inc.
Tenneco Inc.
Thornburg Mortgage Asset
UtiliCorp United Inc.
Westcoast Energy

Other benefits that public companies offer exclusively to their registered shareholders include discounts on travel (British Airways), loans on the value of your stock holdings (Ameritech), and coupons that can be redeemed for product discounts.

10. TEACH YOUR KIDS HOW TO SAVE AND INVEST.

Fee-Free EasyStocks are an unbeatable way to encourage children and young people to invest their allowance or paycheck from a part-time job. Once they are exposed to the awesome benefits of investing in EasyStocks, children and teens may stop and think about whether they really need to buy a DiscMan or a CD player, even if they own shares in Sony, a Fee-Free EasyStock. Let's see how the Michaels family used EasyStocks to interest their children in saving and investing for the future.

LEARN TO EARN

On Saturday morning, after shopping at Wal-Mart with his father, ten-year-old Tommy Michaels eagerly sprinted to the McDonald's located near the back of the giant discount store.

While Tommy was placing his order, Mr. Michaels walked over to the condiment stand and loaded up on ketchup, barbecue sauce, sweet and sour sauce, salt packages, straws, and a pile of napkins. Tommy glanced over at his father with the same stern expression that his teachers often use to single out improper behavior among his classmates.

"Dad, you're gonna mess up my company. If everyone took that much stuff, McDonald's wouldn't do so good," Tommy stated.

A few months before this incident, Tommy's parents introduced him to investing. Mr. and Mrs. Michaels, like all parents, wanted their children to become financially responsible. But how could they ensure their kids wouldn't just take their allowance and newspaper route earnings and run to the arcade? The Michaels agreed that Cindy, 14, and Tommy, 10, weren't too young to start saving and investing for the future.

The Michaels started out by investing in shares of McDonald's, a Fee-Free EasyStock. Every week, Tommy and Cindy were encouraged to contribute a bare minimum of 10% of their allowance toward more shares and their parents invested the balance of McDonald's one hundred dollar monthly minimum requirement for themselves. At the end of the month, the family would calculate how many more shares they could buy, and then make an additional investment. For instance, if each child contributed one dollar per week and McDonald's shares were trading for $65 per share, Tommy and Cindy would be entitled to 0.062 shares within their parents' account ($1 per week × 4 weeks ÷ $65 per share). In this case, Mr. and Mrs. Michaels would have to buy at least $92 in shares for themselves, to fulfill McDonald's monthly minimum requirement.

Now that they owned a stake in the company, Cindy and Tommy would visit the local McDonald's once a week to make sure the company was running smoothly and to keep up with new promotions. It was on one of these regular visits that Tommy became agitated when his father squandered the company's resources and by extension, the returns to its shareholders—Tommy amongst them. Is this ten-year-old or his sister likely to waste his or her money in the future, given that they are now paying attention to the costs and revenues of a Fortune 500 enterprise? Highly unlikely.

Every week, the Michaels family meets around their kitchen table to review their investments and track their growth. They also scout for new EasyStocks to add to the family portfolio by checking if the companies whose products they understand and use offer shares to investors without any fees. (Part Three of this book will show you how to create a portfolio for kids or for yourself.) Their strategy is very similar in style to the one that made Peter Lynch the most successful mutual fund manager years ago and Warren Buffett the most successful investor today. The strategy led the family to make additional investments in Wal-Mart, their favorite store; Compaq Computers, because they own one; Mattel—need I say more? and Disney, "the 'funnest' place on the planet," among other companies.

By investing regularly in these companies, Cindy and Tommy started thinking about gains that could be made by investing in more shares, which puts them on the road to becoming responsible consumers and smart savers in the future. This is also a great way to get kids to save for college or university!

Teachers, too, can use EasyStocks in their classrooms to help their students learn about budgeting, how the stock market works, and how they can save for college. If you are a parent or grandparent, elementary or high school teacher, visit our website at www.easyinvesting.com to obtain free information on how you can bring the EasyStocks program to your classroom. Kids and parents can also go to www.easyinvesting.com/kids.html to get some additional tips and budgeting guides for teaching your children to save, invest, donate, and become an educated consumer.

PART TWO

Getting Started With Fee-Free EasyBonds™

So far, you have discovered how to invest directly in blue-chip stocks, bypassing a traditional broker. But even the most aggressive investor should own some bonds and other debt instruments. So how can you buy bonds without paying any fees? As usual, it's a lot easier than you might think. After reading this section, you will know how to:

- invest in Treasury securities without paying brokerage fees.
- make more money by investing in Fee-Free EasyBonds than with bond mutual funds.
- start buying bonds, bills, and notes with $1,000 or more.
- earn interest that is exempt from state and local U.S. taxes (but not Canadian tax).
- simplify your record keeping.
- convert your current Treasury bonds, bills, and notes to your EasyBonds account through the Treasury Direct Program.
- reinvest your securities without paying any fees.
- receive interest payments directly into your U.S. bank account.

WHAT ARE EASYBONDS?

When an investor buys a bond, bill, or note from the U.S. Treasury, he or she is making a loan to the U.S. government. The money raised is used for paying off maturing debt and for raising funds to operate the government's bureaucracy. Fee-Free EasyBonds™ is simply a term that I coined, which refers to bonds that anyone in any country can buy directly from the U.S. government through their Treasury Direct Program. There is no difference between these bonds and any other treasury security that you can buy through a broker—with the exception that you never pay fees to buy or reinvest securities with the U.S. Treasury. To get started, you need a checking account in a bank within the United States and a thousand dollars to invest.

Before we go on, it is important to understand the different types of securities that are offered by the U.S. Treasury to investors:

Treasury Bonds are long-term obligations of the U.S. government that have a term longer than ten years and that bear a stated interest rate to the holder who receives semi-annual payments.

Treasury Bills are short-term government obligations that are issued with a term of one year or less. Treasury Bills are sold at a discount to par or face value and do not pay interest before maturity. The interest earned on the bill is equal to the difference between the cost paid and the maturity price, or par. All bills are sold in increments of $1,000. (Before 1998, the minimum was much higher.)

Treasury Notes are mid-term obligations of the U.S. government with a term of more than one year but no more than ten years, and like bonds, they bear a stated interest rate to the holder who receives semi-annual payments. For more information on other notes, see the Auction Schedule below. (Notes are sold in increments of $1,000. Before 1998, the minimum was much higher.)

Inflation-Indexed Securities offer long-term investors the ability to own a security that keeps pace with inflation. The Treasury pays holders of this security interest on an inflation-adjusted principal amount. Every six months, interest is paid based on a fixed rate, determined at auction. These securities are also sold in increments of $1,000, but with a term to be announced at auction.

Treasury securities are sold at an auction, only on the dates listed in the following chart. Your money can only be invested at the auction date.

HOW TO GET IN THE GAME

To get started investing in Fee-Free EasyBonds, you can call Treasury Direct at 1-800-366-3144 or visit their website at www.publicdebt.treas.gov to get the required forms to start. You can also visit www.easyinvesting.com to download the forms required to open an account or submit a purchase bid, if you wish. When the forms arrive, just fill out the tender and send a check to your nearest servicing office before the scheduled auction date.

Treasury Direct Auction Information

	Term/Type	Minimum	Multiples	Auction
Treasury Bond	30-Year Bond	$1,000	$1,000	Feb. and Aug.
	Inflation-Indexed Securities	$1,000	$1,000	Jan., April, July, Oct.
Treasury Notes	10-Year Note	$1,000	$1,000	Feb., May, Aug., Nov.
	5-Year Note	$1,000	$1,000	Late in Each Month
	3-Year Note	$1,000	$1,000	Feb., May, Aug., Nov.
	2-Year Note	$1,000	$1,000	Late in Each Month
Treasury Bills	52-Week Bill	$1,000	$1,000	Every Fourth Thursday
	26-Week Bill	$1,000	$1,000	Every Monday
	13-Week Bill	$1,000	$1,000	Every Monday

The following example—which describes how to fill out the above form—should make it easier for you to open an account. Each step corresponds to the numbers on the Treasury Direct form:

STEP ONE: BID INFORMATION

Jane Smith decided that she wanted to invest $1,000 in five-year notes. In the first section of the form, she wrote in the Par Amount of $1,000 U.S. dollars. Since Jane is not a bond market pro—who really is?—she opted for a Non-Competitive Bid, which means that she will accept the prevailing interest rate that is determined by the Treasury auction.

STEP TWO: TREASURY DIRECT ACCOUNT NUMBER

As an investor who wants to open a new account, Jane will simply leave this section blank and an account number will be provided for her and included in her regular account statements. The next time she wants more Treasury securities, she will enter her account number in this space.

Treasury Bill, Note & Bond Tender

PD F 5381
Department of the Treasury
Bureau of the Public Debt

OMB No. 1535-0069

TREASURY DIRECT®

TREASURY BILL, NOTE & BOND TENDER

For Tender Instructions, See PD F 5382

TYPE OR PRINT IN INK ONLY – TENDERS WILL NOT BE ACCEPTED WITH ALTERATIONS OR CORRECTIONS

1. BID INFORMATION *Tender amount must meet or exceed the minimum for the term selected below. (Must Be Completed)*

Par Amount: $

Bid Type: *(Fill in One)*
- ◯ Noncompetitive
- ◯ Competitive at ___.___ %
(Bill bids must end in 0 or 5.)

DEPARTMENT USE
TENDER NO.
RECEIVED BY/DATE

2. TREASURY DIRECT ACCOUNT NUMBER
(If NOT furnished, a new account will be opened.)

3. TAXPAYER ID NUMBER *(Must Be Completed)*
Social Security Number (First-Named Owner) OR Employer ID Number

ENTERED BY

APPROVED BY

4. TERM SELECTION *(Fill in One)*
(Must Be Completed)

Treasury Bill
$10,000 Minimum — Circle the Number of Reinvestments

- ◯ 13-Week.........0 1 2 3 4 5 6 7 8
- ◯ 26-Week.........0 1 2 3 4
- ◯ 52-Week.........0 1 2

Treasury Note/Bond
$5,000 Minimum
- ◯ 2-Year Note
- ◯ 3-Year Note

$1,000 Minimum
- ◯ 5-Year Note
- ◯ 10-Year Note
- ◯ 30-Year Bond
- ◯ Inflation-Indexed ______ Term

5. ACCOUNT NAME Please Type or Print! *(Must Be Completed)*

ISSUE DATE

CUSIP 912794-

CUSIP 912827-

CUSIP 912810-

6. ADDRESS *(For new account or if changed.)* ◯ **New Address?**

City State ZIP Code

FOREIGN

BACKUP

REVIEW

7. TELEPHONE NUMBERS *(For new account or if changed.)* ◯ **New Phone Number?**

Work ( ) - Home ( ) -

8. DIRECT DEPOSIT INFORMATION *(For new account only.)* **Changes? Submit PD F 5178.**

Routing Number

Financial Institution Name

Account Number

Name on Account

Account Type: *(Fill in One)* ◯ Checking ◯ Savings

9. PURCHASE METHOD
(Must Be Completed)

- ◯ ***Automatic Withdrawal*** (Existing Treasury Direct Account Only)
- ◯ Cash: $
- ◯ Checks: $
  $
- ◯ Securities: $

Total Payment Attached: $

CHECKS ARE DEPOSITED IMMEDIATELY

CHECK #

10. AUTHORIZATION *(Must Be Completed – Original Signature Required)*

Tender Submission: I submit this tender pursuant to the provisions of Department of the Treasury Circulars, Public Debt Series Nos. 2-86 (31 CFR Part 357) and 1-93 (31 CFR Part 356), and the applicable offering announcement. As the first-named owner and under penalties of perjury, I certify that the number shown on this form is my correct taxpayer identification number and that I am not subject to backup withholding because (1) I have not been notified that I am subject to backup withholding as a result of a failure to report all interest or dividends, or (2) the Internal Revenue Service has notified me that I am no longer subject to backup withholding. I further certify that all other information provided on this form is true, correct and complete.

Automatic Withdrawal: (If using this purchase method.) I authorize a debit to my account at the financial institution I designated in TREASURY DIRECT to pay for this security. I understand that the purchase price will be charged to my account on or after the settlement date. I also understand that if this transaction cannot be successfully completed, my tender can be rejected and the transaction canceled. If there is a dispute, a copy of this authorization may be provided to my financial institution.

Signature(s) Date

SEE BACK FOR PRIVACY ACT AND PAPERWORK REDUCTION ACT NOTICE

STEP THREE: TAXPAYER ID NUMBER

Next, Jane wrote her social security number (SSN) in the boxes provided. If she were a resident alien, non-resident alien, or non-U.S. investor, the Internal Revenue Service would not require her to fill this section in. However, U.S. partnerships, companies, organizations, and trusts investing in treasury securities should include the employer identification number provided by the IRS.

STEP FOUR: TERM SELECTION

Once those sections were filled out, Jane noted on the form that she was interested in five-year notes by checking the box which specified the term she desired. Although the minimum investment amounts have been lowered to $1,000, the forms have not been changed to reflect this and may still show different minimum investment amounts, so just disregard those. Also, had she requested Treasury bills, Jane could have opted for as many as eight reinvestments, by checking in the appropriate circle. That way, she would be entitled to the current market rate whenever her T-Bills came due. There is no charge for this service.

STEP FIVE: ACCOUNT NAME

Then, she wrote her full name, Jane Margaret Smith, in this field. If Jane had already had an account, she would rewrite her name exactly as it appears on her past statements. Accounts may also be opened for two individuals, an estate, a trust, a corporation, an association, or a natural guardian using this field on the form.

STEP SIX: ADDRESS

Since she doesn't have a Treasury Direct account yet, Jane must include her full mailing address.

STEP SEVEN: TELEPHONE NUMBERS

Jane must also include a phone number, with area code, where she can be reached during business hours. The Bureau of Public Debt requests that you provide this information just in case you fill the form out incorrectly.

STEP EIGHT: DIRECT DEPOSIT INFORMATION

This next important step will ensure that Jane gets her interest payments quickly and without having to run to the bank every few months. (Remember, all interest payments to you are done by direct deposit into your U.S. bank account. Currently, the Treasury Direct program will not allow direct debits from non-U.S. accounts and from accounts in foreign branches of U.S. banks.) First, she filled in her bank's ABA routing number, the nine-digit number that is located at the bottom left corner of her check. Then, she filled in her financial institution's full name, Bank of New York, and her name as it appears on her bank statements, Jane M. Smith. Lastly, Jane filled in her account number, and specified that it is a checking account. As an added precaution, she included a voided check with the application form.

STEP NINE: PURCHASE METHOD

Now Jane entered the total payment being submitted, $1,000, and specified that she was paying by check. In the future, when she has an account set up, Jane can opt to make a direct withdrawal from her bank account. Cash payments, it should be noted, can only be presented in person, while any other payment can be mailed. Treasury securities that are maturing on or before the issue date are also an acceptable form of payment.

STEP TEN: AUTHORIZATION

Once all the above sections were complete, Jane signed on the dotted line, indicating today's date. She retained the customer copy—the last page of the form—as her receipt and sent the original to the Federal Reserve Bank or Branch in her area. To obtain this address, she referred to the list of servicing offices at the back of this book. (Foreign residents with an American bank account can send their form to the Federal Reserve Bank or Branch closest to them.)

Once Ms. Smith opens an account, she will receive a confirmation of accepted tenders in the mail, confirming the deposit of securities to her account. Since she also holds Treasury securities outside of her new account, she plans to add them into her new Treasury Direct account. Termed a Smart Exchange by the people at the Bureau of Public Debt, this free service enables you to consolidate your government securities easily and encourages you to remain a disciplined investor. For more information, request a Security Transfer Form by calling 1-800-366-3144 or visit www.easyinvesting.com.

TAXES AND OTHER NUISANCES

Unfortunately, once you start investing in EasyBonds or any other security, your obligation to pay taxes to the government does not end. Treasury securities, like everything else in life, are subject to federal taxes, including income, estate, gift, or excise taxes. Additionally, foreign investors may be liable for foreign withholding taxes. However, interest earned on Treasury securities is exempt from state and local taxes. Each year, the Bureau of Public Debt reports to the Internal Revenue Service all interest earned by an account holder and the par amount of all matured securities.

As with any other freebie, there are a couple of minor strings attached. When you want to sell a Treasury security that has not yet come due, a $34 fee will be deducted from your transaction. The Bureau of Public Debt will act as your broker, selling your security on the open market and transferring the funds into your bank account.

This final nuisance is somewhat easier to swallow than interest income taxes or early-seller fees, since it only applies to investors whose Treasury Direct account balance exceeds $100,000 in value. In such a case, your account will be subject to a not-so-hefty $25 fee—that's 0.025% or less—in May of each year.

THREE BENEFITS FOR EASY INVESTORS

Now that you know how the Treasury Direct program works, you are probably quite excited to start investing in these Fee-Free EasyBonds without paying any fees. To fan the flame, here are some of the major advantages to this investment approach that haven't been discussed in detail or that should be expanded further:

1. Start investing with $1,000.
2. Make more money with EasyBonds than with bond mutual funds.
3. "Ladder" your portfolio for the best results.

1. START INVESTING WITH $1,000.

Stockbrokers often require account minimums in the thousands of dollars, though many bond mutual funds will lower their initial requirements if you commit to investing on a regular basis. Until 1998, the Treasury Direct program only allowed investors to make an initial purchase of

$1,000 on five-, ten-, and thirty-year securities. Mid-term notes carried a minimum investment of $5,000 and short-term Treasury bills were out of the reach of many investors, with a $10,000 minimum.

But now, any Treasury security can be purchased in increments of $1,000 without any fees. This recent revision is just a testament to how popular the program has become with individual investors. The government doesn't give out too many freebies, so when they do, you'd be foolish not to take them up on the offer.

2. MAKE MORE MONEY WITH EASYBONDS THAN WITH BOND MUTUAL FUNDS.

In Part One, I showed you how much sense it makes to invest in individual blue-chip EasyStocks, instead of buying mutual fund units. Similarly, you will *make more money* by investing in Fee-Free EasyBonds than you can with a government bond mutual fund, comprised of the very same securities that you'd invest in through the Treasury Direct program. To illustrate this point, let's refer back to Adam Smyth, our fictional Easy Investor. Adam knew that a traditional broker might charge him up to two percent to buy and sell government bonds. But he was unsure how much more money he could make by investing in EasyBonds himself instead of parking his money in a similar U.S. government bond fund, managed by a top-ranked mutual fund company.

THE FEE-FREE EASYBONDS ADVANTAGE

How much *more money* can you expect to make with EasyBonds than with mutual funds? Adam Smyth assumed the following in his basic comparison between U.S. government bond funds and EasyBonds:

- $10,000 will be invested today into mutual funds and another $10,000 will be invested into Fee-Free EasyBonds.
- The investment will grow at the annual rate of 6.5%.
- All interest payments will be reinvested.
- The portfolio will be held for thirty years.

- Fee-Free EasyBonds will not charge any commissions, while the bond fund will charge a 1.25% fee, calculated at the end of each year.

Given these assumptions, Mr. Smyth calculated that if he made a $10,000 investment in mutual funds, it would be worth $45,352.51 after growing for thirty years, less 1.25% in fees each year. But he was astounded to discover that the same $10,000 invested into a portfolio of Fee-Free EasyBonds would be worth $66,143.66 thirty years later—46% more money than what the mutual fund would be worth. His portfolio of EasyBonds, which he created by following the instructions on how to ladder your portfolio on page 46, had the same return before expenses as the mutual fund's portfolio, but the total returns to Smyth would be $20,791.15 greater! (See charts on pages 44 to 46.)

As with equity mutual funds, the management expenses for government bond funds significantly decrease an investor's share of gains. If Smyth were to earn a 6.5% return on his bond fund, then a 1.25% annual fee reduces his annual return to only 5.25% before inflation (6.5% return - 1.25% fees = 5.25% return after fees). That means the mutual fund company keeps over 19% of his gains as its annual fees for the year (1.25% overall management fee ÷ 6.5% return × 100% = 19.23% fees as percentage of year's return).

In fact, after thirty years of 6.5% compounded growth, a U.S. government bond fund with annual fees of 1.25%, will have charged a total of $9,105.30 in fees on an initial investment of only $10,000. Worse, the foregone earnings associated with paying the fees would amount to $11,685.83. All these factors, Adam Smyth concluded, make investing in EasyBonds more financially rewarding than investing in U.S. government bond funds, assuming the EasyBonds' performance meets or beats the mutual fund's performance before fees.

As you can see in the graph on the next page, the financial returns posted by a portfolio of EasyBonds keep increasing substantially, while the bond mutual fund gains minus fees are not as impressive.

The following charts compare the returns of U.S. government bond mutual funds and Fee-Free EasyBonds growing at the same annual rate, over thirty years.

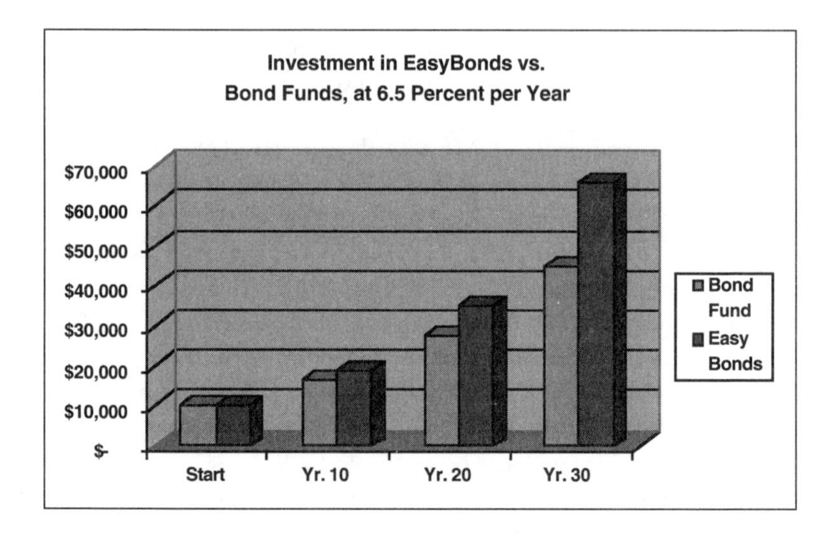

$10,000 GROWING AT 6.5% ANNUALLY OVER 30 YEARS

A) Invested in Mutual Funds (1.25% in Annual Fees)

Year	Start ($)	Gains ($)	Fees ($)	Finish ($)
1	**10,000**	650	133	10,517
2	10,517	684	140	11,060
3	11,060	719	147	11,632
4	11,632	756	155	12,233
5	12,233	795	163	12,866
6	12,866	836	171	13,531
7	13,531	879	180	14,230
8	14,230	925	189	14,966
9	14,966	973	199	15,739
10	15,739	1,023	210	16,553
11	16,553	1,076	220	17,408
12	17,408	1,132	232	18,308
13	18,308	1,190	244	19,254
14	19,254	1,252	256	20,249
15	20,249	1,316	270	21,296
16	21,296	1,384	284	22,397
17	22,397	1,456	298	23,555

18	23,555	1,531	314	24,772
19	24,772	1,610	330	26,052
20	26,052	1,693	347	27,399
21	27,399	1,781	365	28,815
22	28,815	1,873	384	30,305
23	30,305	1,970	403	31,871
24	31,871	2,072	424	33,518
25	33,518	2,179	446	35,251
26	35,251	2,291	469	37,073
27	37,073	2,410	494	38,989
28	38,989	2,534	519	41,004
29	41,004	2,665	546	43,124
30	43,124	2,803	574	**45,353**

B) Invested In Fee-Free EasyBonds

Year	Start ($)	Gains ($)	Fees ($)	Finish ($)
1	**10,000**	650	–	10,650
2	10,650	692	–	11,342
3	11,342	737	–	12,079
4	12,079	785	–	12,865
5	12,865	836	–	13,701
6	13,701	891	–	14,591
7	14,591	948	–	15,540
8	15,540	1,010	–	16,550
9	16,550	1,076	–	17,626
10	17,626	1,146	–	18,771
11	18,771	1,220	–	19,992
12	19,992	1,299	–	21,291
13	21,291	1,384	–	22,675
14	22,675	1,474	–	24,149
15	24,149	1,570	–	25,718
16	25,718	1,672	–	27,390
17	27,390	1,780	–	29,170
18	29,170	1,896	–	31,067
19	31,067	2,019	–	33,086

20	33,086	2,151	–	35,236
21	35,236	2,290	–	37,527
22	37,527	2,439	–	39,966
23	39,966	2,598	–	42,564
24	42,564	2,767	–	45,331
25	45,331	2,946	–	48,277
26	48,277	3,138	–	51,415
27	51,415	3,342	–	54,757
28	54,757	3,559	–	58,316
29	58,316	3,791	–	62,107
30	62,107	4,037	–	**66,144**

Recall that each year a 1.25% annual expense fee diminishes the mutual fund investor's gains. This fee lowers the amount of money available for investing the following year, thereby decreasing the investor's total return. Over thirty years, $10,000 invested in a U.S. government bond fund generated $9,105.30 in management fees that were paid to the mutual fund company, to arrive at the total value of $45,352.51.

On the other hand, Adam Smyth and other Easy Investors never pay a cent in management fees or commissions to maintain their Treasury Direct accounts. Since no commissions are taken out of the account, the full amount of money each year grows at the 6.5% forecasted annual rate, for thirty years. This investor's EasyStocks portfolio would be worth $66,143.66 after thirty years—almost 50% more than a comparable bond mutual fund could be worth. Once again, the Easy Investor triumphs over the no-load mutual fund investor.

3. "LADDER" YOUR PORTFOLIO FOR THE BEST RESULTS.
Generally speaking, as you move into longer maturity dates, from a two-year note to a ten-year note, for example, your yield will increase but so will your interest rate volatility—price swings due to rising or falling interest rates. If interest rates come down, the value of longer-term Treasury securities increases. On the other hand, rising interest rates will have an opposite, negative effect.

So what's an Easy Investor to do? Well, the smartest strategy when investing in stocks is to spread your available cash into regular, periodic investments. That way, you can take advantage of lower prices when the stock market suffers short-term ills, and can avoid investing too much money when prices are high. Similarly, by scheduling or "laddering" your investments in EasyBonds, you can take advantage of higher yields when bond prices fall. This strategy will also allow you to avoid reinvesting all your securities when bond prices are at a high and the yields are at a low.

Laddering your portfolio is a widely accepted method for "diversifying" your maturity dates and protecting yourself against wild interest rate swings. To ladder, simply invest equal amounts in 26-week, 52-week, two-year, three-year, and five-year treasuries. Six months later, invest the same amounts in 52-week, two-year, three-year, and five-year treasuries once again. That way, a security matures almost every six months and the resulting amount can be reinvested into a five-year note when it comes due.

JACOB'S LADDER

For example, Jacob decides to ladder his EasyBonds to protect himself from short-term interest rate swings, committing just under $8,000. Jacob starts by mailing the appropriate Treasury Direct forms with a check to one of the servicing offices whose address he located in Part Four of this book. He purchased $1,000 par value in each of the following securities:

26-week bills
52-week bills
two-year notes
three-year notes
five-year notes

Jacob's total investment so far is just under $5,000, since T-Bills (treasury bills) are sold for less than par and return the par value to investors. Now, Jacob has $3,000 left, which he will also invest in Fee-Free EasyBonds through Treasury Direct. Six months later, once the investment in 26-week bills comes due, the proceeds are wired into Jacob's bank account. He now has about $4,000 left to invest in Treasuries ($3,000 + $1,000 = $4,000). Following the laddering rule, Jacob invests the left-over $4,000 equally by purchasing $1,000 in par value of:

52-week bills
two-year notes
three-year notes
five-year notes

As a result, Jacob's portfolio is properly laddered and one of his securities will mature, on average, every six months. From now on, when any one of his treasury securities matures, Jacob will reinvest the $1,000 par value into a five-year note. (The interest is automatically wired into his bank account.) Note: If Jacob had less money initially to invest in EasyBonds, he could have laddered his bonds by investing only in 52-week bills, 2-year notes, 3-year notes, and 5-year notes.

Laddering ensures that your notes will never yield significantly less or more than current rates since part of your portfolio regularly comes due. Financial planners do not often implement this strategy since the frequent reinvestments would trigger frequent commission charges, frustrating their clients. The laddering strategy is akin to dollar-cost averaging, but uses bonds instead of stocks and interest yields instead of capital gains. As an Easy Investor, you never pay a commission to reinvest your securities, so you can lock in higher yields if rates increase in a few months, taking advantage of lower bond prices to increase the average overall yield in your EasyBond portfolio. Overall, you are never attempting to time the market, just as with stocks. (Even Wall Street gurus have experienced little success and much frustration with market timing.) Regular payments spread out over time will usually shield you from short-term ups and downs in interest rates.

PART THREE

Putting It All Together

In Part One, you learned what Fee-Free EasyStocks are and how you can profit by owning them. In Part Two, you discovered how to participate in the easiest and most profitable way to own Treasury bonds, bills, and notes—the world's lowest-risk investment. But to maintain a regular investment program, you must be able to successfully integrate your stocks and bonds into a portfolio. In this section, it all comes together. You will learn how simple it is to create an Easy Portfolio and how to:

- keep a healthy balance between EasyStocks and EasyBonds.
- select EasyStocks for price performance.
- determine whether to "ladder" your EasyBonds.
- introduce investing to your children and grandchildren.
- invest for your retirement, whether you live in the U.S. or Canada.
- profit from companies that will benefit from an aging population.
- diversify overseas into international EasyStocks.

STOCKS OR BONDS? BOTH

One of the first things you probably think about when you start investing is: "How much money should I allocate to stocks and how much money should I allocate to bonds?" While the question may seem simple enough, Wall Street strategists can't even seem to agree on this one. One strategy that seems to work well is to "invest your age" in bonds, taking it as a percentage that you will subtract from your total investment dollars. Then invest the rest in stocks. So if you are forty-two years old, you will invest roughly 40% in bonds and 60% in stocks. By the time you reach sixty-five, your ideal asset allocation should be closer to 65% bonds and 35% stocks.

The only exception to this rule would be for investors at extreme ends of the age spectrum. A twelve-year-old junior capitalist whose parents got him interested in the stock market cannot be expected to own 10-12% of his portfolio in bonds. Likewise, an eighty-year-old investor may sleep better at night if her entire portfolio is held in Fee-Free EasyBonds.

You can also decide how much of your portfolio should be invested in stocks vs. bonds by figuring out what your time horizon is—when you actually need the money. To accomplish this, take the same age rule as above, but modify it to fit your needs. For instance, Susan Young is forty-two years old but wants to retire by age fifty-five. As a result, Susan's needs and investment requirements will differ from another investor her age who doesn't plan to retire for another twenty-five years.

Aside from investing larger amounts of money to reach her financial goals, Susan should start paring back the riskier stock allocation in her portfolio as she makes the change from living off her income to living off her investments. So when she's fifty, Susan might only be 35-40% invested in the EasyStocks, compared to other investors her age, who might be 50% invested in the stock market.

SELECTING FEE-FREE EASYSTOCKS

Once you have determined how much of your money will be allocated to stocks and how much will go towards bonds, you need to choose individual stocks in which to invest. I do not hold a magical key for selecting superior long-term performers but I can recommend two excellent investment guides that will show you how to choose stocks in general—including Fee-Free EasyStocks—for superior long-term peformance. *The Intelligent Investor*, by Benjamin Graham, with an introduction by Warren Buffett, is probably the third best investment you could ever make—after Fee-Free EasyStocks themselves and this book. Graham states that you should only invest in large companies with a stable earnings growth and dividend record, as well as a low Price/Earnings or P/E ratio—the ratio of the share price to its earnings per share.

Another must-read for anyone who plans to make serious money in EasyStocks is *What Works on Wall Street* by James P. O'Shaughnessy. He studied thirty years of S&P Compustat data (Standard & Poor's historical records for every publicly listed U.S. stock) to prove that the stock market rewards some investment strategies, while it punishes others. O'Shaughnessy found, among other things, that you can do much better than the S&P 500 by concentrating on large, well-known stocks with high dividend yields. (These findings, in fact, verified some of Benjamin Graham's investment rules.) Fee-Free EasyStocks are a great investment because most are large, well-known companies that pay regular dividends.

One final book that should be mentioned is *The Wealthy Barber* by David Chilton, which is very helpful for first-time investors. Books aside, you can also find suitable EasyStocks for your portfolio by following some of the stock screening tools from Investor's Business Daily (1-800-306-9744 in the U.S. and www.investors.com) or the Value Line Investment Survey. (1-800-634-3583 and www.valueline.com). You can research stocks for free by going to the Yahoo! Personal Finance section at www.yahoo.com, where you will find quotes, charts, SEC filings, company profiles, research, and insider sales reports. Other excellent research sites include www.hoovers.com for company profiles, www.zacks.com for analyst coverage, www.edgar-online.com for U.S. company filings, and www.sedar.com for Canadian company filings to securities regulators. Further, TheStreet.com provides excellent stock market commentary by seasoned Wall Street pros and Multex.com offers free and pay-per-view analyst reports for downloading. Canadians will also find Quicken.ca quite useful. If you want to check for changes to a company's EasyStock plan, there is no better place to go than www.netstockdirect.com. And for more money-saving tips for investors, links to all the above-noted websites, and free e-mail notification of new Fee-Free EasyStock plans, surf over to www.easyinvesting.com.

CHOOSING BETWEEN BONDS, BILLS, AND NOTES

Now that your EasyStocks allocation is under way, you need to focus on the EasyBonds portion of your portfolio. Again, through the Treasury Direct program, anyone in any country can invest in U.S. Treasuries without paying a broker's commission, if they have a U.S. bank account.

If you are a Canadian citizen and you have a bank account with a U.S. financial institution, you can start investing in EasyBonds through the Treasury Direct program to fill the bonds section of your portfolio. In the likely case that you do not have a bank account in the United States, you can either open one up the next time you're in the country or you can just stick to Canadian bonds. The most cost-effective way to buy Canadian bonds, bills, and notes is through a discount broker such as TD Waterhouse. Discount brokers are also one source for your first share, which is required before you can participate in the EasyStock plans of Canadian companies.

But how do you decide between bonds, bills, and notes? One method for investing in Fee-Free EasyBonds is to simply ask yourself when you need the money that you are saving. If you plan to buy a house or make another large purchase within the next five or six years, invest in a medium term note that will mature when you require the money. If you plan to buy a car within the next year or sooner, get a shorter-term bill. Otherwise, invest in medium-term notes until you have enough capital to ladder the Treasury portion of your portfolio, as described earlier.

JUNIOR CAPITALIST PORTFOLI-YO™

Just as we discussed in Part One, Fee-Free EasyStocks are a great way to get your children or grandchildren interested in saving and investing for the future. Junior Capitalists will slowly understand how the stock market rewards companies that are leaders in their fields.

So what companies should your kids be invested in? Think about where you take them for a quick meal—McDonald's. Think about where you take them every time they grow out of their clothes—Wal-Mart. Think about what toys they play with every day—Mattel's Barbie or Hot Wheels. These are the companies a lot of children are familiar with.

Canadian investors can get their kids saving and investing in Canadian Fee-Free EasyStocks such as Nortel Networks, BCE, and the Bank of Montreal. But there's no reason why international investors should rule out investing in American companies. Any kid would be excited to own a piece of McDonald's or Mattel. (Remember, foreign investors must request a W-8 Certificate of Foreign Status when they enroll in any U.S. EasyStock plan.)

You might want to encourage your kids to invest part of their allowance in a monthly investment plan. Some parents even find it wise to reward their Junior Capitalists by doubling that part of their allowance that is contributed to the plan. Further, companies that offer their shares directly make it easy to give away a share or shares as a gift to a friend or relative. Though you should always conduct your own research before you invest, the following well-run companies certainly have excellent long-term investment potential for kids and their parents alike. Each one is part of the Fortune 500 and the S&P 500 Index:

Wal-Mart Stores Inc. (NYSE: WMT) is a great start for any portfoli-yo (or portfolio) since you can invest in this EasyStock for just $250 and make monthly investments of $50 or more. The company is the world's largest retailer, operating more than 3,400 Wal-Marts, Sam's Clubs, and Wal-Mart Supercenters around the world. Wal-Mart is part of the Dow Jones Industrial Average.

McDonald's Corp. (NYSE: MCD) is another great company for you and your kids to own. Though the minimum investment is steep at $1,000, the company will waive it if you decide to partake in its $50-minimum monthly automatic investment program, where the funds are debited directly from your bank account. The company is the world's number one fast-food chain, operating more than 23,000 restaurants worldwide and commanding a 42% share of the U.S. fast-food market. McDonald's is part of the Dow Jones Industrial Average.

Mattel Inc. (NYSE: MAT) is the number one toy marketer in the world, making it an obvious choice for any kid's portfoli-yo! For a minimum investment of $500, you and your kids can own part of a company whose major brands include Barbie, Fisher-Price, the Disney lines, Hot Wheels, Matchbox, Cabbage Patch Kids, Skip-Bo, and UNO.

Walt Disney Co. (NYSE: DIS) is a company you should consider owning, if you can swallow the investment minimum of $1,000. Disney is the world's second-largest media conglomerate, after Time Warner, with interests in TV and movie production, theme parks, publishing companies, professional sports franchises, and television network ABC.

Compaq Computer Corp. (NYSE: CPQ) is one final name you might consider, for an initial investment of $250 or more. The company is the number one PC maker in the world, and it recently acquired Digital Equipment to further capture market share.

RETIRE IN STYLE WITH EASYSTOCKS

One of the major reasons people are investing today is to prepare for retirement—even if that goal may be twenty or thirty years away. The Individual Retirement Account (IRA) in the United States and the Registered Retirement Savings Plan (RRSP) in Canada allow individuals to delay paying taxes on their investments until they are withdrawn from the plan decades later. But how do you incorporate Fee-Free EasyStocks into one of these retirement accounts?

Canadian investors can also incorporate Fee-Free EasyStocks into their retirement accounts, even though no Canadian EasyStock offers an RRSP plan for their investors. The process for adding Canadian and U.S. EasyStocks to your RRSP—termed a contribution-in-kind—is easy as one, two, three.

STEP ONE: INVEST

First, make an investment in a Canadian or international EasyStock.

STEP TWO: WITHDRAW

Inform the company's transfer agent that you would like a certain number of whole shares, equivalent in value to the amount you plan to contribute to your RRSP, withdrawn from your EasyStock plan. The share certificates are like a check since they are registered to you but can be signed over to a third party. Be sure to leave some shares in the plan to maintain your account.

STEP THREE: ENDORSE

Finally, when you receive your share certificate in the mail, endorse it to a discount broker to be placed in your self-directed RRSP account.

For example, Michael Wong has $6,500 of contribution room within his RRSP, which has a total current value of $53,000 and no foreign content. He already owned shares in EasyStocks BCE and General Electric outside of his RRSP, so he moved to step two. Michael sent a fax to Montreal Trust, BCE's transfer agent, and informed them well before the RRSP deadline to mail him a certificate for seventy shares.

When his share certificate arrived in the mail, Michael took it to his local Action Direct branch within the Royal Bank. He wasn't sure how to endorse it to Action Direct within his self-directed RRSP account, so the manager of the bank showed him where to sign the stock certificate. Once that was accomplished, the BCE shares were placed into his RRSP account. A few days later, Michael received a tax receipt for his contribution-in-kind. He followed the same process with his General Electric shares.

The downside to this procedure is that Revenue Canada considers a contribution-in-kind to be a sale of your shares. So if Michael purchased EasyStock in BCE for an average price of $47.50 and it was trading at $50.00 when he transferred seventy shares into his RRSP, then he must pay taxes on the capital gains for those seventy shares. (capital gains tax on the $175 gain). On the other hand, if his shares dropped to $45.00 before he made the contribution-in-kind, he would not be entitled to claim a capital loss for those shares.

When it comes to adding EasyStocks to their retirement funds, American investors are presented with two choices. First, you can look for a trustee that will administer a self-directed IRA that contains Fee-Free EasyStocks. One such company is First Trust Corp., (1-800-426-6242 and www.firsttrust.com), which also administers The Low-Cost Plan IRA for members of the National Association of Investors Corporation (NAIC). Otherwise, you can invest in the EasyStocks that offer an IRA program for their investors. The following companies offer an IRA option as part of their EasyStock plan:

Allstate Corp.
Ameritech Corp.
Atmos Energy Corp.
Bell Atlantic Corp.
Chrysler Corp.
Connecticut Energy Corp.
Connecticut Water Service, Inc.
Exxon Corp.
Fannie Mae
Lucent Technologies Inc.
McDonald's Corp.
MCN Energy Group, Inc.
MidSouth Bancorp, Inc.
Mobil Corp.
Morton International, Inc.
Philadelphia Suburban Corp.
Sears, Roebuck and Co.
UtiliCorp United Inc.

Nevertheless, for American and Canadian investors alike, incorporating Fee-Free EasyStocks into a retirement account can be one of the most financially rewarding investments you ever make. Not only will you make tax-deferred capital gains if your shares increase in value, but you'll also save thousands of dollars in brokerage commissions over the life of your account. If you saved just $75 in commissions each year—a very conservative estimate—then over thirty years, with your money growing at 10% per year, your retirement fund would be worth an additional $13,570.76. Who said there's no such thing as free money?

DEMOGRAPHIC INVESTING WITH EASYSTOCKS

You're probably sick of hearing how the Baby Boom will transform the international economy in the coming years. But have you ever thought about how to profit from the aging population? An investment strategy that is increasingly followed by investment firms and mutual fund managers is to pinpoint the companies that are most likely to benefit from these demographic changes.

Boom, Bust and Echo: How to Profit from the Coming Demographic Shift, is a recent book by David K. Foot. He argues that an aging population presents opportunities for investment in financial services companies, travel firms, and health care stocks, among others. It makes sense; as people reach their peak earning years, they start saving and investing more money for retirement.

This means more money for stockbrokers and more money for the investors who own shares in EasyStocks such as American Express and Morgan Stanley, Dean Witter & Company. Later, as the bulk of the population enters their senior years, demand for health care and pharmaceuticals will rise dramatically. That means more money for drug companies such as Merck and Lilly—and, according to the theory, for their investors.

Since demographic investing has become a more widely used strategy, some related EasyStock companies have already seen their shares rise. That said, you might want to add some of the following stocks to your Easy Portfolio if the price is compatible with your investment budget:

American Express
Astra AB
AXA-UAP
Bank of Montreal
CIBC
Eli Lilly & Co.
Luxottica Group S.p.A.,
Merck & Co.
Morgan Stanley, Dean Witter & Co.
Pharmacia & Upjohn
SmithKline Beecham
Warner-Lambert Co.
Zeneca Group PLC

Refer to the directory of Fee-Free EasyStocks and the Directory of Canadian Fee-Free EasyStocks for investment details.

Granted, this selection of EasyStock companies looks more like a basket of financial and health care stocks than a diversified portfolio. These stocks would be best utilized as additions to your already existing Easy Portfolio, and not as a starting point. Investing in these firms cannot guarantee you financial success, but they all have powerful demographic trends working in their favor.

INTERNATIONAL INVESTING WITH EASYSTOCKS

Once you have assembled your Easy Portfolio, you might want to consider adding some international stocks, including those that have already been mentioned. European companies are just starting to implement the technology and restructuring programs that have resulted in dramatic profit increases for their North American counterparts. As a result, European EasyStocks might at some point outperform the largest and most respected Dow stocks. Further, some Latin American companies can be purchased for a fraction of the cost of similar North American companies, albeit with added political risk.

All of the international companies—excluding some Canadian firms—listed in the directory in Part Four trade on the New York Stock Exchange as American Depository Receipts (ADR). Here are a few of these international EasyStocks that you might want to research further:

ABN Amro Holdings (Netherlands)
AXA-UAP (France)
Coca-Cola Femsa S.A. de C.V.(Mexico)
Fiat S.p.A. (Italy)
National Westminster Bank PLC (U.K.)
SmithKline Beecham PLC (U.K.)
Telebras HOLDR (Brazil)
Telecom Italia S.p.A. (Italy)
Zeneca Group PLC (U.K.)

Refer to the directory of Fee-Free EasyStocks and the Directory of Canadian Fee-Free EasyStocks for investment details.

For more about international EasyStocks, refer to Part One: Ten Benefits for Easy Investors. It must be noted, however, that international stock markets can be more volatile than North American markets, so investors should exercise caution and conduct thorough research before investing in any of these companies.

I hope you have found this book to be a useful source of financial information and new investment ideas. Early in the book, I showed you how to assemble a $10,000 portfolio of Fee-Free EasyStocks that could be worth $174,494 after thirty years, compared with $88,162 invested in no-load mutual funds, growing at the same rate. You also saw how a $10,000 investment in Fee-Free EasyBonds could grow to $66,144 after thirty years, compared to just $43,353 invested in a U.S. Treasury Bond Fund. I also showed you how to get your kids interested in saving and investing. If you can save just $50 per year by implementing the strategies detailed in this book, and invest that amount at a 10% annual return, you will earn an extra $9,047.17 after thirty years. For help putting together your portfolio or for new money-saving and money-making tips, visit our website at www.easyinvesting.com. You will find links to all the financial information you need to make an informed investment. You can also receive free e-mail notification when new EasyStocks become available to investors.

PART FOUR

Directories

Now that you understand what EasyStocks are and how they function, you obviously want to know which companies offer this unbeatable plan. In this directory, you will find almost five hundred American, Canadian, and international Fee-Free EasyStocks, plus additional information about each company.

USING THE DIRECTORY

Each company's full name, stock ticker symbol, and address are included for your reference. The group of letters that appears before the ticker symbol represents the stock exchange upon which the company is listed. For example, American Express, which is traded on the New York Stock Exchange and has the ticker symbol AXP, will appear in the directory as NYSE: AXP. In contrast, BCE Inc. is listed on the Toronto and New York stock exchanges with the ticker symbol BCE, so it appears in the directory as TSE/NYSE: BCE. For clarification purposes:

- AMEX represents the American Stock Exchange
- NASDAQ represents the NASDAQ Stock Exchange
- NYSE represents the New York Stock Exchange
- TSE represents the Toronto Stock Exchange (Canadian stocks)

The firm's Internet address is also included, if applicable. Further, you can request enrollment forms and an annual report from the company's transfer agent, whose number is listed in this directory. Canadian and international investors, who do not have U.S. social security numbers, should simply press their phone's * key, # key, dial 0, or wait for assistance while on the line with an automated attendant for a U.S. stock. Most importantly, each company's plan differs from the next, so the complete information for each is included in order. Even with this information, you should still request a copy of the prospectus, which describes the company's program.

The following information is provided for each Fee-Free EasyStock listing:

- Initial minimum investment is the amount of money required to enroll in the plan. Usually, this amount is $250 or less for U.S. and international stocks, and one share for Canadian EasyStocks.
- Minimum per month (optional) is the minimum additional investment the company will allow you to make per month. Some companies let you make additional investments each week, but Canadian firms usually allow quarterly investments only.
- Maximum Annual Investment is the maximum amount of money the company will allow you to commit to their investment plan per year. Usually this amount is over $100,000 per EasyStock.
- Whether the company pays cash dividends, allows partial reinvestment, and provides a discount on the reinvestment of dividends or the purchase of more shares.
- If the company offers an Individual Retirement Account (IRA) option for American investors, this information will be stated.
- If the company permits direct debits from your bank account, either for the direct deposit of cash dividends—if you choose not to reinvest them—or for regular monthly investments, this information will also be clearly laid out.
- Some companies' plans allow you to take out a loan by using the value of your shares as collateral. While rare, this option is available in some cases.
- Finally, some companies allow you to enroll online for their Easy Investment Programs, at www.netstockdirect.com. This guide will let you know which ones allow online enrollment. Due to the explosive growth of the Internet, many companies that did not allow online enrollment at the time of publication will likely offer that service in the future. Check www.netstockdirect.com to see if you can view a company's plan materials online, enroll online, or even have the materials mailed to you through an online request.
- Optional Cash purchases denotes whether the company allows you to make additional investments on a monthly, quarterly, or yearly basis.

FIND WHAT YOU'RE LOOKING FOR

To help you find what you're looking for easily, this section has been divided into four parts:

- U.S. and International Fee-Free EasyStocks contains all the information on those investment plans. This section begins on page 66.
- Canadian Fee-Free EasyStocks contains all the information on EasyStocks from Canada. These are the only companies that require ownership of one share before you can participate in the plan. This section begins on page 214.
- Fee-Free EasyStocks Listed by Industry Group shows all the EasyStocks, regardless of their country of origin, by their industry classification. This section begins on page 228.
- Fee-Free EasyStocks Listed by Home Country shows all the EasyStocks by their country of origin. This section begins on page 237.

Once again, it is important to note that while great care has been taken to ensure the reliability of this data, you should still read prospectus for each plan before investing. Some companies might make periodic changes to their Easy Investment Plan (which they will likely refer to as a Direct Stock Purchase Plan or a Dividend Reinvestment Program), so take the time to read the information that the company's transfer agent sends you.

The list of Fee-Free EasyStocks is expanding quickly. Some experts are predicting that the number will double within a few years or less. For an updated list of EasyStocks that have been added since publication, visit our Internet site at **www.easyinvesting.com**.

U.S. AND INTERNATIONAL FEE-FREE EASYSTOCKS

ABN AMRO Holdings N.V.
Netherlands: Banking
NYSE: AAN
c/o Morgan Guaranty Trust Company
PO Box 9073
Boston, MA 02205-9948
www.abnamro.com

ABN Amro Holdings is the Netherlands' biggest bank and the largest foreign bank with branches in the U.S. and Japan, providing standard commercial banking services from about 1,700 branches worldwide.

Phone to enroll:
Morgan Guaranty Trust Company
800-997-8970

EasyStock Investment Plan:
- Initial minimum investment: $250
- Minimum per month (optional): $50
- Maximum annual investment: $100,000
- No cash dividends paid.
- Partial dividend reinvestment.
- No discount is available.
- No IRA option is available.
- Optional cash purchases allowed.
- Direct debits are available.

ABT Building Products Corp.
United States: Manufacturing
NASDAQ: ABTC
One Neenah Center, Suite 600
Neenah, WI 54956
www.abtco.com
414-751-8611

ABT Building Products manufactures specialty building supplies and other materials for construction and remodeling.

Phone to enroll:
Harris Bank
800-286-9178

EasyStock Investment Plan:
- Initial minimum investment: $250
- Minimum per month (optional): $50
- Maximum annual investment: $100,000
- No cash dividends paid.
- No partial dividend reinvestment.
- No discount is available.
- No IRA option is available.
- Optional cash purchases allowed.
- Direct debits are available.

Adecco S.A.
Switzerland: Staffing Services
NASDAQ: ADIAY
c/o Morgan Guaranty Trust Company
PO Box 9073
Boston, MA 02205-9948
www.adecco.com

Adecco is one of the two largest employment agencies in the world (the other is Manpower), supplying temporary and permanent personnel to 200,000 clients.

Phone to enroll:
Morgan Guaranty Trust Company
800-997-8970

EasyStock Investment Plan:
- Initial minimum investment: $250
- Minimum per month (optional): $50
- Maximum annual investment: $100,000
- Cash dividends are offered.
- Partial dividend reinvestment.

- No discount is available.
- No IRA option is available.
- Optional cash purchases allowed.
- Direct debits are available.

AEGON N.V.
Netherlands: Insurance
NYSE: AEG
Mariahoeveplein 50, Postbus 202
The Hague 2501 CE
www.aegonrealty.com

AEGON is the Netherlands' second largest insurance company and one of the ten largest in the world, providing service in the Netherlands, Spain, the U.K., and the U.S.

Phone to enroll:
Citibank
800-808-8010

EasyStock Investment Plan:
- Initial minimum investment: $250
- Minimum per month (optional): $50
- Maximum annual investment: $100,000
- Cash dividends are offered.
- Partial dividend reinvestment.
- No discount is available.
- No IRA option is available.
- Optional cash purchases allowed.
- Direct debits are available.

Aetna Inc.
United States: Health care
NYSE: AET
151 Farmington Avenue
Hartford, CT 06156
www.aetna.com
203-273-3977

Aetna is a leader in managed health care, providing group and individual health care products, including standard indemnity, preferred provider plans, and health maintenance organizations. Aetna also sells life and health insurance and financial services abroad through subsidiaries and joint ventures.

Phone to enroll:
First Chicago Trust Company
800-446-2617

EasyStock Investment Plan:
- Initial minimum investment: $500
- Minimum per month (optional): $50
- Maximum annual investment: $250,000
- Cash dividends are offered.
- Partial dividend reinvestment.
- No discount is available.
- No IRA option is available.
- Optional cash purchases allowed.
- Direct debits are available.
- View materials and enroll online at www.netstockdirect.com.

AFLAC, Inc.
United States: Insurance Carriers
NYSE: AFL
1932 Wynnton Road
Columbus, GA 31999
www.aflac.com
706-323-3431

AFLAC sells supplemental medical insurance policies that cover special conditions, primarily cancer. It is America's largest seller of supplemental insurance and the leading cancer-expense insurance company in Japan, which accounts for more than 80% of company revenues.

Phone company to enroll:
800-235-2667

EasyStock Investment Plan:
- Initial minimum investment: $750
- Minimum per month (optional): $50

- Maximum annual investment: $120,000
- Cash dividends are offered.
- Partial dividend reinvestment.
- No discount is available.
- No IRA option is available.
- Optional cash purchases allowed.
- Direct debits are available.

AFP Provida
Chile: Investment Management
NYSE: PVD
c/o Bank of New York
48 Wall Street
New York, NY 10286
www.provida.cl

Administradora de Fondos de Pensiones Provida manages the assets of 5.5 million Chilean workers. With about 20% of the market, AFP Provida is Chile's leading pension fund administrator. Its assets total about $27.5 billion.

Phone to enroll:
Bank of New York
888-BNY-ADRS or 888-269-2377

EasyStock Investment Plan:
- Initial minimum investment: $250
- Minimum per month (optional): $50
- Maximum per transaction: $250,000
- Maximum annual investment: $250,000
- No cash dividends paid.
- Partial dividend reinvestment.
- No discount is available.
- No IRA option is available.
- Optional cash purchases allowed.
- Direct debits are available.

AGL Resources, Inc.
United States: Utilities
NYSE: ATG
303 Peachtree Street NE
Atlanta, GA 30308
www.aglr.com
404-584-3714

AGL Resources is a holding company for Atlanta Gas and Light, a distribution utility that sells natural gas to more than 1.4 million customers in the metropolitan Atlanta area.

Phone to enroll:
Wachovia Bank of North Carolina
800-866-1543

EasyStock Investment Plan:
- Initial minimum investment: $250
- Minimum per month (optional): $25
- Maximum monthly investment: $5,000
- Cash dividends are offered.
- Partial dividend reinvestment.
- No discount is available.
- No IRA option is available.
- Optional cash purchases allowed.
- Direct debits are available.

Air Products and Chemicals, Inc.
United States: Chemicals
NYSE: APD
7201 Hamilton Blvd
Allentown, PA 18195
www.airproducts.com
610-481-4911

Air Products and Chemicals produces industrial gases and chemicals. Gases account for nearly 60% of sales.

Phone to enroll:
First Chicago Trust Company of New York
888-694-9458

EasyStock Investment Plan:

- Initial minimum investment: $500
- Minimum per month (optional): $100
- Maximum annual investment: $200,000
- Cash dividends are offered.
- Partial dividend reinvestment.
- No discount is available.
- No IRA option is available.
- Optional cash purchases allowed.
- Direct debits are available.
- View materials and enroll online at www.netstockdirect.com.

AirTouch Communications, Inc.
United States: Telecommunications
NYSE: ATI
One California Street
San Francisco, CA 94111
www.airtouch.com
415-658-2232

AirTouch Communications provides wireless communications to more than 13 million customers in the U.S. and in 11 countries in Asia and Europe. Its operations include cellular telephone service, paging, and personal communication service, or PCS.

Phone to enroll:
Bank of New York
800-432-0140

EasyStock Investment Plan:

- Initial minimum investment: $500
- Minimum per month (optional): $100
- Maximum per transaction: $10,000
- No cash dividends paid.
- No partial dividend reinvestment.
- No discount is available.
- No IRA option is available.
- Optional cash purchases allowed.
- No direct debit option.

Aktiebolaget Electrolux AB
Sweden: Appliances
NASDAQ: ELUXY
c/o Morgan Guaranty Trust Company
PO Box 9073
Boston, MA 02205-9948
www.electrolux.se

Electrolux is the world's number one producer of large appliances. Especially dominant in Europe, the company is number four in the U.S., through its subsidiary Frigidaire. U.S. brand names include Frigidaire, Tappan, and Kelvinator.

Phone to enroll:
Morgan Guaranty Trust Company
800-997-8970

EasyStock Investment Plan:

- Initial minimum investment: $250
- Minimum per month (optional): $50
- Maximum annual investment: $100,000
- Cash dividends are offered.
- Partial dividend reinvestment.
- No discount is available.
- No IRA option is available.
- Optional cash purchases allowed.
- Direct debits are available.

Akzo Nobel N.V.
Netherlands: Chemicals
NASDAQ: AKZOY
c/o Morgan Guaranty Trust Company
PO Box 9073
Boston, MA 02205-9948
www:akzonobel.com

Chemicals giant Akzo Nobel is one of Europe's largest paint manufacturers and is a major producer of salt.

Phone to enroll:
Morgan Guaranty Trust Company
800-997-8970

EasyStock Investment Plan:
- Initial minimum investment: $250
- Minimum per month (optional): $50
- Maximum annual investment: $100,000
- Cash dividends are offered.
- Partial dividend reinvestment.
- No discount is available.
- No IRA option is available.
- Optional cash purchases allowed.
- Direct debits are available.

Alcatel Alsthom
France: Telecommunications Equipment
NYSE: ALA
c/o Bank of New York
48 Wall Street
New York, NY 10286
www.alcatel.com

Alcatel Alsthom, one of France's largest industrial companies, supplies high-tech equipment for global telecommunications, power, and transportation industries.

Phone to enroll:
Bank of New York
888-BNY-ADRS or 888-269-2377

EasyStock Investment Plan:
- Initial minimum investment: $250
- Minimum per month (optional): $50
- Maximum per transaction: $250,000
- Cash dividends are offered.
- Partial dividend reinvestment.
- No discount is available.
- No IRA option is available.
- Optional cash purchases allowed.
- Direct debits are available.

Allied Irish Banks, PLC
Ireland: Banking
NYSE: AIB
c/o Bank of New York
48 Wall Street
New York, NY 10286
www.aib.ie

Allied Irish Banks provides banking and related services in Ireland, the U.S., and the U.K. The company provides retail and commercial banking services, installment and variable-rate loans, leasing services, life insurance, pension and trust services.

Phone to enroll:
Bank of New York
888-BNY-ADRS or 888-269-2377

EasyStock Investment Plan:
- Initial minimum investment: $200
- Minimum per month (optional): $50
- Maximum annual investment: $250,000
- Cash dividends are offered.
- Partial dividend reinvestment.
- No discount is available.
- No IRA option is available.
- Optional cash purchases allowed.
- Direct debits are available.

Allstate Corp.
United States: Insurance
NYSE: ALL
2775 Sanders Road
Northbrook, IL 60062
www.allstate.com
800-402-5000

Allstate is the second-largest U.S. personal lines insurer behind State Farm, and sells life, property and casualty insurance in North America and Asia.

Phone to enroll:
First Chicago Trust Company of New York
800-355-5191

EasyStock Investment Plan:
- Initial minimum investment: $500
- Minimum per month (optional): $50
- Maximum annual investment: $150,000
- Cash dividends are offered.
- Partial dividend reinvestment.
- No discount is available.
- AN IRA Option is available.
- Optional cash purchases allowed.
- Direct debits are available.

Amcor Limited
Australia: Conglomerates
NASDAQ: AMCRY
c/o Morgan Guaranty Trust Company
PO Box 9073
Boston, MA 02205-9948
www.amcor.com.au

Amcor subsidiaries grow grapes, develop real estate, and perform natural waste recycling.

Phone to enroll:
Morgan Guaranty Trust Company
800-997-8970

EasyStock Investment Plan:
- Initial minimum investment: $250
- Minimum per month (optional): $50
- Maximum annual investment: $100,000
- Cash dividends are offered.
- Partial dividend reinvestment.
- No discount is available.
- No IRA option is available.
- Optional cash purchases allowed.
- Direct debits are available.

American Express Co.
United States: Financial Services
NYSE: AXP
200 Vesey Street
New York, NY 10285
www.americanexpress.com
212-640-2000

American Express is one of America's largest financial services companies and is the largest corporate travel agency. Investor Warren Buffett's Berkshire Hathaway owns about 10% of the company.

Phone to enroll:
Chase Mellon
800-842-7629

EasyStock Investment Plan:
- Initial minimum investment: $1,000
- Minimum per month (optional): $50
- Maximum monthly investment: $10,000
- Cash dividends are offered.
- Partial dividend reinvestment.
- No discount is available.
- No IRA option is available.
- Optional cash purchases allowed.
- Direct debits are available.

American Water Works Co., Inc.
United States: Utilities
NYSE: AWK
1025 Laurel Oak Road
Voorhees, NJ 08043
www.amwater.com
609-346-8200

American Water Works is the largest regulated water utility in the U.S., serving an aggregate population of over seven million people in more than 860 communities in twenty-two states.

Phone to enroll:
First National Bank of Boston
609-346-8200

EasyStock Investment Plan:
- Initial minimum investment: $100
- Minimum per month (optional): $100
- Maximum per transaction: $5,000
- Maximum annual investment: -
- Cash dividends are offered.
- Partial dividend reinvestment.
- No discount is available.
- No IRA option is available.
- Optional cash purchases allowed.
- No direct debit option.

Ameritech Corporation
United States: Telecommunications
NYSE: AIT
30 South Wacker Drive
Chicago, IL 60606-7402
www.ameritech.com
312-750-5000

Ameritech, a regional Bell operating company, which has agreed to be acquired by SBC Communications, focuses on local telephone and cellular telecommunications services in the Great Lakes region of Illinois, Indiana, Michigan, Ohio and Wisconsin.

Phone to enroll:
First Chicago Trust Company of New York
888-PLAN-AIT

EasyStock Investment Plan:
- Initial minimum investment: $1,000
- Minimum per month (optional): $100
- Maximum annual investment: $150,000
- Maximum per transaction: $150,000
- Cash dividends are offered.
- Partial dividend reinvestment.
- No discount is available.
- An IRA option is available.
- Optional cash purchases allowed.
- Direct debits are available.
- Get a loan secured by your shares.
- View materials and enroll online at www.netstockdirect.com

AMVESCAP PLC
United Kingdom: Investment Management
NYSE: AVZ
c/o Morgan Guaranty Trust Company
PO Box 9073
Boston, MA 02205-9948
www.amvescap.com

AMVESCAP manages mutual funds in Europe, Asia, North America, and South America. AMVESCAP was created by the 1997 merger of INVESCO and AIM Management Group, and recently purchased LGT Asset Management.

Phone to enroll:
Morgan Guaranty Trust Company
800-997-8970

EasyStock Investment Plan:
- Initial minimum investment: $250
- Minimum per month (optional): $50
- Maximum annual investment: $100,000
- Cash dividends are offered.
- Partial dividend reinvestment.
- No discount is available.
- No IRA option is available.
- Optional cash purchases allowed.
- Direct debits are available.

Amway Asia Pacific, Ltd.
Hong Kong: Consumer Products
NYSE: AAP
c/o Bank of New York
48 Wall Street
New York, NY 10286
www.amway.com

Amway Asia Pacific is the exclusive distributor for Amway in all areas of the Pacific Rim excluding Japan, selling more than two hundred different Amway products.

Phone to enroll:
Bank of New York
888-BNY-ADRS or 888-269-2377

EasyStock Investment Plan:
- Initial minimum investment: $500
- Minimum per month (optional): $50
- Maximum per transaction: $10,000
- No cash dividends paid.
- Partial dividend reinvestment.
- No discount is available.
- No IRA option is available.
- Optional cash purchases allowed.
- Direct debits are available.

Amway Japan Limited
Japan: Consumer Products
NYSE: AJL
c/o Morgan Guaranty Trust Company
PO Box 9073
Boston, MA 02205-9948
www.amway.co.jp

The exclusive distributor of Amway products in Japan, Amway Japan sells some 160 different products directly through more than one million independent distributors.

Phone to enroll:
Morgan Guaranty Trust Company
800-997-8970

EasyStock Investment Plan:
- Initial minimum investment: $250
- Minimum per month (optional): $50
- Maximum annual investment: $100,000
- Cash dividends are offered.
- Partial dividend reinvestment.
- No discount is available.
- No IRA option is available.
- Optional cash purchases allowed.
- Direct debits are available.

APT Satellite Co., Ltd.
Hong Kong: Telecommunications
NYSE: ATS
c/o Bank of New York
48 Wall Street
New York, NY 10286
www.apstar.com

APT Satellite Co. is a Hong Kong based satellite broadcaster.

Phone to enroll:
Bank of New York
888-BNY-ADRS or 888-269-2377

EasyStock Investment Plan:
- Initial minimum investment: $250
- Minimum per month (optional): $50
- Maximum per transaction: $250,000
- No cash dividends paid.
- No partial dividend reinvestment.
- No discount is available.
- No IRA option is available.
- Optional cash purchases allowed.
- Direct debits are available.

Aracruz Celulose S.A.
Brazil: Lumber/Paper
NYSE: ARA
c/o Morgan Trust Guaranty Company
PO Box 9073
Boston, MA 02205-9948
www.aracruz.com.br

Brazil's Aracruz is the world's leading producer of bleached eucalyptus market pulp, supplying 22% of worldwide demand.

Phone to enroll:
Morgan Guaranty Trust Company
800-997-8970

EasyStock Investment Plan:
- Initial minimum investment: $250
- Minimum per month (optional): $50
- Maximum annual investment: $100,000
- No cash dividends paid.
- Partial dividend reinvestment.
- No discount is available.
- No IRA option is available.
- Optional cash purchases allowed.
- Direct debits are available.

ARCADIS N.A.
Netherlands: Construction
NASDAQ: ARCAF
c/o Bank of New York
48 Wall Street
New York, NY 10286
www.arcadis.nl

ARCADIS, formerly Heidemij N.V., is an international consulting, engineering, and contracting company. The company offers large-scale construction, waste management, and air quality services, as well as urban and rural development consulting.

Phone to enroll:
Bank of New York
888-BNY-ADRS or 888-269-2377

EasyStock Investment Plan:
- Initial minimum investment: $250
- Minimum per month (optional): $50
- Maximum per transaction: $250,000
- Cash dividends are offered.
- Partial dividend reinvestment.
- No discount is available.
- No IRA option is available.
- Optional cash purchases allowed.
- Direct debits are available.

Arrow Financial Corp.
United States: Financial Services
NASDAQ: AROW
1250 Glen Strret
PO Box 216
Glen Falls, NY 12801
518-745-1000
www.gfnational.com

Arrow Financial is the holding company for Glen Falls National Bank and Saratoga National Bank. The

banks focus on residential and installment loans, which make up about 80% of their loan portfolio.

Phone to enroll:
American Stock Transfer & Trust
518-745-1000

EasyStock Investment Plan:
- Initial minimum investment: $300
- Minimum per month (optional): $50
- Maximum quarterly investment: $10,000
- Cash dividends are offered.
- Partial dividend reinvestment.
- No discount is available.
- No IRA option is available.
- Optional cash purchases allowed.
- No direct debits option.

Ascent Entertainment Group, Inc.
United States: Entertainment
NASDAQ: GOAL
1200 Seventeenth Street
Denver, CO 80202
303-626-7000

Ascent Entertainment is the largest provider of on-demand in-room entertainment services to the domestic lodging industry, including movies, video games, and other interactive entertainment.

Phone to enroll:
Bank of New York
800-4320140

EasyStock Investment Plan:
- Initial minimum investment: $100
- Minimum per month (optional): $20
- Maximum per transaction: $250,000
- No cash dividends paid.
- No partial dividend reinvestment.
- No discount is available.
- No IRA option is available.
- Optional cash purchases allowed.
- Direct debits are available.

Asia Pulp & Paper Co., Ltd.
Singapore: Paper
c/o Bank of New York
48 Wall Street
New York, NY 10286
www.asiapulpaper.com

Asia Pulp & Paper, the world's lowest-cost paper producer, is a vertically integrated pulp and paper company that produces approximately 900,000 tons of cultural and industrial paper per year.

Phone to enroll:
Bank of New York
888-BNY-ADRS or 888-269-2377

EasyStock Investment Plan:
- Initial minimum investment: $250
- Minimum per month (optional): $50
- Maximum per transaction: $250,000
- No cash dividends paid.
- Partial dividend reinvestment.
- No discount is available.
- No IRA option is available.
- Optional cash purchases allowed.
- Direct debits are available.

Asia Satellite Telecommunications Holdings Ltd.
Hong Kong: Aerospace/Defense
NYSE:SAT
c/o Morgan Guaranty Trust Company
PO Box 9073
Boston, MA 02205-9948
www.asiasat.com

Asia Satellite Telecommunications operates the AsiaSat satellite system, covering more than fifty countries in Asia, about two-thirds of the world's population.

Phone to enroll:
Morgan Guaranty Trust Company
800-997-8970

EasyStock Investment Plan:
- Initial minimum investment: $250
- Minimum per month (optional): $50
- Maximum annual investment: $100,000
- Cash dividends are offered.
- Partial dividend reinvestment.
- No discount is available.
- No IRA option is available.
- Optional cash purchases allowed.
- Direct debits are available.

Astra AB
Sweden: Pharmaceuticals
NYSE: A
c/o Bank of New York
48 Wall Street
New York, NY 10286
www.astra.com

Astra is a leading pharmeceudicals company that develops anti-infectives, cardiovascualr agents, gastrointestinal agents, pain control drugs, and agents for respiratory disease. Its peptic ulcer remedy, Losec, is the best-selling prescription drug in the world.

Phone to enroll:
Bank of New York
888-BNY-ADRS or 888-269-2377

EasyStock Investment Plan:
- Initial minimum investment: $250
- Minimum per month (optional): $50
- Maximum per transaction: $250,000
- Cash dividends are offered.
- Partial dividend reinvestment.
- No discount is available.
- No IRA option is available.
- Optional cash purchases allowed.
- Direct debits are available.

Atlas Pacific Ltd.
Australia: Pearl Farming
NASDAQ:APCFY
c/o Bank of New York
48 Wall Street
New York, NY 10286
www.atlaspacific.com.au

Atlas Pacific has taken a dive—deep into the exotic South Sea pearl industry—by buying a 75% interest in Indonesian pearl company P.T. Cendana Indopearls.

Phone to enroll:
Bank of New York
888-BNY-ADRS or 888-269-2377

EasyStock Investment Plan:
- Initial minimum investment: $250
- Minimum per month (optional): $50
- Maximum per transaction: $250,000
- No cash dividends paid.
- Partial dividend reinvestment.
- No discount is available.
- No IRA option is available.
- Optional cash purchases allowed.
- Direct debits are available.

Atmos Energy Corp.
United States: Utilities/Natural Gas
NYSE: ATO
5430 Lyndon B. Johnson Freeway
Dallas, TX 75240-0205
www.atmosenergy.com
800-382-8667

Atmos Energy distributes natural gas and propane to more than one million customers in the midwestern United States.

Phone to enroll:
Boston Equiserve LP
800-543-3038

EasyStock Investment Plan:
- Initial minimum investment: $200
- Minimum per month (optional): $25
- Maximum annual investment: $100,000
- Cash dividends are offered.
- Partial dividend reinvestment.
- Discounts on share purchases.
- AN IRA option is available.
- Optional cash purchases allowed.
- Direct debits are available.

AXA-UAP Inc.
France: Financial Services
NYSE: AXA
c/o Bank of New York
48 Wall Street
New York, NY 10286
www.axa.com

AXA-UAP is the world's largest insurance firm measured by assets. The company also owns a controlling stake in the Equitable Companies and most of Donaldson, Lufkin & Jenrette.

Phone to enroll:
Bank of New York
888-BNY-ADRS or 888-269-2377

EasyStock Investment Plan:
- Initial minimum investment: $250
- Minimum per month (optional): $50
- Maximum annual investment: $250,000
- Cash dividends are offered.
- Partial dividend reinvestment.
- No discount is available.
- No IRA option is available.
- Optional cash purchases allowed.
- Direct debits are available.

B

Baan Company N.V.
Netherlands: Computer Software
NASDAQ: BAANF
c/o Morgan Guaranty Trust Company
PO Box 9073
Boston, MA 02205-9948
www.baan.com

Baan is a leading maker of enterprise resource planning software, which allows companies to monitor and manage operations.

Phone to enroll:
Morgan Guaranty Trust Company
800-997-8970

EasyStock Investment Plan:
- Initial minimum investment: $250
- Minimum per month (optional): $50
- Maximum annual investment: $100,000
- Cash dividends are offered.
- Partial dividend reinvestment.
- No discount is available.
- No IRA option is available.
- Optional cash purchases allowed.
- Direct debits are available.

Banco BHIF, S.A.
Chile: Banking
NYSE: BB
c/o Bank of New York
48 Wall Street
New York, NY 10286
www.bhif.cl

Banco BHIF is a Chilean bank offering financial products and services to individuals and to the corporate market.

Phone to enroll:
Bank of New York
888-BNY-ADRS or 888-269-2377

EasyStock Investment Plan:
- Initial minimum investment: $250
- Minimum per month (optional): $50
- Maximum per transaction: $250,000
- Cash dividends are offered.
- Partial dividend reinvestment.
- No discount is available.
- No IRA option is available.
- Optional cash purchases allowed.
- Direct debits are available.

Banco Bilbao Vizcaya S.A.
Spain: Banking
NYSE: BBV
c/o Bank of New York
48 Wall Street
New York, NY 10286
www.bbv.es

Banco Bilbao Vizcaya is an international commercial bank offering retail and wholesale banking.

Phone to enroll:
Bank of New York
888-BNY-ADRS or 888-269-2377

EasyStock Investment Plan:
- Initial minimum investment: $250
- Minimum per month (optional): $50
- Maximum per transaction: $250,000
- Cash dividends are offered.
- Partial dividend reinvestment.
- No discount is available.
- No IRA option is available.
- Optional cash purchases allowed.
- Direct debits are available.

Banco de Galicia y Buenos Aires
Argentina: Banking
NASDAQ: BGALY
c/o Bank of New York
48 Wall Street
New York, NY 10286
www.bancogalicia.com.ar

Banco de Galicia y Buenos Aires has more than two hundred banking offices in Argentina, five in Uruguay, and one in New York; it also has representative offices in Brazil and Chile.

Phone to enroll:
Bank of New York
888-BNY-ADRS or 888-269-2377

EasyStock Investment Plan:
- Initial minimum investment: $250
- Minimum per month (optional): $50
- Maximum per transaction: $250,000
- Cash dividends are offered.
- Partial dividend reinvestment.
- No discount is available.
- No IRA option is available.
- Optional cash purchases allowed.
- Direct debits are available.

Banco de Santander S.A.
Spain: Banking/Financial Services
NYSE: STD
c/o Morgan Guaranty Trust Company
PO Box 9073
Boston, MA 02205-9948
www.bsantander.com

Phone to enroll:
Morgan Guaranty Trust Company
800-997-8970

EasyStock Investment Plan:
- Initial minimum investment: $250
- Minimum per month (optional): $50
- Maximum annual investment: $100,000
- Cash dividends are offered.
- Partial dividend reinvestment.
- No discount is available.
- No IRA option is available.
- Optional cash purchases allowed.
- Direct debits are available.

Banco Ganadero S.A.
Colombia: Banking
NYSE: BGA
c/o Bank of New York
48 Wall Street
New York, NY 10286
www.bancoganadero.com

In a time of political and economic uncertainty, Colombia's Banco Ganadero is trying to improve loan quality and to manage vast liquid assets resulting from lowered reserve requirements.

Phone to enroll:
Bank of New York
888-BNY-ADRS or 888-269-2377

EasyStock Investment Plan:
- Initial minimum investment: $250
- Minimum per month (optional): $50
- Maximum per transaction: $250,000
- Cash dividends are offered.
- Partial dividend reinvestment.
- No discount is available.
- No IRA option is available.
- Optional cash purchases allowed.
- Direct debits are available.

Banco Industrial Colombiano, S.A.
Colombia: Banking
NYSE: CIB
c/o Bank of New York
48 Wall Street
New York, NY 10286
www.bic.com.co

Phone to enroll:
Bank of New York
888-BNY-ADRS or 888-269-2377

EasyStock Investment Plan:
- Initial minimum investment: $250
- Minimum per month (optional): $50
- Maximum per transaction: $250,000
- Cash dividends are offered.
- Partial dividend reinvestment.
- No discount is available.
- No IRA option is available.
- Optional cash purchases allowed.
- Direct debits are available.

Banco Popular Inc.
United States: Banking
NASDAQ: BPOP
209 Munoz Rivera Avenue
Hato Rey, Puerto Rico
809-765-9800

Banco Popular de Puerto Rico is the largest bank in the commonwealth, serving individuals and businesses from more than two hundred branches and nearly four hundred ATMs on the island, as well as thirty branches in New York and an agency in Chicago.

Phone company to enroll:
787-765-9800

EasyStock Investment Plan:
- Initial minimum investment: $25
- Minimum per month (optional): $50
- Maximum per transaction: $250,000
- No cash dividends paid.
- Partial dividend reinvestment.
- No discount is available.
- No IRA option is available.
- Optional cash purchases allowed.
- Direct debits are available.

Banco Rio de la Plata, S.A.
Argentina: Banking
NYSE: BRS
c/o Bank of New York
48 Wall Street
New York, NY 10286
www.bancorio.com.ar

Banco Rio de la Plata provides commercial and investment banking to large corporations, small and mid-sized companies, and individuals. It has 163 full-service branches (62 in Bueno Aires) and serves more than 700,000 domestic clients.

Phone to enroll:
Bank of New York
888-BNY-ADRS or 888-269-2377

EasyStock Investment Plan:
- Initial minimum investment: $250
- Minimum per month (optional): $50
- Maximum per transaction: $250,000
- No cash dividends paid.
- Partial dividend reinvestment.
- No discount is available.
- No IRA option is available.
- Optional cash purchases allowed.
- Direct debits are available.

Banco Santiago S.A.
Chile: Banking
NYSE: SAN
c/o Morgan Guaranty Trust Company
PO Box 9073
Boston, MA 02205-9948
www.bsantiag.cl

Banco Santiago operates 159 branches throughout Chile. By itself, the bank claims to control nearly 10% of the Chilean loan market. That figure rose to more than 16% following the bank's 1997 merger with Banco O'Higgins.

Phone to enroll:
Morgan Guaranty Trust Company
800-997-8970

EasyStock Investment Plan:
- Initial minimum investment: $250
- Minimum per month (optional): $50
- Maximum annual investment: $100,000
- Cash dividends are offered.
- Partial dividend reinvestment.
- No discount is available.
- No IRA option is available.

- Optional cash purchases allowed.
- Direct debits are available.

Banco Wiese Ltdo.
Peru: Banking/Financial Services
NYSE: BWP
c/o Morgan Guaranty Trust Company
PO Box 9073
Boston, MA 02205-9948
www.bancowiese.com.pe

Banco Wiese Limitado is one of the largest commercial banks in Peru. The bank has almost a 20% market share of total bank deposits and loans made in Peru, with more than 85% of those loans going to businesses.

Phone to enroll:
Morgan Guaranty Trust Company
800-997-8970

EasyStock Investment Plan:
- Initial minimum investment: $250
- Minimum per month (optional): $50
- Maximum annual investment: $100,000
- Cash dividends are offered.
- Partial dividend reinvestment.
- No discount is available.
- No IRA option is available.
- Optional cash purchases allowed.
- Direct debits are available.

Bank of Ireland PLC
Ireland: Banking
NYSE: IRE
c/o Bank of New York
48 Wall Street
New York, NY 10286
www.bank-of-ireland.co.uk

The Bank of Ireland is a financial services group serving personal, commercial, and industrial customers in Ireland, the U.K., and the U.S. through over three hundred branches.

Phone to enroll:
Bank of New York
888-BNY-ADRS or 888-269-2377

EasyStock Investment Plan:
- Initial minimum investment: $250
- Minimum per month (optional): -
- Maximum annual investment: -
- Cash dividends are offered.
- Partial dividend reinvestment.
- No discount is available.
- No IRA option is available.
- Optional cash purchases allowed.
- Direct debits are available.

Bank of New York Co., Inc.
United States: Banking
NYSE: BK
48 Wall Street
New York, NY 10286
www.bankofny.com
212-495-1784

The Bank of New York (BNY) is one of the top retail banking organizations in the New York metropolitan area, with about 375 branches in the tri-state area. It offers a complete range of consumer and small-business banking services.

Phone to enroll:
Bank of New York
800-432-0140

EasyStock Investment Plan:
- Initial minimum investment: -
- Minimum per month (optional): $50
- Maximum per transaction: $250,000
- Cash dividends are offered.
- No partial dividend reinvestment.

- No discount is available.
- No IRA option is available.
- Optional cash purchases allowed.
- No direct debit option.

Bank of Tokyo-Mitsubishi
Japan: Banking
OTC: BTKYY
c/o Bank of New York
48 Wall Street
New York, NY 10286
www.btm.co.jp/index_e.htm

The Bank of Tokyo-Mitsubishi is the world's largest bank, with 360 branches in Japan and more than four hundred offices in about forty-five countries. About 50% of the bank's business is derived from overseas sources.

Phone to enroll:
Bank of New York
888-BNY-ADRS or 888-269-2377

EasyStock Investment Plan:
- Initial minimum investment: $250
- Minimum per month (optional): $25
- Maximum monthly investment: $10,000
- Cash dividends are offered.
- Partial dividend reinvestment.
- No discount is available.
- No IRA option is available.
- Optional cash purchases allowed.
- Direct debits are available.

Barclays Bank PLC
United Kingdom: Banking
NYSE: BCS
c/o Morgan Guaranty Trust Company
PO Box 9073
Boston, MA 02205-9948
www.barclays.com

Barclays is the second largest U.K. banking company behind HSBC. The company has more than 3000 branches worldwide and its Barclays Global Investors is the world's largest manager of funds for institutions.

Phone to enroll:
Morgan Guaranty Trust Company
800-997-8970

EasyStock Investment Plan:
- Initial minimum investment: $250
- Minimum per month (optional): $50
- Maximum annual investment: $100,000
- Cash dividends are offered.
- Partial dividend reinvestment.
- No discount is available.
- No IRA option is available.
- Optional cash purchases allowed.
- Direct debits are available.

Becton, Dickinson and Co.
United States: Medical Supplies
NYSE: BDX
One Becton Drive
Franklin Lakes, NJ 07417
www.bd.com
201-847-6800

Becton, Dickinson is a leading global medical technology firm. Its Medical Supplies and Devices segment makes diabetes care, infusion therapy, and drug injection products, while its Diagnostic Systems segment makes flow cytometry (cell analysis) supplies, and similar products.

Phone to enroll:
First Chicago Trust Company
800-955-4743 or 800-446-2617

EasyStock Investment Plan:
- Initial minimum investment: $250

- Minimum per month (optional): $50
- Maximum annual investment: -
- Cash dividends are offered.
- Partial dividend reinvestment.
- No discount is available.
- No IRA option is available.
- Optional cash purchases allowed.
- Direct debits are available.

Bedford Property Investors, Inc.
United States: Real Estate Investment Trust
NYSE: BED
270 Lafayette Circle
Lafayette, CA 94549
www.bedfordproperty.com
510-283-8910

Bedford Property Investors is a real estate investment trust with investments in seven industrial and five suburban office properties concentrated in the western U.S.

Phone to enroll:
Chase Mellon
800-842-7629

EasyStock Investment Plan:
- Initial minimum investment: $1,000
- Minimum per month (optional): $100
- Maximum annual investment: $5,000
- Cash dividends are offered.
- Partial dividend reinvestment.
- Discounts on share purchases.
- No IRA option is available.
- Optional cash purchases allowed.
- No direct debit option.

Beijing Yanhua Petrochemical Co. Ltd.
China: Chemicals
NYSE: BYH
c/o Bank of New York
48 Wall Street
New York, NY 10286
www.yanshanpcg.com

Beijing Yanhua Petrochemical is China's largest producer of resins, plastics, and ethylene for the agricultural, industrial, construction, automotive, and manufacturing industries.

Phone to enroll:
Bank of New York
888-BNY-ADRS or 888-269-2377

EasyStock Investment Plan:
- Initial minimum investment: $250
- Minimum per month (optional): $50
- Maximum per transaction: $250,000
- No cash dividends paid.
- Partial dividend reinvestment.
- No discount is available.
- No IRA option is available.
- Optional cash purchases allowed.
- Direct debits are available.

Bell Atlantic Corp.
United States: Telecommunications
NYSE: BEL
1717 Arch Street
Philadelphia, PA 19103
www.bell-atl.com
212-395-2121

Bell Atlantic, which became a $29 billion company with its 1997 purchase of fellow Baby Bell NYNEX, provides local telephone service through forty million access lines in thirteen Northeastern states and Washington, D.C.

Phone to enroll:
Boston Equiserve LP
800-736-3001

EasyStock Investment Plan:
- Initial minimum investment: $1,000
- Minimum per month (optional): $50
- Maximum annual investment: $200,000
- Cash dividends are offered.
- Partial dividend reinvestment.
- No discount is available.
- AN IRA option is available.
- Optional cash purchases allowed.
- Direct debits are available.

BellSouth Corp.
United States: Telecommunications
NYSE: BLS
1155 Peachtree Street N.E.
Atlanta, GA 30309
www.bellsouth.com
404-249-2000

BellSouth provides local telephone service in nine Southeastern states, wireless service to more than 5.3 million customers in the U.S., and international telecommunications services in fourteen countries, serving almost two million customers.

Phone to enroll:
Chase Mellon
888-887-2965

EasyStock Investment Plan:
- Initial minimum investment: $500
- Minimum per month (optional): $50
- Maximum annual investment: $100,000
- Cash dividends are offered.
- Partial dividend reinvestment.
- No discount is available.
- No IRA option is available.
- Optional cash purchases allowed.
- Direct debits are available.

Benetton Group S.p.A.
Italy: Clothing/Merchandising
NYSE: BNG
c/o Morgan Guaranty Trust Company
PO Box 9073
Boston, MA 02205-9948
www.benetton.com

Benetton is a global, family-run enterprise, selling United Colors of Benetton, Sisley, and other products in more than 120 countries.

Phone to enroll:
Morgan Guaranty Trust Company
800-997-8970

EasyStock Investment Plan:
- Initial minimum investment: $250
- Minimum per month (optional): $50
- Maximum annual investment: $100,000
- Cash dividends are offered.
- Partial dividend reinvestment.
- No discount is available.
- No IRA option is available.
- Optional cash purchases allowed.
- Direct debits are available.

Biora AB
Sweden: Biotechnology
NASDAQ: BIORY
c/o Bank of New York
48 Wall Street
New York, NY 10286
www.biora.se

Biora AB develops and manufactures products for treatment of periodontal disease and for use during oral surgery.

Phone to enroll:
Bank of New York
888-BNY-ADRS or 888-269-2377

EasyStock Investment Plan:
- Initial minimum investment: $250
- Minimum per month (optional): $50
- Maximum per transaction: $250,000
- No cash dividends paid.
- Partial dividend reinvestment.
- No discount is available.
- No IRA option is available.
- Optional cash purchases allowed.
- Direct debits are available.

Blue Square-Israel Ltd.
Israel: Supermarkets
NYSE: BSI
c/o Bank of New York
48 Wall Street
New York, NY 10286
www.coop.co.il

Blue Square is Israel's largest grocer, with nearly 160 supermarkets. The company will open an IKEA store in Tel Aviv.

Phone to enroll:
Bank of New York
888-BNY-ADRS or 888-269-2377

EasyStock Investment Plan:
- Initial minimum investment: $250
- Minimum per month (optional): $50
- Maximum per transaction: $250,000
- No cash dividends paid.
- Partial dividend reinvestment.
- No discount is available.
- No IRA option is available.
- Optional cash purchases allowed.
- Direct debits are available.

Bob Evans Farms, Inc.
United States: Restaurants
NASDAQ: BOBE
3776 South High Street
Columbus, OH 43207
www.bobevans.com
614-491-2225

Bob Evans Farms owns and operates almost four hundred restaurants in eighteen states in the Midwest, Mid-Atlantic, and Southeast.

Phone company to enroll:
614-492-4952

EasyStock Investment Plan:
- Initial minimum investment: $50
- Minimum per month (optional): $10
- Maximum monthly investment: $10,000
- Cash dividends are offered.
- Partial dividend reinvestment.
- No discount is available.
- No IRA option is available.
- Optional cash purchases allowed.
- Direct debits are available.

BOC Group PLC
United States: Chemicals
NYSE: BOX
c/o Morgan Guaranty Trust Company
PO Box 9073
Boston, MA 02205-9948
www.boc.com

The BOC Group is a producer of industrial and specialty gases, and also makes vacuum pumps and distributes consumer goods.

Phone to enroll:
Morgan Guaranty Trust Company
800-997-8970

EasyStock Investment Plan:
- Initial minimum investment: $250
- Minimum per month (optional): $50
- Maximum annual investment: $100,000
- Cash dividends are offered.
- Partial dividend reinvestment.
- No discount is available.
- No IRA option is available.
- Optional cash purchases allowed.
- Direct debits are available.

Boral Limited
Argentina: Construction Materials
NASDAQ: BORAY
c/o Bank of New York
48 Wall Street
New York, NY 10286
www.boral.com.au

Boral produces building materials, which it sells to engineering and construction companies in Asia, Australia, Europe, and the U.S.

Phone to enroll:
Bank of New York
888-BNY-ADRS or 888-269-2377

EasyStock Investment Plan:
- Initial minimum investment: $250
- Minimum per month (optional): $50
- Maximum per transaction: $250,000
- Cash dividends are offered.
- Partial dividend reinvestment.
- No discount is available.
- No IRA option is available.
- Optional cash purchases allowed.
- Direct debits are available.

Borg-Warner Automotive, Inc.
United States: Automotive Parts
NYSE: BWA
200 South Michigan Avenue
Chicago, IL 60604
www.bwauto.com
312-322-8500

A major beneficiary of the automotive outsourcing trend, Borg-Warner Automotive is the world's leading independent maker of four-wheel-drive transfer cases (installed in popular sport utility vehicles) and automatic transmission components.

Phone to enroll:
Bank of New York
800-842-7629

EasyStock Investment Plan:
- Initial minimum investment: $500
- Minimum per month (optional): $50
- Maximum annual investment: $120,000
- Cash dividends are offered.
- Partial dividend reinvestment.
- No discount is available.
- No IRA option is available.
- Optional cash purchases allowed.
- Direct debits are available.

Boston Beer Co., Inc.
United States: Beverages
NYSE: SAM
75 Arlington Street
Boston, MA 02116
www.samadams.com
617-368-5000

Boston Beer produces more than seventeen seasonal and year-round varieties of craft-brewed beers, including its flagship Samuel Adams Boston Lager brand. It sells nearly

1.2 million barrels of lager, ales, and cider a year, more than the next five largest microbreweries combined.

Phone to enroll:
Chase Mellon
888-266-6780

EasyStock Investment Plan:
- Initial minimum investment: $500
- Minimum per month (optional): $50
- Maximum monthly investment: $10,000
- Cash dividends are offered.
- No partial dividend reinvestment.
- No discount is available.
- No IRA option is available.
- Optional cash purchases allowed.
- Direct debits are available.

Bowne & Co., Inc.
United States: Information
AMEX: BNE
345 Hudson St.
New York, NY 10014
www.bowne.com
212-924-5500

Bowne, the world's largest financial printer, is an information empowerment company helping major corporations and professional firms apply the latest technologies to manage their information flows worldwide.

Phone to enroll:
Bank of New York
800-432-0140

EasyStock Investment Plan:
- Initial minimum investment: $500
- Minimum per month (optional): $50
- Maximum annual investment: $100,000
- Cash dividends are offered.
- Partial dividend reinvestment.
- No discount is available.
- No IRA option is available.
- Optional cash purchases allowed.
- Direct debits are available.
- View materials and enroll online at www.netstockdirect.com.

Brahma S.A.
Brazil: Beverages
NYSE: BRHC
c/o Bank of New York
48 Wall Street
New York, NY 10286
www.brahma.com.br

Companhia Cervejaria Brahma is Latin America's largest brewery and the fifth largest in the world. The company controls about 50% of the Brazilian beer market with its Brahma and Skol brands. Outside Brazil, it brews and sells beer in Argentina and Venezuela.

Phone to enroll:
Bank of New York
800-524-4458

EasyStock Investment Plan:
- Initial minimum investment: $250
- Minimum per month (optional): $50
- Maximum per transaction: $250,000
- Maximum annual investment: $250,000
- No cash dividends paid.
- Partial dividend reinvestment.
- No discount is available.
- No IRA option is available.
- Optional cash purchases allowed.
- Direct debits are available.

BP Amoco PLC
United Kingdom: International Refiners
NYSE: BPA
c/o Morgan Guaranty Trust Company
PO Box 9073
Boston, MA 02205-9948
www.bpamoco.com

BP Amoco is the U.K.'s largest company and one of the world's largest oil firms, due to its recent merger. The company explores for, develops, and produces oil and chemicals.

Phone to enroll:
Morgan Guaranty Trust Company
800-997-8970

EasyStock Investment Plan:
- Initial minimum investment: $250
- Minimum per month (optional): $50
- Maximum annual investment: $100,000
- No cash dividends paid.
- Partial dividend reinvestment.
- No discount is available.
- No IRA option is available.
- Optional cash purchases allowed.
- Direct debits are available.
- View materials and enroll online at www.netstockdirect.com.

BRE Properties, Inc.
United States: Real Estate Investment Trust
NYSE: BRE
One Montgomery Street
Suite 2500
San Francisco, CA 94104
www.breproperties.com
415-445-6530

BRE Properties is a real estate investment trust that owns, acquires, develops, rehabilitates, and manages apartment communities in the western U.S. Its portfolio consists of almost 85 apartment complexes with approximately 20,000 units.

Phone to enroll:
Chase Mellon
800-842-7629

EasyStock Investment Plan:
- Initial minimum investment: $500
- Minimum per month (optional): $100
- Maximum monthly investment: $10,000
- Cash dividends are offered.
- Partial dividend reinvestment.
- No discount is available.
- No IRA option is available.
- Optional cash purchases allowed.
- Direct debits are available.

British Airways PLC
United Kingdom: Airlines
NYSE: BAB
c/o Morgan Guaranty Trust Company
PO Box 9073
Boston, MA 02205-9948
www.british-airways.com

British Airways is one of the world's largest airlines. Based at London's Heathrow, the busiest airport in the world for international flights, BA serves over 170 destinations in more than eighty countries.

Phone to enroll:
Morgan Guaranty Trust Company
800-997-8970
EasyStock Investment Plan:
- Initial minimum investment: $250
- Minimum per month (optional): $50

- Maximum annual investment: $100,000
- Cash dividends are offered.
- Partial dividend reinvestment.
- No discount is available.
- No IRA option is available.
- Optional cash purchases allowed.
- Direct debits are available.

British Telecommunications PLC
United Kingdom: Telecommunications
NYSE: BTY
c/o Morgan Guaranty Trust Company
PO Box 9073
Boston, MA 02205-9948
www.bt.com

British Telecommunications is the U.K.'s dominant phone company. Formerly a state-owned monopoly, BT offers local, long-distance, international, and mobile service.

Phone to enroll:
Morgan Guaranty Trust Company
800-997-8970

EasyStock Investment Plan:
- Initial minimum investment: $250
- Minimum per month (optional): $50
- Maximum annual investment: $100,000
- Cash dividends are offered.
- Partial dividend reinvestment.
- No discount is available.
- No IRA option is available.
- Optional cash purchases allowed.
- Direct debits are available.

Bufete Industrial, S.A.
Mexico: Construction
NYSE: GBI
c/o Bank of New York
48 Wall Street
New York, NY 10286
www.bufete.com

Bufete Industrial S.A. is Mexico's largest firm specializing in engineering, procurement, and construction. The company executes projects in categories including the oil and petrochemical industry, power generation, and manufacturing and processing plants.

Phone to enroll:
Bank of New York
888-BNY-ADRS or 888-269-2377

EasyStock Investment Plan:
- Initial minimum investment: $250
- Minimum per month (optional): $50
- Maximum per transaction: $250,000
- No cash dividends paid.
- Partial dividend reinvestment.
- No discount is available.
- No IRA option is available.
- Optional cash purchases allowed.
- Direct debits are available.

C

C.R. Bard, Inc.
United States: Medical Supplies
NYSE: BCR
730 Central Avenue
Murray Hill, NJ 07974-1139
www.crbard.com
908-277-8000

C. R. Bard is a leading multinational producer of urological, cardiovascular, and surgical products. Bard is best known for its urological devices.

Phone to enroll:
First Chicago Trust Company
800-446-2617

EasyStock Investment Plan:
- Initial minimum investment: $250
- Minimum per month (optional): $25
- Maximum annual investment: -
- Cash dividends are offered.
- Partial dividend reinvestment.
- No discount is available.
- No IRA option is available.
- Optional cash purchases allowed.
- Direct debits are available.
- View materials and enroll online at www.netstockdirect.com.

Cadbury Schweppes PLC
United Kingdom: Food/Beverages
NYSE: CSG
c/o Morgan Guaranty Trust Company
PO Box 9073
Boston, MA 02205-9948
www.cadbury.co.uk

Cadbury Schweppes makes candy and soft drinks. The world's number three soft drink vendor, after Coca-Cola and PepsiCo, Cadbury produces such labels as 7Up (in the U.S. only), A&W Root Beer, plus Motts apple products and Clamato.

Phone to enroll:
Morgan Guaranty Trust Company
800-997-8970

EasyStock Investment Plan:
- Initial minimum investment: $250
- Minimum per month (optional): $50
- Maximum annual investment: $100,000
- Cash dividends are offered.
- Partial dividend reinvestment.
- No discount is available.
- No IRA option is available.
- Optional cash purchases allowed.
- Direct debits are available.

Canon, Inc.
Japan: Computer Systems
NASDAQ: CANNY
c/o Morgan Guaranty Trust Company
PO Box 9073
Boston, MA 02205-9948
www.canon.com

Canon is one of the world's top makers of business machines, cameras, and optical products and the world's leading seller of cameras and color copiers.

Phone to enroll:
Morgan Guaranty Trust Company
800-997-8970

EasyStock Investment Plan:
- Initial minimum investment: $250
- Minimum per month (optional): $50
- Maximum annual investment: $100,000
- Cash dividends are offered.
- Partial dividend reinvestment.
- No discount is available.
- No IRA option is available.
- Optional cash purchases allowed.
- Direct debits are available.

Cantab Pharmaceuticals PLC
United Kingdom: Pharmaceuticals
NASDAQ: CNTBY
c/o Bank of New York
48 Wall Street
New York, NY 10286
www.cantab.co.uk

Cantab Pharmaceuticals is a biotechnology company that develops pharmaceuticals primarily using

immunogenics, a method that uses genetically engineered drugs and vaccines to treat patients' immune systems.

Phone to enroll:
Bank of New York
888-BNY-ADRS or 888-269-2377

EasyStock Investment Plan:
- Initial minimum investment: $250
- Minimum per month (optional): $50
- Maximum per transaction: $250,000
- No cash dividends paid.
- Partial dividend reinvestment.
- No discount is available.
- No IRA option is available.
- Optional cash purchases allowed.
- Direct debits are available.

Capstead Mortgage Corp.
United States: Real Estate
NYSE: CMO
2711 North Haskell Avenue
Dallas, TX 75204
www.capstead.com
214-874-2323

Capstead Mortgage is a mortgage banking firm that invests in mortgage-backed securities. The company qualifies as a REIT since it distributes all its income to unit holders.

Phone to enroll:
Norwest Bank Minnesota
800-358-2323

EasyStock Investment Plan:
- Initial minimum investment: $250
- Minimum per month (optional): $50
- Maximum monthly investment: $10,000
- Cash dividends are offered.
- Partial dividend reinvestment.
- Discounts on share purchases.
- No IRA option is available.
- Optional cash purchases allowed.
- Direct debits are available.

Carey Diversified, LLC
United States: Real Estate Investment Trust
NYSE: CDC
50 Rockefeller Plaza
New York, NY 10020
www.cdllc.com
212-492-1100

Carey Diversified buys, manages, and leases real estate for commercial use, including office space and distribution and industrial facilities. Carey Diversified was formed by the consolidation of nine real estate partnerships.

Phone to enroll:
Chase Mellon
800-842-8432

EasyStock Investment Plan:
- Initial minimum investment: $500
- Minimum per month (optional): $500
- Maximum monthly investment: $25,000
- Cash dividends are offered.
- Partial dividend reinvestment.
- No discount is available.
- No IRA option is available.
- Optional cash purchases allowed.
- Maximum per transaction: $25,000
- Direct debits are available.

Carlton Communications PLC
United Kingdom: Entertainment
NASDAQ: CCTVY
c/o Morgan Guaranty Trust Company
PO Box 9073
Boston, MA 02205-9948
www.carltonplc.co.uk

A producer and broadcaster of TV programming in the U.K., Carlton Communications also provides extensive production services to the film, video, and television industries worldwide.

Phone to enroll:
Morgan Guaranty Trust Company
800-997-8970

EasyStock Investment Plan:
- Initial minimum investment: $250
- Minimum per month (optional): $50
- Maximum annual investment: $100,000
- Cash dividends are offered.
- Partial dividend reinvestment.
- No discount is available.
- No IRA option is available.
- Optional cash purchases allowed.
- Direct debits are available.

Carolina Power & Light Co.
United States: Electric Services
NYSE: CPL
411 Fayetteville Street
Raleigh, NC 27601
www.cplc.com
919-546-6111

Carolina Power & Light (CP&L) generates and distributes electricity to consumers in North and South Carolina. CP&L retails electricity in about 220 communities.

Phone to enroll:
Wachovia Bank of North Carolina
800-662-7232

EasyStock Investment Plan:
- Initial minimum investment: $20
- Minimum per month (optional): $20
- Maximum monthly investment: $2,000
- Cash dividends are offered.
- Partial dividend reinvestment.
- No discount is available.
- No IRA option is available.
- Optional cash purchases allowed.
- Direct debits are available.

Carpenter Technology Corp.
United States: Manufacturing
NYSE: CRS
101 West Bern Street
Reading, PA 19612
www.cartech.com
610-208-2000

Carpenter Technology manufactures and markets specialty metals, primarily specialty steels (corrosion resistant) and special alloys (heat resistant or with special magnetic properties).

Phone to enroll:
First Chicago Trust Company
800-446-2617

EasyStock Investment Plan:
- Initial minimum investment: $500
- Minimum per month (optional): $25
- Maximum annual investment: $60,000
- Cash dividends are offered.
- Partial dividend reinvestment.
- No discount is available.
- No IRA option is available.
- Optional cash purchases allowed.

- Direct debits are available.
- View materials and enroll online at www.netstockdirect.com.

Cascade Natural Gas Corp.
United States: Natural Gas
NYSE: CGC
222 Fairview Avenue North
Seattle, WA 98109
206-624-3900

Cascade Natural Gas is a regulated public utility that distributes natural gas to about 60,000 residential, commercial, and industrial customers in Washington and Oregon.

Phone to enroll:
Bank of New York
800-432-0140

EasyStock Investment Plan:
- Initial minimum investment: $250
- Minimum per month (optional): $50
- Maximum annual investment: $20,000
- Cash dividends are offered.
- Partial dividend reinvestment.
- No discount is available.
- No IRA option is available.
- Optional cash purchases allowed.
- No direct debit option.

CBT Group PLC
Ireland: Office Equipment
NASDAQ: CBTSY
c/o Bank of New York
48 Wall Street
New York, NY 10286
www.cbtsvs.com

CBT Group provides interactive software used to educate and train business staffs in the latest information technology. The company develops, publishes, and markets a library of over 550 software titles that focus on client/server technologies.

Phone to enroll:
Bank of New York
888-BNY-ADRS or 888-269-2377

EasyStock Investment Plan:
- Initial minimum investment: $250
- Minimum per month (optional): $50
- Maximum per transaction: $250,000
- No cash dividends paid.
- Partial dividend reinvestment.
- No discount is available.
- No IRA option is available.
- Optional cash purchases allowed.
- Direct debits are available.

Central and South West Corp.
United States: Electric Services
NYSE: CSR
P.O. Box 660164
1616 Woodall Rodgers Freeway
Dallas, TX 75266-0164
www.csw.com
214-777-1000

Central and South West Corporation (CSW) is a holding company for four electric-utility subsidiaries: Central Power and Light (South Texas), Public Service Company of Oklahoma, Southwestern Electric Power (Arkansas and Louisiana), and West Texas Utilities.

Phone company to enroll:
800-527-5797

EasyStock Investment Plan:
- Initial minimum investment: $250
- Minimum per month (optional): $25
- Maximum annual investment: $100,000
- Cash dividends are offered.
- Partial dividend reinvestment.

- No discount is available.
- No IRA option is available.
- Optional cash purchases allowed.
- Direct debits are available.
- View materials and enroll online at www.netstockdirect.com.

Central Hudson Gas & Electric
United States: Natural Gas
NYSE: CNH
284 South Avenue
Poughkeepsie, NY 12601-4879
www.cenhud.com
914-452-2000

Central Hudson Gas & Electric supplies electricity and gas to customers in New York's Hudson Valley region (with a population of about 600,000). Approximately 80% of the company's sales come from electricity and 20% from gas.

Phone company to enroll:
888-280-3848

EasyStock Investment Plan:
- Initial minimum investment: $100
- Minimum per month (optional): $50
- Maximum annual investment: $150,000
- Cash dividends are offered.
- Partial dividend reinvestment.
- No discount is available.
- No IRA option is available.
- Optional cash purchases allowed.
- Direct debits are available.
- View materials and enroll online at www.netstockdirect.com.

Central Vermont Public Service
United States: Electric Services
NYSE: CV
77 Grove Street
Rutland, VT 05701
www.cvps.com
802-773-2711

Central Vermont Public Service Corporation provides electric utility services and nonregulated energy services. It serves approximately 135,000 consumers in 175 of the 245 towns in Vermont.

Phone to enroll:
Boston Equiserve LP
800-736-3001

EasyStock Investment Plan:
- Initial minimum investment: $250
- Minimum per month (optional): $100
- Maximum monthly investment: $2,000
- Maximum quarterly investment: $6,000
- Cash dividends are offered.
- No partial dividend reinvestment.
- No discount is available.
- No IRA option is available.
- Optional cash purchases allowed.
- No direct debit option.

Chevron Corp.
United States: Petroleum Refiner
NYSE: CHV
225 Bush Street
San Francisco, CA 94104
www.chevron.com
415-894-7700

Chevron has net reserves of more than four billion barrels of oil. The integrated oil giant has operations that run the gamut from the well-head to the self-service pump. The

company is pursuing an aggressive exploration and production initiative.

Phone to enroll:
Chase Mellon
800-842-7629

EasyStock Investment Plan:
- Initial minimum investment: $250
- Minimum per month (optional): $50
- Maximum annual investment: $100,000
- No cash dividends paid.
- No partial dividend reinvestment.
- No discount is available.
- No IRA option is available.
- Optional cash purchases allowed.
- No direct debit option.

Chicago Bridge & Iron Co. N.V.
Netherlands: Construction
NYSE: CBI
c/o Bank of New York
48 Wall Street
New York, NY 10286
www.chicago-bridge.com

Chicago Bridge & Iron is building a new future as well as constructing and erecting steel tanks, pressure vessels, cryogenic storage facilities, and other steel-plate structures for the petroleum, pulp and paper, mining, and chemical industries.

Phone to enroll:
Bank of New York
888-BNY-ADRS or 888-269-2377

EasyStock Investment Plan:
- Initial minimum investment: $250
- Minimum per month (optional): $50
- Maximum annual investment: $250,000
- Cash dividends are offered.
- Partial dividend reinvestment.
- No discount is available.
- No IRA option is available.
- Optional cash purchases allowed.
- Direct debits are available.

China Southern Airlines Co. Ltd.
China: Aircraft
NYSE: ZNH
c/o Bank of New York
48 Wall Street
New York, NY 10286

With its fleet of Boeing and Airbus aircraft, China Southern Airlines carries more than 10 million passengers annually and operates 270 routes serving nearly seventy Chinese destinations.

Phone to enroll:
Bank of New York
888-BNY-ADRS or 888-269-2377

EasyStock Investment Plan:
- Initial minimum investment: $250
- Minimum per month (optional): $50
- Maximum per transaction: $250,000
- Cash dividends are offered.
- Partial dividend reinvestment.
- No discount is available.
- No IRA option is available.
- Optional cash purchases allowed.
- Direct debits are available.

Chock Full O' Nuts Corp.
United States: Food Products
NYSE: CHF
370 Lexington Avenue
New York, NY 10017
www.chockfullonuts.com
212-532-0300

Chock Full O' Nuts roasts, packs, and markets a wide range of regular, instant, decaffeinated, ground roast, and specialty coffees. The company sells its beverages regionally across

the U.S. and Canada under brand names such as Cains, LaTouraine, and Chock Full O' Nuts.

Phone to enroll:
American Stock & Transfer Trust
212-936-5100

EasyStock Investment Plan:
- Initial minimum investment: $100
- Minimum per month (optional): $50
- Maximum per transaction: $10,000
- Maximum annual investment: $100,000
- No cash dividends paid.
- Partial dividend reinvestment.
- No discount is available.
- No IRA option is available.
- Optional cash purchases allowed.
- Direct debits are available.

Cilcorp Inc.
United States: Utilities
NYSE: CER
300 Hamilton Boulevard, Suite 300
Peoria, IL 61602
www.cilco.com
309-675-8810

Cilcorp is the holding company for Central Illinois Light, which generates, transmits, and sells electricity to about 193,000 retail customers in Central and East-Central Illinois. Electricity sales account for more than 60% of revenues.

Phone company to enroll:
800-654-1685

EasyStock Investment Plan:
- Initial minimum investment: $250
- Minimum per month (optional): $25
- Maximum quarterly investment: $25,000
- Cash dividends are offered.
- Partial dividend reinvestment.
- No discount is available.
- No IRA option is available.
- Optional cash purchases allowed.
- No direct debit option.

CLP Holdings Limited
Hong Kong: Utilities
OTC: CLPWY
c/o Morgan Guaranty Trust Company
PO Box 9073
Boston, MA 02205-9948
www.chinalightandpower.com.hk
Phone to enroll:
Morgan Guaranty Trust Company
800-997-8970

EasyStock Investment Plan:
- Initial minimum investment: $250
- Minimum per month (optional): $50
- Maximum annual investment: $100,000
- Cash dividends are offered.
- Partial dividend reinvestment.
- No discount is available.
- No IRA option is available.
- Optional cash purchases allowed.
- Direct debits are available.

CMS Energy Corp.
United States: Utilities
NYSE: CMS
212 West Michigan Avenue
Jackson, MI 49201-2236
www.cmsenergy.com
313-436-9200

CMS Energy is the holding company for Consumers Energy Company, operating in Michigan's Lower Peninsula, and CMS Enterprises (nonutility energy-related businesses). Consumers Energy owns and operates twenty-eight power plants in Michigan.

Phone company to enroll:
800-774-4177

EasyStock Investment Plan:
- Initial minimum investment: $500
- Minimum per month (optional): $25
- Maximum annual investment: $120,000
- Cash dividends are offered.
- Partial dividend reinvestment.
- No discount is available.
- No IRA option is available.
- Optional cash purchases allowed.
- Direct debits are available.

Coastal Corp.
United States: Petroleum Refiner
NYSE: CGP
9 Greenway Plaza
Houston, TX 77046-0995
www.coastalcorp.com
713-877-1400

The Coastal Corporation is a diversified energy giant whose business segments include natural gas, petroleum, chemicals, power plants, and trucking. It engages in exploration, production, refining, and marketing of petroleum and natural gas products worldwide.

Phone to enroll:
First Chicago Trust Company
800-788-2500

EasyStock Investment Plan:
- Initial minimum investment: $250
- Minimum per month (optional): $50
- Maximum annual investment: $120,000
- Cash dividends are offered.
- Partial dividend reinvestment.
- No discount is available.
- No IRA option is available.
- Optional cash purchases allowed.
- No direct debit option.

Coca-Cola FEMSA
Mexico: Beverages
NYSE: KOF
c/o Bank of New York
48 Wall Street
New York, NY 10286
www.femsa.com/cocacola.html

Coca-Cola FEMSA is a bottler for the Coca-Cola Company in Latin America. Its territories include Mexico City and surrounding areas, Southeast Mexico, and a significant part of the Buenos Aires metropolitan area.

Phone to enroll:
Bank of New York
888-BNY-ADRS or 888-269-2377

EasyStock Investment Plan:
- Initial minimum investment: $250
- Minimum per month (optional): $50
- Maximum per transaction: $250,000
- No cash dividends paid.
- Partial dividend reinvestment.
- No discount is available.
- No IRA option is available.
- Optional cash purchases allowed.
- Direct debits are available.

Companhia Brasileira De Distribucao S.A.
Brazil: Distributors
NYSE: GPASY
c/o Bank of New York
48 Wall Street
New York, NY 10286

Companhia Brasileira De Distribucao S.A. distributes goods in the Brazilian market.

Phone to enroll:
Bank of New York
888-BNY-ADRS or 888-269-2377

EasyStock Investment Plan:
- Initial minimum investment: $250
- Minimum per month (optional): $50
- Maximum per transaction: $250,000
- Cash dividends are offered.
- Partial dividend reinvestment.
- No discount is available.
- No IRA option is available.
- Optional cash purchases allowed.
- Direct debits are available.

Compañia Cervecerias Unidas S.A.
Chile: Beverages
NASDAQ: CCUUY
c/o Morgan Guaranty Trust Company
PO Box 9073
Boston, MA 02205-9948
www.ccu-sa.com

Compañia Cervecerias Unidas distributes foreign beers and controls over 80% of the domestic beer market in Chile. The company also owns about half of a large Chilean winery.

Phone to enroll:
Morgan Guaranty Trust Company
800-997-8970

EasyStock Investment Plan:
- Initial minimum investment: $250
- Minimum per month (optional): $50
- Maximum annual investment: $100,000
- Cash dividends are offered.
- Partial dividend reinvestment.
- No discount is available.
- No IRA option is available.
- Optional cash purchases allowed.
- Direct debits are available.

Compañia de Minas Buenaventura S.A.
Peru: Mining/Minerals
NYSE: BVN
c/o Bank of New York
48 Wall Street
New York, NY 10286
www.buenaventura.com

Compañia de Minas Buenaventura owns more than 40% of Latin America's largest gold mine, Minera Yanacocha, in northwest Peru.

Phone to enroll:
Bank of New York
888-BNY-ADRS or 888-269-2377

EasyStock Investment Plan:
- Initial minimum investment: $250
- Minimum per month (optional): $50
- Maximum per transaction: $250,000
- Cash dividends are offered.
- Partial dividend reinvestment.
- No discount is available.
- No IRA option is available.
- Optional cash purchases allowed.
- Direct debits are available.

Compaq Computer Corp.
United States: Computer Systems
NYSE: CPQ
PO Box 692000
Houston, TX 77269
www.compaq.com
281-370-0670

Compaq is the number one PC maker in the world. The company's line of desktop PCs includes the Deskpro business series and Presario home series. Its portable computers

include the Armada line, and its network systems include the ProSignia and ProLiant server families.

Phone to enroll:
Bank of New York
800-432-0140

EasyStock Investment Plan:
- Initial minimum investment: $250
- Minimum per month (optional): $50
- Maximum monthly investment: $10,000
- Cash dividends are offered.
- Partial dividend reinvestment.
- No discount is available.
- No IRA option is available.
- Optional cash purchases allowed.
- Direct debits are available.

COMSAT Corp.
United States: Telecommunications
NYSE: CQ
6560 Rock Spring Drive
Bethesda, MD 20817
www.comsat.com
301-214-3000

COMSAT provides satellite capacity into and out of the U.S. for such customers as AT&T, MCI, and Sprint; broadcasters; multinational corporations; news-gathering organizations; and the U.S. government.

Phone to enroll:
Boston Equiserve LP
301-214-3200

EasyStock Investment Plan:
- Initial minimum investment: $250
- Minimum per month (optional): $50
- Maximum per transaction: $10,000
- Maximum annual investment: $40,000
- Cash dividends are offered.
- Partial dividend reinvestment.
- No discount is available.
- No IRA option is available.
- Optional cash purchases allowed.
- No direct debit option.

Connecticut Energy Corp.
United States: Natural Gas
NYSE: CNE
855 Main Street
Bridgeport, CT 06604
www.connenergy.com
800-760-7776

Connecticut Energy, a public-utility holding company, primarily operates through its retail gas distribution subsidiary, Southern Connecticut Gas, which serves about 160,000 residential, commercial, and industrial customers in 22 Connecticut towns.

Phone to enroll:
Bank of New York
800-736-3001

EasyStock Investment Plan:
- Initial minimum investment: $250
- Minimum per month (optional): $50
- Maximum annual investment: $50,000
- Cash dividends are offered.
- Partial dividend reinvestment.
- No discount is available.
- An IRA option is available.
- Optional cash purchases allowed.
- Direct debits are available.

Connecticut Water Service, Inc.
United States: Water Services
NASDAQ: CTWS
93 West Main Street
Clinton, CT 06413
860-669-8636

Connecticut Water Service is the parent company of the Connecticut Water Co. (CWC), a regulated public utility. CWC supplies water and fire protection in thirty-one towns. It serves a total of 60,325 residential, commercial, industrial, and public authority customers.

Phone to enroll:
Boston Equiserve LP
203-669-8636

EasyStock Investment Plan:
- Initial minimum investment: $100
- Minimum per month (optional): $25
- Maximum monthly investment: $1,000
- Maximum quarterly investment: $3,000
- Cash dividends are offered.
- Partial dividend reinvestment.
- No discount is available.
- AN IRA option is available.
- Optional cash purchases allowed.
- No direct debit option.

Consolidated Freightways Corp.
United States: Transportation
NASDAQ: CFWY
175 Linfield Drive
Menlo Park, CA 94025
www.cfwy.com
415-326-1700

Consolidated Freightways is America's third largest long-haul, less-than-truckload (under 10,000 pounds) trucking company, after Yellow Corp. and Roadway Express. It operates more than 40,000 tractors, trailers, and other vehicles and more than 350 terminals.

Phone to enroll:
Bank of New York
800-432-0140

EasyStock Investment Plan:
- Initial minimum investment: $100
- Minimum per month (optional): $25
- Maximum annual investment: $50,000
- No cash dividends paid.
- No partial dividend reinvestment.
- No discount is available.
- No IRA option is available.
- Optional cash purchases allowed.
- No direct debit option.

Consorcio G Grupo Dina, S.A. de C.V.
Mexico: Automotive Parts
NYSE: DIN
c/o Morgan Guaranty Trust Company
PO Box 9073
Boston, MA 02205-9948
www.motorcoach.com

Dina is a Mexican automotive parts company with major U.S. operations.

Phone to enroll:
Morgan Guaranty Trust Company
800-997-8970

EasyStock Investment Plan:
- Initial minimum investment: $250
- Minimum per month (optional): $50
- Maximum annual investment: $100,000
- Cash dividends are offered.
- Partial dividend reinvestment.
- No discount is available.
- No IRA option is available.

- Optional cash purchases allowed.
- Direct debits are available.

COPEL S.A.
Brazil: Utilities
NYSE: ELP
c/o Bank of New York
48 Wall Street
New York, NY 10286
www.copel.br

Companhia Paranaense de Energia (Copel) generates and transmits electricity for 2.6 million customers in the Parana state.

Phone to enroll:
Bank of New York
800-218-4373

EasyStock Investment Plan:
- Initial minimum investment: $250
- Minimum per month (optional): $50
- Maximum annual investment: $250,000
- No cash dividends paid.
- No partial dividend reinvestment.
- No discount is available.
- No IRA option is available.
- Optional cash purchases allowed.
- Direct debits are available.

Corporacion Bancaria de Espana, S.A. Argentarian
Spain: Banking
NYSE: AGR
c/o Morgan Guaranty Trust Company
PO Box 9073
Boston, MA 02205-9948
www.argentarian.es

Corporacion Bancaria de Espana Argentarian is a large bank with almost 2,000 branches throughout Spain.

Phone to enroll:
Morgan Guaranty Trust Company
800-997-8970

EasyStock Investment Plan:
- Initial minimum investment: $250
- Minimum per month (optional): $50
- Maximum annual investment: $100,000
- Cash dividends are offered.
- Partial dividend reinvestment.
- No discount is available.
- No IRA option is available.
- Optional cash purchases allowed.
- Direct debits are available.

Cresud S.A.C.I.F. y A.
Argentina: Agricultural
NYSE: CRESY
c/o Bank of New York
48 Wall Street
New York, NY 10286

As Argentina's largest landowner, Cresud raises beef and dairy cattle on over a million acres, and cultivates grains, including corn, soybeans, sunflowers, and wheat. Cresud is in a partnership to build and run Argentine feedlots with Cactus Feeders of Texas, the second biggest feedlot in the U.S.

Phone to enroll:
Bank of New York
888-BNY-ADRS or 888-269-2377

EasyStock Investment Plan:
- Initial minimum investment: $250
- Minimum per month (optional): $50
- Maximum per transaction: $250,000
- No cash dividends paid.
- Partial dividend reinvestment.
- No discount is available.
- No IRA option is available.
- Optional cash purchases allowed.
- Direct debits are available.

CRIIMI MAE Inc.
United States: Real Estate Investment Trust
NYSE: CMM
11200 Rockville Pike
Rockville, MD 20852

CRIIMI MAE is a real estate investment trust (REIT) specializing in investments that are secured by multi-family housing complexes, retail, and other commercial real estate properties located throughout the U.S.

Phone to enroll:
Bank of New York
800-998-9151

EasyStock Investment Plan:
- Initial minimum investment: $500
- Minimum per month (optional): $100
- Maximum monthly investment: $10,000
- Cash dividends are offered.
- Partial dividend reinvestment.
- Discounts on share purchases.
- No IRA option is available.
- Optional cash purchases allowed.
- Direct debits are available.

Cross Timbers Oil Co.
United States: Petroleum Refiners
NYSE: XTO
810 Houston Street
Suite 2000
Fort Worth, TX 76102
www.crosstimbers.com
817-870-2800

Cross Timbers Oil Company acquires, exploits, and develops quality, long-lived producing oil and gas properties. The company's properties are located in East and West Texas, Kansas, Louisiana, New Mexico, Oklahoma, and Wyoming.

Phone to enroll:
Registrar and Transfer Company
800-938-6387

EasyStock Investment Plan:
- Initial minimum investment: $500
- Minimum per month (optional): $50
- Maximum per transaction: $100,000
- Maximum monthly investment: $10,000
- Cash dividends are offered.
- Partial dividend reinvestment.
- No discount is available.
- No IRA option is available.
- Optional cash purchases allowed.
- Direct debits are available.

Crown American Realty Trust
United States: Real Estate Investment Trust
NYSE: CWN
Pasquerilla Plaza
Johnstown, PA 15907
www.crownam.com
814-536-4441

Crown American Realty Trust is involved primarily in the ownership, operation, management, acquisition, leasing, and development of enclosed shopping malls.

Phone to enroll:
Chase Mellon
800-278-4353

EasyStock Investment Plan:
- Initial minimum investment: $100
- Minimum per month (optional): $100

- Maximum quarterly investment: $5,000
- Cash dividends are offered.
- Partial dividend reinvestment.
- No discount is available.
- No IRA option is available.
- Optional cash purchases allowed.
- No direct debit option.

CSR Limited
Australia: Building Materials
OTC: CSRLY
c/o Morgan Guaranty Trust Company
PO Box 9073
Boston, MA 02205-9948
www.csr.com.au

Phone to enroll:
Morgan Guaranty Trust Company
800-997-8970

EasyStock Investment Plan:
- Initial minimum investment: $250
- Minimum per month (optional): $50
- Maximum annual investment: $100,000
- Cash dividends are offered.
- Partial dividend reinvestment.
- No discount is available.
- No IRA option is available.
- Optional cash purchases allowed.
- Direct debits are available.

CSX Corporation
United States: Railroads/Shipping
NYSE: CSX
One James Center
Richmond, VA 23219
www.csx.com
804-782-1400

CSX operates the third-largest rail system in America, after Union Pacific and Burlington Northern, linking twenty U.S. states in the East, the Midwest, and the South. CSX also engages in ocean shipping, inland barging, and logistics operations.

Phone to enroll:
Harris Trust and Savings Bank
888-261-6800

EasyStock Investment Plan:
- Initial minimum investment: $500
- Minimum per month (optional): $50
- Maximum monthly investment: $10,000
- Cash dividends are offered.
- Partial dividend reinvestment.
- No discount is available.
- No IRA option is available.
- Optional cash purchases allowed.
- Direct debits are available.

Curtiss-Wright Corp.
United States: Equipment/Parts
NYSE: CW
1200 Wall Street West
Lyndhurst, NJ 07071
www.curtisswright.com
201-896-8400

Curtiss-Wright Corporation is a diversified multinational manufacturing company that produces and markets precision components and systems. Curtiss-Wright also provides engineered services to aerospace, industrial, and flow control and marine markets.

Phone to enroll:
Harris Bank
888-266-6793

EasyStock Investment Plan:
- Initial minimum investment: $200
- Minimum per month (optional): $100
- Maximum monthly investment: $10,000

- Cash dividends are offered.
- Partial dividend reinvestment.
- No discount is available.
- No IRA option is available.
- Optional cash purchases allowed.
- Direct debits are available.

D

DaimlerChrysler AG
Germany: Automotive
NYSE: DCX
c/o Bank of New York
48 Wall Street
New York, NY 10286
www.daimlerchrysler.com

DaimlerChrysler, resulting from the merger of Daimler-Benz AG and Chrysler Corp., is one of the world's largest automakers. The combined company produces about four million vehicles a year.

Phone to enroll:
Bank of New York
888-BNY-ADRS or 888-269-2377

EasyStock Investment Plan:
- Initial minimum investment: $1,000
- Minimum per month (optional): $50
- Maximum annual investment: $350,000
- Cash dividends are offered.
- Partial dividend reinvestment.
- No discount is available.
- An IRA option is available.
- Optional cash purchases allowed.
- Direct debits are available.
- View materials and enroll online at www.netstockdirect.com.

Darden Restaurants, Inc.
United States: Restaurants
NYSE: DRI
5900 Lake Ellenor Drive
Orlando, FL 32809
407-245-4000

Darden Restaurants, the largest casual-dining restaurant group in the world, operates three distinct restaurant concepts: Red Lobster, Olive Garden, and Bahama Breeze.

Phone to enroll:
Chase Mellon
800-829-8432

EasyStock Investment Plan:
- Initial minimum investment: $1,000
- Minimum per month (optional): $50
- Maximum quarterly investment: $25,000
- Maximum annual investment: $100,000
- Cash dividends are offered.
- Partial dividend reinvestment.
- No discount is available.
- No IRA option is available.
- Optional cash purchases allowed.
- No direct debit option.

Dassault Systems S.A.
France: Computer Systems
NASDAQ: DASTY
c/o Morgan Guaranty Trust Company
PO Box 9073
Boston, MA 02205-9948
www.dsweb.com
Phone to enroll:
Morgan Guaranty Trust Company
800-997-8970

EasyStock Investment Plan:
- Initial minimum investment: $250

- Minimum per month (optional): $50
- Maximum annual investment: $100,000
- Cash dividends are offered.
- Partial dividend reinvestment.
- No discount is available.
- No IRA option is available.
- Optional cash purchases allowed.
- Direct debits are available.

Dayton Hudson Corp.
United States: Department Stores
NYSE: DH
777 Nicollet Mall
Minneapolis, MN 55402
www.dhc.com
612-370-6948

Dayton Hudson operates more than 1,100 stores in three retail formats, including Target, the third-largest discount chain; Mervyn's, mid-range department stores operating in the west and southwest; and Marshall Fields.

Phone to enroll:
Morgan Guaranty Trust Company
888-268-0203

EasyStock Investment Plan:
- Initial minimum investment: $500
- Minimum per month (optional): $50
- Maximum annual investment: $100,000
- Cash dividends are offered.
- Partial dividend reinvestment.
- No discount is available.
- No IRA option is available.
- Optional cash purchases allowed.
- Direct debits are available.
- View materials and enroll online at www.netstockdirect.com.

De Rigo S.p.A.
Italy: Eyewear
NYSE: DER
c/o Bank of New York
48 Wall Street
New York, NY 10286
www.derigo.com

De Rigo is one of the world's largest makers of medium- to high-end sunglasses. The company has about 670 models of sunglasses and regular eyeglasses under its own brands and licensed names.

Phone to enroll:
Bank of New York
888-BNY-ADRS or 888-269-2377

EasyStock Investment Plan:
- Initial minimum investment: $250
- Minimum per month (optional): $50
- Maximum per transaction: $250,000
- No cash dividends paid.
- Partial dividend reinvestment.
- No discount is available.
- No IRA option is available.
- Optional cash purchases allowed.
- Direct debits are available.

Deere & Company Inc.
United States: Heavy Machinery
NYSE: DE
John Deere Road
Moline, IL 61265
www.deere.com
309-765-8000

Deere & Company is the world's largest maker of farm equipment and a leading producer of industrial and lawn care equipment.

Phone to enroll:
Bank of New York
800-268-7369

EasyStock Investment Plan:
- Initial minimum investment: $500
- Minimum per month (optional): $100
- Maximum annual investment: $10,000
- Cash dividends are offered.
- Partial dividend reinvestment.
- No discount is available.
- No IRA option is available.
- Optional cash purchases allowed.
- Direct debits are available.

Delta Natural Gas Co., Inc.
United States: Natural Gas
NASDAQ: DGAS
3617 Lexington Road
Winchester, KY 40391
www.deltagas.com
606-744-6171

Delta Natural Gas is a regulated public utility that provides gas in twenty counties in central and southeastern Kentucky. More than 99% of its approximately 36,000 customers are residential or commercial.

Phone to enroll:
Bank of New York
606-744-6171

EasyStock Investment Plan:
- Initial minimum investment: $100
- Minimum per month (optional): $25
- Maximum annual investment: $50,000
- Cash dividends are offered.
- Partial dividend reinvestment.
- No discount is available.
- No IRA option is available.
- Optional cash purchases allowed.
- No direct debit option.

Diageo PLC
United Kingdom: Beverages
NYSE: DEO
c/o Bank of New York
48 Wall Street
New York, NY 10286
www.diageo.com

Diageo, created by the merger of Grand Metropolitan and Guinness, is the world's largest drinks group, offering three of the five best-selling Scotch brands in America (J&B, Johnnie Walker, and Scoresby).

Phone to enroll:
Bank of New York
888-BNY-ADRS or 888-269-2377

EasyStock Investment Plan:
- Initial minimum investment: $250
- Minimum per month (optional): $50
- Maximum per transaction: $250,000
- Cash dividends are offered.
- Partial dividend reinvestment.
- No discount is available.
- No IRA option is available.
- Optional cash purchases allowed.
- Direct debits are available.

Digitale Telekabel AG
Germany: Media
NASDAQ: DTAGY
c/o Bank of New York
48 Wall Street
New York, NY 10286
www.dta-ag.de

Digitale Telekabel wires apartment buildings and condominiums to a satellite network or to Deutsche Telekom. The company's cables allow for future expansion into the Internet-access market.

Phone to enroll:
Bank of New York
888-BNY-ADRS or 888-269-2377

EasyStock Investment Plan:
- Initial minimum investment: $250
- Minimum per month (optional): $50
- Maximum per transaction: $250,000
- No cash dividends paid.
- Partial dividend reinvestment.
- No discount is available.
- No IRA option is available.
- Optional cash purchases allowed.
- Direct debits are available.

Dominion Resources, Inc.
United States: Electric Services
NYSE: D
901 East Byrd Street
PO Box 26532
Richmond, VA 23261-4072
www.domres.com
804-775-5700

Dominion Resources, through primary subsidiary Virginia Electric and Power, provides electricity to two million customers in North Carolina and Virginia.

Phone to enroll:
Bank of New York
800-552-4034

EasyStock Investment Plan:
- Initial minimum investment: $250
- Minimum per month (optional): $40
- Maximum quarterly investment: $100,000
- Cash dividends are offered.
- Partial dividend reinvestment.
- No discount is available.
- No IRA option is available.
- Optional cash purchases allowed.
- Direct debits are available.

Dow Jones & Co., Inc.
United States: Newspapers
NYSE: DJ
200 Liberty Street
New York, NY 10281
www.dowjones.com
212-416-2000

Dow Jones, a multinational media company, specializes in business news, dispensing it in print and electronically. Its flagship publication, *The Wall Street Journal*, is America's number one daily newspaper in terms of circulation. Dow Jones recently combined its online operations with those of Reuters.

Phone company to enroll:
800-247-0400

EasyStock Investment Plan:
- Initial minimum investment: $1,000
- Minimum per month (optional): $100
- Maximum per transaction: $10,000
- Maximum monthly investment: $10,000
- Maximum quarterly investment: $30,000
- Maximum annual investment: $120,000
- Cash dividends are offered.
- Partial dividend reinvestment.
- No discount is available.
- No IRA option is available.
- Optional cash purchases allowed.
- Direct debits are available.

DQE, Inc.
United States: Electric Services
NYSE: DQE
500 Cherrington Pkwy.
Coraopolis, PA 15108
www.dqe.com
412-262-4700

DQE is an energy services holding company. Its main subsidiary, Duquesne Light, produces, transmits, distributes, and sells electricity to approximately 580,000 customers in an 817-square-mile area in western Pennsylvania.

Phone to enroll:
Chase Mellon
800-247-0400

EasyStock Investment Plan:
- Initial minimum investment: $100
- Minimum per month (optional): $10
- Maximum annual investment: $60,000
- Cash dividends are offered.
- Partial dividend reinvestment.
- No discount is available.
- No IRA option is available.
- Optional cash purchases allowed.
- Direct debits are available.
- View materials and enroll online at www.netstockdirect.com.

Dr. Solomon's Group PLC
United Kingdom: Computer Software
NASDAQ: SOLLY
c/o Bank of New York
48 Wall Street
New York, NY 10286
www.drsolomon.com

As computer viruses have spread, so has Dr. Solomon's software, the world leader in computer virus detection, identification, and repair. Success is mainly attributed to the Anti-Virus Toolkit, which detects over 14,000 currently known viruses and variants.

Phone to enroll:
Bank of New York
888-BNY-ADRS or 888-269-2377

EasyStock Investment Plan:
- Initial minimum investment: $250
- Minimum per month (optional): $50
- Maximum per transaction: $250,000
- No cash dividends paid.
- Partial dividend reinvestment.
- No discount is available.
- No IRA option is available.
- Optional cash purchases allowed.
- Direct debits are available.

DTE Energy Co. Inc.
United States: Electric Services
NYSE: DTE
2000 Second Avenue
Detroit, MI 48226
www.dteenergy.com
313-235-4000

DTE Energy is the holding company for Detroit Edison, which generates electricity and sells it to two million customers in southeastern Michigan.

Phone to enroll:
Bank of New York
800-432-0140

EasyStock Investment Plan:
- Initial minimum investment: $100
- Minimum per month (optional): $25
- Maximum annual investment: $100,000
- Cash dividends are offered.
- Partial dividend reinvestment.
- No discount is available.

- No IRA option is available.
- Optional cash purchases allowed.
- No direct debit option.

Duke Energy Corp.
United States: Electric Services
NYSE: DUK
422 South Church Street
Charlotte, NC 28242
www.duke-energy.com
704-594-6200

Duke Energy was formed from the merger of electric utility company Duke Power Co. and natural gas pipeline operator PanEnergy Corp. Duke Power transmits electricity to 1.8 million customers in North and South Carolina.

Phone company to enroll:
800-488-3853

EasyStock Investment Plan:
- Initial minimum investment: $25
- Minimum per month (optional): $25
- Maximum quarterly investment: $20,000
- Cash dividends are offered.
- Partial dividend reinvestment.
- No discount is available.
- No IRA option is available.
- Optional cash purchases allowed.
- Direct debits are available.

Duke Realty Investments, Inc.
United States: Real Estate Investment Trust
NYSE: DRE
8888 Keystone Crossing
Indianapolis, IN 46240
www.dukereit.com
317-846-4700

Duke Realty Investments is a self-administered and self-managed real estate investment trust. It owns a diversified portfolio of about 380 industrial, office, and retail rental properties containing almost 46 million rentable square feet.

Phone company to enroll:
800-937-5449

EasyStock Investment Plan:
- Initial minimum investment: $250
- Minimum per month (optional): $100
- Maximum monthly investment: $5,000
- Cash dividends are offered.
- No partial dividend reinvestment.
- Discounts on share purchases.
- No IRA option is available.
- Optional cash purchases allowed.
- Direct debits are available.

Durbam Roodeport Deep Ltd.
South Africa: Mining
NASDAQ: DROOY
c/o Bank of New York
48 Wall Street
New York, NY 10286
www.drd.co.za

Durban Roodepoort Deep has been mining gold in South Africa since 1895, converting it into bullion.

Phone to enroll:
Bank of New York
888-BNY-ADRS or 888-269-2377

EasyStock Investment Plan:
- Initial minimum investment: $250
- Minimum per month (optional): $50
- Maximum per transaction: $250,000
- No cash dividends paid.

- Partial dividend reinvestment.
- No discount is available.
- No IRA option is available.
- Optional cash purchases allowed.
- Direct debits are available.

E

Eastern Company Ltd.
United States: Manufacturing
AMEX: EML
112 Bridge Street
Naugatuck, CT 06770
www.easterncompany.com
203-729-2255

The Eastern Company makes locks and security hardware for use in industry, underground mining, and commercial construction. The company's lock subsidiaries include CCL, World Lock, and Illinois Lock.

Phone to enroll:
Bank of New York
800-633-3455

EasyStock Investment Plan:
- Initial minimum investment: $250
- Minimum per month (optional): $50
- Maximum annual investment: $150,000
- Cash dividends are offered.
- Partial dividend reinvestment.
- No discount is available.
- No IRA option is available.
- Optional cash purchases allowed.
- Direct debits are available.

Eastman Kodak Co.
United States: Film/Camera
NYSE: EK
343 State Street
Rochester, NY 14650
www.kodak.com
716-724-4000

Image-conscious Eastman Kodak makes cameras, copiers, film, and projectors. The company is aggressively expanding and improving its digital imaging products and services for consumers and professionals in the U.S. and its film products in the developing world.

Phone to enroll:
Boston Equiserve LP
800-253-6057

EasyStock Investment Plan:
- Initial minimum investment: $150
- Minimum per month (optional): $50
- Maximum annual investment: $60,000
- Cash dividends are offered.
- Partial dividend reinvestment.
- No discount is available.
- No IRA option is available.
- Optional cash purchases allowed.
- No direct debit option.

ECsoft Group PLC
United Kingdom: Technology
NASDAQ: ECSGY
c/o Bank of New York
48 Wall Street
New York, NY 10286
www.ecsoft-group.com

ECsoft Group is a London-based information technology (IT) services company that helps European corporations implement or upgrade their IT systems.

Phone to enroll:
Bank of New York
888-BNY-ADRS or 888-269-2377

EasyStock Investment Plan:
- Initial minimum investment: $250
- Minimum per month (optional): $50
- Maximum per transaction: $250,000
- No cash dividends paid.
- Partial dividend reinvestment.
- No discount is available.
- No IRA option is available.
- Optional cash purchases allowed.
- Direct debits are available.

Elan Corporation PLC
Ireland: Pharmaceuticals
NYSE: ELN
c/o Bank of New York
48 Wall Street
New York, NY 10286

Elan Corporation designs oral, microparticulate, and transdermal delivery systems; develops drugs for Alzheimer's disease; and conducts extensive research.

Phone to enroll:
Bank of New York
888-BNY-ADRS or 888-269-2377

EasyStock Investment Plan:
- Initial minimum investment: $250
- Minimum per month (optional): $50
- Maximum per transaction: $250,000
- No cash dividends paid.
- Partial dividend reinvestment.
- No discount is available.
- No IRA option is available.
- Optional cash purchases allowed.
- Direct debits are available.

Elf Aquitaine
France: Integrated Oils
NYSE: ELF
c/o Bank of New York
48 Wall Street
New York, NY 10286
www.elf.fr

Elf Aquitaine operates worldwide, exploring for and producing petroleum in nearly thirty countries, with major activity in the North Sea and Africa. Elf operates refineries and sells gasoline through its retail distribution network.

Phone to enroll:
Bank of New York
888-BNY-ADRS or 888-269-2377

EasyStock Investment Plan:
- Initial minimum investment: $250
- Minimum per month (optional): $50
- Maximum per transaction: $250,000
- No cash dividends paid.
- Partial dividend reinvestment.
- No discount is available.
- No IRA option is available.
- Optional cash purchases allowed.
- Direct debits are available.

Eli Lilly and Co. Inc.
United States: Pharmacueticals
NYSE: LLY
Lilly Corporate Center
Indianapolis, IN 46285
www.elililly.com
317-276-2000

Eli Lilly makes Prozac, the world's best-selling antidepressant. It also makes Gemzar, a treatment for pancreatic cancer and associated pain; Humalog, an injectible insulin; and ReoPro, a blood-clot inhibitor widely used in angioplasties.

Phone to enroll:
Bank of New York
800-432-0140

EasyStock Investment Plan:
- Initial minimum investment: $1,000
- Minimum per month (optional): $50
- Maximum annual investment: $150,000
- Cash dividends are offered.
- Partial dividend reinvestment.
- No discount is available.
- No IRA option is available.
- Optional cash purchases allowed.
- Direct debits are available.
- View materials and enroll online at www.netstockdirect.com.

Emcee Broadcast Products, Inc.
United States: Telecommunications
NASDAQ: ECIN
Susquehonna Street
White Haven, PA 18661
www.emcee-brd.com
717-443-9575

Emcee Broadcast Products makes and sells microwave transmitters for the wireless cable television industry and, to a lesser extent, the low-power television industry.

Phone to enroll:
First Chicago Trust Company
888-200-3167

EasyStock Investment Plan:
- Initial minimum investment: $100
- Minimum per month (optional): $100
- Maximum per transaction: $10,000
- Maximum monthly investment: $10,000
- Maximum annual investment: $100,000
- No cash dividends paid.
- Partial dividend reinvestment.
- No discount is available.
- No IRA option is available.
- Optional cash purchases allowed.
- Direct debits are available.

Emerging Markets Telecommunications Fund, Inc.
United States: Telecommunications
NYSE: ETF
c/o Boston Equiserve
InvestLink Program, PO Box 1681
Boston, MA 02205

The Emerging Markets Telecommunications Fund invests in international telecommunications companies in emerging markets.

Phone to enroll:
Boston Equiserve LP
800-730-6001

EasyStock Investment Plan:
- Initial minimum investment: $250
- Minimum per month (optional): $100
- Maximum annual investment: $150,000
- Cash dividends are offered.
- Partial dividend reinvestment.
- No discount is available.
- No IRA option is available.
- Optional cash purchases allowed.
- Direct debits are available.

Empresas ICA, S.A. de C.V.
Mexico: Construction
NYSE: ICA
c/o Bank of New York
48 Wall Street
New York, NY 10286
www.ica.com.mx

Empresas ICA Sociedad Controladora is the largest construction company in Mexico. ICA and Sofregaz U.S. are building underground petroleum storage projects in Mexico.

Phone to enroll:
Bank of New York
888-BNY-ADRS or 888-269-2377

EasyStock Investment Plan:
- Initial minimum investment: $250
- Minimum per month (optional): $50
- Maximum per transaction: $250,000
- Cash dividends are offered.
- Partial dividend reinvestment.
- No discount is available.
- No IRA option is available.
- Optional cash purchases allowed.
- Direct debits are available.

Empresas La Moderna S.A. de C.V.
Mexico: Tobacco
NYSE: ELM
c/o Bank of New York
48 Wall Street
New York, NY 10286

Empresas La Moderna makes and sells seeds and produce. The company's Seminis subsidiary is the largest producer of vegetable seeds in the world, with a 20% market share. La Moderna also distributes fresh produce in Mexico, Europe, and the Middle East.

Phone to enroll:
Bank of New York
888-BNY-ADRS or 888-269-2377

EasyStock Investment Plan:
- Initial minimum investment: $250
- Minimum per month (optional): $50
- Maximum per transaction: $250,000
- Cash dividends are offered.
- Partial dividend reinvestment.
- No discount is available.
- No IRA option is available.
- Optional cash purchases allowed.
- Direct debits are available.

Empresas Telex-Chile
Chile: Telecommunications
NYSE: TL
c/o Bank of New York
48 Wall Street
New York, NY 10286
www.chilesat.net/web/com/telex/ingles.html

Telex-Chile is a telecommunications company that provides long-distance telephone service in Chile, other Latin American countries, and the U.S.

Phone to enroll:
Bank of New York
888-BNY-ADRS or 888-269-2377

EasyStock Investment Plan:
- Initial minimum investment: $250
- Minimum per month (optional): $50
- Maximum per transaction: $250,000
- Cash dividends are offered.
- Partial dividend reinvestment.
- No discount is available.
- No IRA option is available.
- Optional cash purchases allowed.
- Direct debits are available.

Endesa, S.A.
Spain: Electric Services
NYSE: ELE
c/o Morgan Guaranty Trust Company
PO Box 9073
Boston, MA 02205-9948
www.endesa.es/english/index.htm

Endesa (formerly Empresa Nacional de Electricidad, S.A.) supplies power to over nine million customers as the largest electricity producer in Spain.

Phone to enroll:
Morgan Guaranty Trust Company
800-997-8970

EasyStock Investment Plan:
- Initial minimum investment: $250
- Minimum per month (optional): $50
- Maximum annual investment: $100,000
- Cash dividends are offered.
- Partial dividend reinvestment.
- No discount is available.
- No IRA option is available.
- Optional cash purchases allowed.
- Direct debits are available.

Energen Corp.
United States: Natural Gas
NYSE: EGN
2101 Sixth Avenue North
Birmingham, AL 35203
www.energen.com
205-326-2700

Energen is an energy holding company in the natural gas and oil exploration and production business. Its Alabama Gas (Alagasco) subsidiary is a publicly regulated gas utility with about 19,000 miles of service lines.

Phone to enroll:
Morgan Guaranty Trust Company
800-286-9178

EasyStock Investment Plan:
- Initial minimum investment: $250
- Minimum per month (optional): $25
- Maximum annual investment: $100,000
- Cash dividends are offered.
- Partial dividend reinvestment.
- No discount is available.
- No IRA option is available.
- Optional cash purchases allowed.
- Direct debits are available.

Enron Corporation
United States: Natural Gas
NYSE: ENE
1400 Smith Street
Houston, TX 77002
www.enron.com
713-853-6161

Enron, North Americas largest buyer and seller of natural gas, also builds and manages worldwide natural gas transportation, power generation, liquids, and clean fuel facilities.

Phone to enroll:
First Chicago Trust Company
800-662-7662

EasyStock Investment Plan:
- Initial minimum investment: $250
- Minimum per month (optional): $25
- Maximum annual investment: $120,000
- Cash dividends are offered.
- Partial dividend reinvestment.
- No discount is available.
- No IRA option is available.
- Optional cash purchases allowed.
- Direct debits are available.
- View materials and enroll online at www.netstockdirect.com.

Entergy Corp.
United States: Electric Services
NYSE: ETR
639 Loyola Avenue
New Orleans, LA 70113
www.entergy.com
504-529-5262

Entergy generates electricity and transmits and distributes it to about 2.4 million customers in Arkansas, Louisiana, Mississippi, and Texas.

Phone to enroll:
First Chicago Trust Company
800-225-1721

EasyStock Investment Plan:
- Initial minimum investment: $1,000
- Minimum per month (optional): $100
- Maximum monthly investment: $3,000
- Cash dividends are offered.
- Partial dividend reinvestment.
- Discounts on share purchases.
- No IRA option is available.
- Optional cash purchases allowed.
- No direct debit option.

Equitable Companies, Inc.
United States: Financial Services
NYSE: EQ
787 Seventh Avenue
New York, NY 10019
www.equitable.com
212-554-1234

The Equitable Companies own a controlling stake in Donaldson, Lufkin & Jenrette and Alliance Capital Management, in addition to several insurance and financial services businesses, and have a sales force of 7,200 career agents.

Phone to enroll:
Chase Mellon
800-923-6782

EasyStock Investment Plan:
- Initial minimum investment: $500
- Minimum per month (optional): $25
- Maximum monthly investment: $5,000
- Maximum annual investment: $60,000
- Cash dividends are offered.
- No partial dividend reinvestment.
- No discount is available.
- No IRA option is available.
- Optional cash purchases allowed.
- No direct debit option.
- View materials and enroll online at www.netstockdirect.com.

Equity Residential Properties Trust
United States: Real Estate Investment Trust
NYSE: EQR
Two North Riverside Plaza
Chicago, IL 60606
www.eqr.com
312-474-1300

Equity Residential Properties Trust owns 500 apartment properties containing over 140,000 units located in 35 states throughout the U.S.

Phone to enroll:
First Chicago Trust Company

EasyStock Investment Plan:
- Initial minimum investment: $250
- Minimum per month (optional): $250
- Maximum monthly investment: $5,000
- Cash dividends are offered.
- Partial dividend reinvestment.

- Discounts on share purchases.
- No IRA option is available.
- Optional cash purchases allowed.
- No direct debit option.

Esprit Telecom PLC
United Kingdom: Telecommunications
NASDAQ: ESPRY
c/o Bank of New York
48 Wall Street
New York, NY 10286
www.esprittele.com/esprit.htm

Esprit Telecom provides domestic and international telecommunication services to large- and medium-sized companies throughout Europe.

Phone to enroll:
Bank of New York
888-BNY-ADRS or 888-269-2377

EasyStock Investment Plan:
- Initial minimum investment: $250
- Minimum per month (optional): $50
- Maximum per transaction: $250,000
- No cash dividends paid.
- Partial dividend reinvestment.
- No discount is available.
- No IRA option is available.
- Optional cash purchases allowed.
- Direct debits are available.

Exxon Corp.
United States: Integrated Oils
NYSE: XON
225 East John W. Carpenter Freeway
Irving, TX 75062
www.exxon.com

The world's number two oil company, behind Royal Dutch/Shell, Exxon has oil reserves of 6.6 billion barrels and gas reserves of 42.2 trillion cubic feet. The company operates or markets products in more than 100 countries. Each day Exxon sells about 65 million gallons of gasoline. When Exxon completes its acquisition of Mobil, the merged entity will become the world's largest oil company.

Phone to enroll:
Bank of New York
800-432-0140

EasyStock Investment Plan:
- Initial minimum investment: $250
- Minimum per month (optional): $50
- Maximum annual investment: $100,000
- Cash dividends are offered.
- Partial dividend reinvestment.
- No discount is available.
- AN IRA option is available.
- Optional cash purchases allowed.
- Direct debits are available.

F

FAI Insurances Limited
Australia: Insurance
NYSE: FAI
c/o Bank of New York
48 Wall Street
New York, NY 10286
www.fai.com.au

Deep within the core of the South Pacific is FAI Insurances, an insurance company that derives 14% of its revenues from mining.

Phone to enroll:
Bank of New York
888-BNY-ADRS or 888-269-2377

EasyStock Investment Plan:
- Initial minimum investment: $250
- Minimum per month (optional): $50
- Maximum per transaction: $250,000
- Cash dividends are offered.
- Partial dividend reinvestment.
- No discount is available.
- No IRA option is available.
- Optional cash purchases allowed.
- Direct debits are available.

Fannie Mae Corp.
United States: Mortgage Finance
NYSE: FNM
3900 Wisconsin Avenue NW
Washington, DC 20016
www.fanniemae.com
202-752-7000

Fannie Mae, formerly the Federal National Mortgage Association, is mandated by the U.S. government. Its purpose is to provide liquidity in the mortgage market by buying mortgages from lenders and packaging them for re-sale.

Phone to enroll:
Bank of New York
888-BNY-ADRS or 888-269-2377
800-BUY-FANNIE or 800-289-3266

EasyStock Investment Plan:
- Initial minimum investment: $250
- Minimum per month (optional): $25
- Maximum annual investment: $250,000
- Cash dividends are offered.
- Partial dividend reinvestment.
- No discount is available.
- An IRA option is available.
- Optional cash purchases allowed.
- Direct debits are available.
- View materials and enroll online at www.netstockdirect.com.

FIAT S.p.A.
Italy: Automotive
NYSE: FIA
c/o Morgan Guaranty Trust Company
PO Box 9073
Boston, MA 02205-9948
www.fiat.com

Fiat is Italy's largest carmaker and is second in Europe, behind Volkswagen. Its automobile brands range from compacts and sedans such as the Fiat Siena and Fiat Palio to sports cars offered by Alfa Romeo and Ferrari.

Phone to enroll:
Morgan Guaranty Trust Company
800-997-8970

EasyStock Investment Plan:
- Initial minimum investment: $250
- Minimum per month (optional): $50
- Maximum annual investment: $100,000
- Cash dividends are offered.
- Partial dividend reinvestment.
- No discount is available.
- No IRA option is available.
- Optional cash purchases allowed.
- Direct debits are available.

Fila Holdings S.p.A.
Italy: Clothing/Footwear
NYSE: FHL
c/o Bank of New York
48 Wall Street
New York, NY 10286
www.fila.com

Fila Holdings is the world's fourth largest shoemaker, after Nike, Reebok, and Adidas. Fila's footwear collection offers products ranging from active sports styles designed

for basketball, running, hiking, and tennis to canvas deck shoes and walking shoes.

Phone to enroll:
Bank of New York
888-BNY-ADRS or 888-269-2377

EasyStock Investment Plan:
- Initial minimum investment: $250
- Minimum per month (optional): $50
- Maximum per transaction: $250,000
- Cash dividends are offered.
- Partial dividend reinvestment.
- No discount is available.
- No IRA option is available.
- Optional cash purchases allowed.
- Direct debits are available.

Finova Group, Inc.
United States: Finance
NYSE: FNV
1850 North Central Avenue
Phoenix, AZ 85004
www.finova.com
602-207-4900

The Finova Group, formerly known as GFC Financial Corporation, is one of the nation's top commercial finance companies. The Finova Group provides secured financing and leasing to small- and medium-sized businesses.

Phone to enroll:
Bank of New York
800-286-9178

EasyStock Investment Plan:
- Initial minimum investment: $500
- Minimum per month (optional): $50
- Maximum quarterly investment: $25,000
- No cash dividends paid.
- No partial dividend reinvestment.
- No discount is available.
- No IRA option is available.
- Optional cash purchases allowed.
- Direct debits are available.

First Energy Corporation
United States: Utilities
NYSE: FE
76 South Main Street
Akron, OH 44308
www.firstenergycorp.com
330-384-5100

FirstEnergy holds four electric utilities and serves 2.2 million customers in Ohio and western Pennsylvania.

Phone to enroll:
First Commercial Trust Company
800-736-3402

EasyStock Investment Plan:
- Initial minimum investment: $250
- Minimum per month (optional): $50
- Maximum annual investment: $100,000
- Cash dividends are offered.
- Partial dividend reinvestment.
- No discount is available.
- No IRA option is available.
- Optional cash purchases allowed.
- No direct debit option.

First Financial Holdings, Inc.
United States: Savings and Loan
NASDAQ: FFCH
34 Broad Street
Charleston, SC 29401
www.firstfederal.com
803-529-5800

First Financial Holdings owns First Federal Savings and Loan and Peoples Federal Savings and Loan. The banks have thirty-five branches in South Carolina.

Phone company to enroll:
800-998-9151

EasyStock Investment Plan:
- Initial minimum investment: $250
- Minimum per month (optional): $100
- Maximum monthly investment: $5,000
- Cash dividends are offered.
- Partial dividend reinvestment.
- No discount is available.
- No IRA option is available.
- Optional cash purchases allowed.
- Direct debits are available.

First Israel Fund, Inc.
Israel: Investment Management
NYSE: ISL
c/o Boston Equiserve LP
InvestLink Program,
PO Box 1681
Boston, MA 02105-1681

First Israel Fund invests in Israeli companies, creating an Israeli investment fund.

Phone to enroll:
Boston Equiserve LP
800-730-6001

EasyStock Investment Plan:
- Initial minimum investment: $250
- Minimum per month (optional): $100
- Maximum annual investment: $100,000
- Cash dividends are offered.
- Partial dividend reinvestment.
- No discount is available.
- No IRA option is available.
- Optional cash purchases allowed.
- Direct debits are available.

First Plus Financial Group, Inc.
United States: Financial Services
NASDAQ: FPFG
1600 Viceroy Drive
Dallas, TX 75235
www.firstplus.com

A specialized consumer finance company, First Plus Financial Group makes home improvement and debt-consolidating home equity loans through about two hundred locations in the U.S.

Phone to enroll:
Bank of New York
800-742-7629

EasyStock Investment Plan:
- Initial minimum investment: $1,000
- Minimum per month (optional): $100
- Maximum per transaction: $5,000
- Maximum monthly investment: $5,000
- No cash dividends paid.
- Partial dividend reinvestment.
- Discounts on share purchases.
- No IRA option is available.
- Optional cash purchases allowed.
- No direct debit option.

Flamel Technologies S.A.
France: Pharmaceuticals
NASDAQ: FLMLY
c/o Bank of New York
48 Wall Street
New York, NY 10286
www.flamel-technologies.fr

Flame Technologies is a French pharmaceutical company.

Phone to enroll:
Bank of New York
888-BNY-ADRS or 888-269-2377

EasyStock Investment Plan:
- Initial minimum investment: $250
- Minimum per month (optional): $50
- Maximum per transaction: $250,000
- No cash dividends paid.
- Partial dividend reinvestment.
- No discount is available.
- No IRA option is available.
- Optional cash purchases allowed.
- Direct debits are available.

Florida Progress Corp.
United States: Electric Services
NYSE: FPC
One Progress Plaza
St. Petersburg, FL 33701
www.fpc.com
727-824-6400

Florida Progress is a utility holding company whose primary subsidiary, Florida Power, is the second largest electric utility in the state. Florida Power serves 1.3 million customers in the north and central parts of the state.

Phone to enroll:
Bank of New York
813-824-6416

EasyStock Investment Plan:
- Initial minimum investment: $100
- Minimum per month (optional): $10
- Maximum annual investment: $100,000
- Cash dividends are offered.
- Partial dividend reinvestment.
- No discount is available.
- No IRA option is available.
- Optional cash purchases allowed.
- No direct debit option.

Food Lion, Inc.
United States: Food/Supermarkets
NASDAQ: FDLNA
2110 Executive Drive
Salisbury, NC 28145
www.foodlion.com
704-633-8250

Food Lion operates more than 1,150 general food supermarkets under the Food Lion and Kash 'n' Karry names in eleven states. Food Lion emphasizes low prices and private-label brands.

Phone to enroll:
Boston Equiserve LP
888-232-9530

EasyStock Investment Plan:
- Initial minimum investment: $250
- Minimum per month (optional): $50
- Maximum monthly investment: $2,500
- Cash dividends are offered.
- Partial dividend reinvestment.
- No discount is available.
- No IRA option is available.
- Optional cash purchases allowed.
- Direct debits are available.
- View materials and enroll online at www.netstockdirect.com.

Ford Motor Company Limited
United States: Automotive
NYSE: F
The American Road
Dearborn, MI 481211899
www.ford.com
313-322-3000

Ford is the world's largest truck maker and the number two manufacturer of cars and trucks combined, behind GM. It makes vehicles under

the Aston Martin, Ford, Jaguar, Lincoln, and Mercury brands and markets over seventy different models.

Phone to enroll:
First Chicago Trust Company
800-955-4791

EasyStock Investment Plan:
- Initial minimum investment: $1,000
- Minimum per month (optional): $50
- Maximum annual investment: $250,000
- Cash dividends are offered.
- Partial dividend reinvestment.
- No discount is available.
- No IRA option is available.
- Optional cash purchases allowed.
- Direct debits are available.
- View materials and enroll online at www.netstockdirect.com.

Formula Systems Inc.
Israel: Computer Software and Systems
NYSE: FORTY
c/o Bank of New York
48 Wall Street
New York, NY 10286
www.formula.co.il

Through its subsidiaries and affiliates, Israel-based Formula Systems provides a wide range of software and computer-based business services.

Phone to enroll:
Bank of New York
888-BNY-ADRS or 888-269-2377

EasyStock Investment Plan:
- Initial minimum investment: $250
- Minimum per month (optional): $50
- Maximum per transaction: $250,000
- Maximum annual investment: $250,000
- Cash dividends are offered.
- Partial dividend reinvestment.
- No discount is available.
- No IRA option is available.
- Optional cash purchases allowed.
- Direct debits are available.

Formulab Neuronetics Inc.
Australia: Computer Software
NYSE: FNCLY
c/o Bank of New York
48 Wall Street
New York, NY 10286

Formulab Neuronetics creates products that combine voice mail, intercom, and Internet telephony.

Phone to enroll:
Bank of New York
888-BNY-ADRS or 888-269-2377

EasyStock Investment Plan:
- Initial minimum investment: $250
- Minimum per month (optional): $50
- Maximum per transaction: $250,000
- No cash dividends paid.
- Partial dividend reinvestment.
- No discount is available.
- No IRA option is available.
- Optional cash purchases allowed.
- Direct debits are available.

Fresenius Medical Care AG
Germany: Health-care Facilities
NYSE: FRN
c/o Morgan Guaranty Trust Company
PO Box 9073
Boston, MA 02205-9948

Fresenius Medical Care is the largest dialysis service provider in the U.S. and the world. The company treats

more than 56,000 patients, 82% of them in the U.S. It provides these services through more than 780 dialysis clinics in sixteen countries.

Phone to enroll:
Morgan Guaranty Trust Company
800-997-8970

EasyStock Investment Plan:
- Initial minimum investment: $250
- Minimum per month (optional): $50
- Maximum annual investment: $100,000
- Cash dividends are offered.
- Partial dividend reinvestment.
- No discount is available.
- No IRA option is available.
- Optional cash purchases allowed.
- Direct debits are available.

Frontier Insurance Group, Inc.
United States: Insurance
NYSE: FTR
195 Lake Louise Marie Road
Rock Hill, NY 12775
www.frontierins.com
914-796-2100

Frontier Insurance Group sells specialty property and casualty insurance through its subsidiaries, including Frontier Insurance, Medical Professional Liability Agency, Lyndon Property Insurance, and Pioneer Claim Management.

Phone to enroll:
Morgan Guaranty Trust Company
888-200-3162

EasyStock Investment Plan:
- Initial minimum investment: $100
- Minimum per month (optional): $50
- Maximum per transaction: $10,000
- Maximum annual investment: $100,000
- Cash dividends are offered.
- Partial dividend reinvestment.
- No discount is available.
- No IRA option is available.
- Optional cash purchases allowed.
- Direct debits are available.

G

Gallaher Group PLC
United Kingdom: Tobacco
NYSE: GLH
c/o Bank of New York
48 Wall Street
New York, NY 10286
www.gallaher-group.com

Gallaher Group is the largest U.K. cigarette company, having been spun off to shareholders by Fortune Brands.

Phone to enroll:
Bank of New York
888-BNY-ADRS or 888-269-2377

EasyStock Investment Plan:
- Initial minimum investment: $250
- Minimum per month (optional): $50
- Maximum per transaction: $250,000
- Cash dividends are offered.
- Partial dividend reinvestment.
- No discount is available.
- No IRA option is available.
- Optional cash purchases allowed.
- Direct debits are available.

GenCorp Inc.
United States: Chemicals
NYSE: GY
175 Ghent Road
Fairlawn, OH 44333-3300
www.gencorp.com
330-869-4200

GenCorp makes specialty polymers, tennis balls and racquetballs, decorative and building products, vehicle sealants, and rocket systems. The company's specialty polymers unit makes latex coatings and adhesives.

Phone to enroll:
Bank of New York
800-432-0140

EasyStock Investment Plan:
- Initial minimum investment: $500
- Minimum per month (optional): $50
- Maximum annual investment: -
- Cash dividends are offered.
- Partial dividend reinvestment.
- No discount is available.
- No IRA option is available.
- Optional cash purchases allowed.
- Direct debits are available.

General Cable PLC
United Kingdom: Telecommunications
NASDAQ: GCABY
c/o Bank of New York
48 Wall Street
New York, NY 10286
www.generalcable.co.uk

General Cable develops, manufactures, and sells more than 11,000 copper wire and cable products for the transmission of voice, data, video, and control signals and electrical currents.

Phone to enroll:
Bank of New York
888-BNY-ADRS or 888-269-2377

EasyStock Investment Plan:
- Initial minimum investment: $250
- Minimum per month (optional): $50
- Maximum per transaction: $250,000
- No cash dividends paid.
- Partial dividend reinvestment.
- No discount is available.
- No IRA option is available.
- Optional cash purchases allowed.
- Direct debits are available.

General Electric Co. Ltd.
United States: Electrical Equipment
Financial Services/Media/Utilities
NYSE: GE
3135 Easton Turnpike
Fairfield, CT 06431
www.ge.com
203-373-2211

General Electric operates a wide array of businesses, from TV network NBC, to GE Capital, to power plant parts manufacturing. GE is known for its commitment to be the top-ranked firm in every business it operates.

Phone to enroll:
Bank of New York
800-786-2543

EasyStock Investment Plan:
- Initial minimum investment: $250
- Minimum per month (optional): $10
- Maximum per transaction: $10,000
- Cash dividends are offered.
- Partial dividend reinvestment.

- No discount is available.
- No IRA option is available.
- Optional cash purchases allowed.
- Direct debits are available.

General Growth Properties, Inc.
United States: Real Estate Investment Trust
NYSE: GGP
55 West Monroe
Suite 3100
Chicago, IL 60603
www.generalgrowth.com
312-960-5000

General Growth Properties is the second-largest owner and operator of regional malls in the U.S., behind the Simon DeBartolo Group. It owns, develops, or operates more than 105 shopping malls.

Phone to enroll:
Norwest Bank Minnesota
888-291-3713

EasyStock Investment Plan:
- Initial minimum investment: $200
- Minimum per month (optional): $50
- Maximum per quarter: $125,000
- Cash dividends are offered.
- Partial dividend reinvestment.
- No discount is available.
- No IRA option is available.
- Optional cash purchases allowed.
- Direct debits are available.

Gillette Co. Ltd.
United States: Consumer Products
NYSE: G
Prudential Tower Building
Boston, MA 02199
www.gillette.com
617-421-7000

Although best known for its razors and blades, Gillette is also a leader in batteries (Duracell), dental care (Oral-B), toiletries (Right Guard, White Rain), and writing products (Parker).

Phone to enroll:
Boston Equiserve LP
800-643-6989

EasyStock Investment Plan:
- Initial minimum investment: $1,000
- Minimum per month (optional): $100
- Maximum annual investment: $120,000
- No cash dividends paid.
- No partial dividend reinvestment.
- No discount is available.
- No IRA option is available.
- Optional cash purchases allowed.
- Direct debits are available.

Glenborough Realty Trust, Inc.
United States: Real Estate Investment Trust
NYSE: GLB
400 South El Camino Real
San Mateo, CA 94402
650-343-9300

Glenborough Realty Trust's portfolio contains about 130 industrial, office, hotel, retail, and multi-family properties in twenty-three states.

Phone to enroll:
Boston Equiserve LP
800-998-9151

EasyStock Investment Plan:
- Initial minimum investment: $250
- Minimum per month (optional): $100
- Maximum monthly investment: $10,000
- Cash dividends are offered.
- Partial dividend reinvestment.
- No discount is available.
- No IRA option is available.
- Optional cash purchases allowed.
- Direct debits are available.

Glimcher Realty Trust
United States: Real Estate Investment Trust
NYSE: GRT
20 South Third Street
Columbus, OH 43215
614-621-9000

Glimcher Realty owns, manages, acquires, and develops regional malls, community shopping centers, and single-tenant retail properties. The trust owns and manages more than 115 properties.

Phone to enroll:
Registrar and Transfer Company
800-286-9178

EasyStock Investment Plan:
- Initial minimum investment: -
- Minimum per month (optional): -
- Maximum annual investment: -
- Cash dividends are offered.
- No partial dividend reinvestment.
- No discount is available.
- No IRA option is available.
- Optional cash purchases allowed.
- Direct debits are available.

Goodyear Tire & Rubber Co. Ltd.
United States: Tires and Rubber
NYSE: GT
1144 East Market Street
Akron, OH 44316
www.goodyear.com
330-796-2121

Goodyear Tire & Rubber is the number one maker of car and truck tires in the U.S. and is ranked third in the world, behind Michelin and Bridgestone. Other products include auto hoses and belts, and industrial chemicals.

Phone to enroll:
Harris Bank
800-317-4445

EasyStock Investment Plan:
- Initial minimum investment: $250
- Minimum per month (optional): $25
- Maximum annual investment: $150,000
- Cash dividends are offered.
- Partial dividend reinvestment.
- No discount is available.
- No IRA option is available.
- Optional cash purchases allowed.
- Direct debits are available.
- View materials and enroll online at www.netstockdirect.com.

Great Central Mines
Australia: Precious Metals
NASDAQ: GTCMY
c/o Bank of New York
48 Wall Street
New York, NY 10286
www.ausgold.com/gcm

From both open pit mines and deep underground shafts, Great Central Mines digs gold in Australia. The company's mines have proven gold

reserves of more than 1.5 million ounces.

Phone to enroll:
Bank of New York
888-BNY-ADRS or 888-269-2377

EasyStock Investment Plan:
- Initial minimum investment: $250
- Minimum per month (optional): $50
- Maximum per transaction: $250,000
- Cash dividends are offered.
- Partial dividend reinvestment.
- No discount is available.
- No IRA option is available.
- Optional cash purchases allowed.
- Direct debits are available.

Green Mountain Power Corp.
United States: Electric Services
NYSE: GMP
25 Green Mountain Drive
South Burlington, VT 05403
www.gmpvt.com
802-864-5731

Green Mountain Power is a public utility that supplies electric energy and related services to approximately 83,000 customers in Vermont. Residential customers account for about 34% of total sales, while commercial and industrial customers account for 54% of sales.

Phone to enroll:
Bank of New York
802-864-5731

EasyStock Investment Plan:
- Initial minimum investment: $50
- Minimum per month (optional): $50
- Maximum annual investment: $40,000
- Cash dividends are offered.
- Partial dividend reinvestment.
- Discounts on share purchases.
- No IRA option is available.
- Optional cash purchases allowed.
- No direct debit option.

GreenPoint Financial Corp.
United States: Banking
NYSE: GPT
90 Park Avenue
New York, NY 10016
www.greenpoint.com
212-834-1711

GreenPoint Financial is a financial services holding company for a bank, a mortgage company, and a community development corporation. Subsidiary GreenPoint Bank serves New York City through seventy-five banking offices.

Phone to enroll:
Chase Mellon
800-842-7629

EasyStock Investment Plan:
- Initial minimum investment: $2,000
- Minimum per month (optional): $100
- Maximum monthly investment: $10,000
- Cash dividends are offered.
- Partial dividend reinvestment.
- No discount is available.
- No IRA option is available.
- Optional cash purchases allowed.
- Direct debits are available.

Groupe AB
France: Media
NYSE: ABG
c/o Bank of New York
48 Wall Street
New York, NY 10286
www.abweb.com/abid/index.html

Groupe AB produces and distributes TV programming in France, other French-speaking regions of Europe, and more than forty-five other countries. The company owns a library of more than 30,000 hours of programming, including cartoons, TV movies, sitcoms, and documentaries.

Phone to enroll:
Bank of New York
888-BNY-ADRS or 888-269-2377

EasyStock Investment Plan:
- Initial minimum investment: $250
- Minimum per month (optional): $50
- Maximum per transaction: $250,000
- No cash dividends paid.
- Partial dividend reinvestment.
- No discount is available.
- No IRA option is available.
- Optional cash purchases allowed.
- Direct debits are available.

Grupo Casa Autrey, S.A. de C.V.
Mexico: Drug Stores
NYSE: ATY
c/o Morgan Guaranty Trust Company
PO Box 9073
Boston, MA 02205-9948
www.autrey.com

Grupo Casa Autrey distributes pharmaceuticals, health and beauty aids, non-perishable foods, magazines, books, videos, consumer products, and office supplies throughout Mexico.

Phone to enroll:
Morgan Guaranty Trust Company
800-997-8970

EasyStock Investment Plan:
- Initial minimum investment: $250
- Minimum per month (optional): $50
- Maximum annual investment: $100,000
- Cash dividends are offered.
- Partial dividend reinvestment.
- No discount is available.
- No IRA option is available.
- Optional cash purchases allowed.
- Direct debits are available.

Grupo Elektra S.A. de C.V.
Mexico: Merchandising
NYSE: EKT
c/o Bank of New York
48 Wall Street
New York, NY 10286
www.elektra.com.mx

Mexico-based Grupo Elektra is a specialty retailer offering brand-name consumer electronics, major appliances, and household furniture.

Phone to enroll:
Bank of New York
888-BNY-ADRS or 888-269-2377

EasyStock Investment Plan:
- Initial minimum investment: $250
- Minimum per month (optional): $50
- Maximum per transaction: $250,000
- No cash dividends paid.
- Partial dividend reinvestment.
- No discount is available.
- No IRA option is available.
- Optional cash purchases allowed.
- Direct debits are available.

Grupo Imsa, S.A. de C.V.
Mexico: Steel
NYSE: IMY
c/o Bank of New York
48 Wall Street
New York, NY 10286
www.grupoimsa.com

Steel, batteries, and construction products constitute the business segments of Mexico's Grupo IMSA. Subsidiary Imsa Acero owns plants that produce steel, while EnerMex makes automotive batteries.

Phone to enroll:
Bank of New York
888-BNY-ADRS or 888-269-2377

EasyStock Investment Plan:
- Initial minimum investment: $250
- Minimum per month (optional): $50
- Maximum per transaction: $250,000
- Cash dividends are offered.
- Partial dividend reinvestment.
- No discount is available.
- No IRA option is available.
- Optional cash purchases allowed.
- Direct debits are available.

Grupo Industrial Durango S.A .de C.V.
Mexico: Packaging/Printing
NYSE: GID
c/o Bank of New York
48 Wall Street
New York, NY 10286

Grupo Industrial Durango is Mexico's largest paper-packaging company and is aggressively expanding into the United States.

Phone to enroll:
Bank of New York
888-BNY-ADRS or 888-269-2377

EasyStock Investment Plan:
- Initial minimum investment: $250
- Minimum per month (optional): $50
- Maximum per transaction: $250,000
- No cash dividends paid.
- Partial dividend reinvestment.
- No discount is available.
- No IRA option is available.
- Optional cash purchases allowed.
- Direct debits are available.

Grupo Iusacell S.A. de C.V.
Mexico: Telecommunications
NYSE: CEL.D
c/o Bank of New York
48 Wall Street
New York, NY 10286
www.iusacell.com.mx

Grupo Iusacell offers cellular phone, long-distance, paging, and wireless data services in Mexico. Bell Atlantic owns a large part of this company, which has over 500,000 subscribers.

Phone to enroll:
Bank of New York
888-BNY-ADRS or 888-269-2377

EasyStock Investment Plan:
- Initial minimum investment: $250
- Minimum per month (optional): $50
- Maximum per transaction: $250,000
- No cash dividends paid.
- Partial dividend reinvestment.
- No discount is available.
- No IRA option is available.
- Optional cash purchases allowed.
- Direct debits are available.

Grupo Tribasa, S.A. de C.V.
Mexico: Construction
NYSE: GTR
c/o Bank of New York
48 Wall Street
New York, NY 10286
www.tribasa.com.mx

Grupo Tribasa builds roads, highways, and bridges throughout Mexico. The company also builds tunnels, drainage systems, waste-management systems, and parking facilities in addition to its demolition and excavation services.

Phone to enroll:
Bank of New York
888-BNY-ADRS or 888-269-2377

EasyStock Investment Plan:
- Initial minimum investment: $250
- Minimum per month (optional): $50
- Maximum per transaction: $250,000
- No cash dividends paid.
- Partial dividend reinvestment.
- No discount is available.
- No IRA option is available.
- Optional cash purchases allowed.
- Direct debits are available.

Guangshen Railway Co. Limited
China: Railroad
NYSE: GSH
c/o Morgan Guaranty Trust Company
PO Box 9073
Boston, MA 02205-9948

Guangshen Railway runs south China's main rail system, providing passenger, freight, and high-speed train services between the Guangdong region and Hong Kong.

Phone to enroll:
Morgan Guaranty Trust Company
800-997-8970

EasyStock Investment Plan:
- Initial minimum investment: $250
- Minimum per month (optional): $50
- Maximum annual investment: $100,000
- Cash dividends are offered.
- Partial dividend reinvestment.
- No discount is available.
- No IRA option is available.
- Optional cash purchases allowed.
- Direct debits are available.

Guidant Corp.
United States: Equipment/Supplies
NYSE: GDT
307 East McCarty Street
Indianapolis, IN 46225
www.guidant.com
317-971-2000

Guidant manufactures cardiovascular devices and related products, including pacemakers. The company also develops minimally invasive surgical devices.

Phone to enroll:
Morgan Guaranty Trust Company
800-537-1677

EasyStock Investment Plan:
- Initial minimum investment: $250
- Minimum per month (optional): $50
- Maximum annual investment: -
- Cash dividends are offered.
- Partial dividend reinvestment.
- No discount is available.
- No IRA option is available.
- Optional cash purchases allowed.
- Direct debits are available.
- View materials and enroll online at www.netstockdirect.com.

H

Harmony Gold Mining Co. Ltd.
South Africa: Precious Metals
NASDAQ: HGMCY
c/o Bank of New York
48 Wall Street
New York, NY 10286
www.mbendi.co.za/orgs/cb37.htm

Harmony Gold Mining extracts gold from seven deep-level shafts, processes and smelts the ore, then sells the finished product to the South African Reserve Bank. The company also owns three metallurgical plants.

Phone to enroll:
Morgan Guaranty Trust Company
800-997-8970

EasyStock Investment Plan:
- Initial minimum investment: $250
- Minimum per month (optional): $50
- Maximum per transaction: $250,000
- Maximum annual investment:
- No cash dividends paid.
- Partial dividend reinvestment.
- No discount is available.
- No IRA option is available.
- Optional cash purchases allowed.
- Direct debits are available.

Hawaiian Electric Industries, Inc.
United States: Electric Services
NYSE: HE
900 Richards Street
Honolulu, HI 96813
www.hei.com
808-543-5662

Hawaiian Electric Industries operates utilities, savings banks, freight transportation, real estate, and other businesses. Subsidiary Hawaiian Electric Company is the sole Hawaiian electric public utility.

Phone to enroll:
American Stock Transfer & Trust
808-532-5841

EasyStock Investment Plan:
- Initial minimum investment: $100
- Minimum per month (optional): $25
- Maximum annual investment: $100,000
- Cash dividends are offered.
- Partial dividend reinvestment.
- No discount is available.
- No IRA option is available.
- Optional cash purchases allowed.
- Direct debits are available.

Hillenbrand Industries, Inc.
United States: Manufacturing
NYSE: HB
700 State Route 46 East
Batesville, IN 47006
www.hillenbrand.com
812-934-7000

Hillenbrand Industries has a lock on several niche markets in the health care, funeral services, and high-security industries through four major subsidiaries.

Phone company to enroll:
800-286-9178

EasyStock Investment Plan:
- Initial minimum investment: $250
- Minimum per month (optional): $100
- Maximum annual investment: $50,000
- Cash dividends are offered.

- Partial dividend reinvestment.
- No discount is available.
- No IRA option is available.
- Optional cash purchases allowed.
- Direct debits are available.

The Home Depot, Inc.
United States: Hardware Stores
NYSE: HD
2727 Paces Ferry Road
Atlanta, GA 30339
www.homedepot.com

The Home Depot is the largest home improvement retailer in the U.S. and has a significant presence in Canada. Overall, from its start in the mid-1990s Home Depot has grown to more than eight hundred stores in North America, including over forty in Canada.

Phone to enroll:
Harris Bank
800-928-0380

EasyStock Investment Plan:
- Initial minimum investment: $250
- Minimum per month (optional): $25
- Maximum annual investment: $100,000
- Cash dividends are offered.
- Partial dividend reinvestment.
- No discount is available.
- No IRA option is available.
- Optional cash purchases allowed.
- Direct debits are available.

Home Properties of New York, Inc.
United States: Real Estate Investment Trust
NYSE: HME
850 Clinton Square
Rochester, NY 14604
716-546-4900

Home Properties of New York owns and manages apartment properties in over 230 communities with more than 26,000 apartment units.

Phone to enroll:
Boston Equiserve LP
800-278-4353

EasyStock Investment Plan:
- Initial minimum investment: $2,000
- Minimum per month (optional): $50
- Maximum monthly investment: $5,000
- Cash dividends are offered.
- Partial dividend reinvestment.
- Discounts on share purchases.
- No IRA option is available.
- Optional cash purchases allowed.
- No direct debit option.

Huaneng Power International
China: Utilities
NYSE: HNP
c/o Morgan Guaranty Trust Company
PO Box 9073
Boston, MA 02205-9948

Huaneng Power constructs, owns, and operates power plants in China. The company operates five coal-burning plants and one oil-fueled plant in five coastal provinces (Fujian, Guangdong, Hebei, Jiangsu, and Liaoning).

Phone to enroll:
Morgan Guaranty Trust Company
800-997-8970

EasyStock Investment Plan:
- Initial minimum investment: $250
- Minimum per month (optional): $50
- Maximum annual investment: $100,000
- Cash dividends are offered.
- Partial dividend reinvestment.
- No discount is available.
- No IRA option is available.
- Optional cash purchases allowed.
- Direct debits are available.

Huntingdon Life Sciences Group
United Kingdom: Pharmaceuticals
NASDAQ: HTD
c/o Bank of New York
48 Wall Street
New York, NY 10286
www.huntingdon.com

Huntingdon Life Sciences Group performs safety tests for the pharmaceutical and chemical industries.

Phone to enroll:
Morgan Guaranty Trust Company
800-997-8970

EasyStock Investment Plan:
- Initial minimum investment: $250
- Minimum per month (optional): $50
- Maximum per transaction: $250,000
- No cash dividends paid.
- Partial dividend reinvestment.
- No discount is available.
- No IRA option is available.
- Optional cash purchases allowed.
- Direct debits are available.

I

Idacorp Inc.
United States: Electric Services
NYSE: IDA
1221 West Idaho Street
Boise, ID 83702-5627
www.idacorpinc.com
208-388-2200

Idacorp is the holding company that owns Idaho Power, which generates and sells electric energy to more than 363,000 retail customers in southern Idaho, eastern Oregon, and northern Nevada. Residential customers account for more than 25% of revenues.

Phone to enroll:
Bank of New York
800-635-5406

EasyStock Investment Plan:
- Initial minimum investment: $10
- Minimum per month (optional): $10
- Maximum quarterly investment: $15,000
- Cash dividends are offered.
- Partial dividend reinvestment.
- No discount is available.
- No IRA option is available.
- Optional cash purchases allowed.
- No direct debit option.

Illinova Corp.
United States: Multi-Service
NYSE: ILN
500 South 27th Street
PO Box 511
Decatur, IL 62525
www.illinova.com
217-424-6600

Illinova is the holding company for Illinois Power and Illinova Generat-

ing. Illinois Power contributes more than 70% of Illinova's sales, generating and selling electric energy and transporting and selling natural gas. Coal fuels most of its electricity.

Phone company to enroll:
800-750-7011

EasyStock Investment Plan:
- Initial minimum investment: $250
- Minimum per month (optional): $25
- Maximum quarterly investment: $5,000
- Maximum annual investment: $60,000
- Cash dividends are offered.
- Partial dividend reinvestment.
- No discount is available.
- No IRA option is available.
- Optional cash purchases allowed.
- Direct debits are available.

Imperial Chemical Industries PLC
United Kingdom: Chemicals
NYSE: ICI
c/o Morgan Guaranty Trust Company
PO Box 9073
Boston, MA 02205-9948
www.demon.co.uk/ici

Imperial Chemical Industries is one of the largest specialty chemical, materials, and coatings companies in the world. It makes CFC replacements and catalysts and is the world's number one maker of paints.

Phone to enroll:
Morgan Guaranty Trust Company
800-997-8970

EasyStock Investment Plan:
- Initial minimum investment: $250
- Minimum per month (optional): $50
- Maximum annual investment: $100,000
- Cash dividends are offered.
- Partial dividend reinvestment.
- No discount is available.
- No IRA option is available.
- Optional cash purchases allowed.
- Direct debits are available.

Indonesia Fund, Inc.
Indonesia: Investment Management
NYSE: IF
c/o Boston Equiserve LP
InvestLink Program
PO Box 1681
Boston, MA 02105-1681

The Indonesia Fund invests in Indonesian companies.

Phone to enroll:
Boston Equiserve LP
800-730-6001

EasyStock Investment Plan:
- Initial minimum investment: $250
- Minimum per month (optional): $100
- Maximum annual investment: $100,000
- Cash dividends are offered.
- Partial dividend reinvestment.
- No discount is available.
- No IRA option is available.
- Optional cash purchases allowed.
- Direct debits are available.

Industrias Bachoco S.A. de C.V.
Mexico: Food Products
NYSE: IBA
c/o Bank of New York
48 Wall Street
New York, NY 10286
www.bachoco.com.mx

Industrias Bachoco, Mexico's leading poultry producer, doesn't care if the chicken or the egg came first, as long as they both keep coming. The company operates 400 chicken farms, four processing units, seven feeding facilities, and eleven incubation plants.

Phone to enroll:
Bank of New York
888-BNY-ADRS or 888-269-2377

EasyStock Investment Plan:
- Initial minimum investment: $250
- Minimum per month (optional): $50
- Maximum per transaction: $250,000
- No cash dividends paid.
- Partial dividend reinvestment.
- No discount is available.
- No IRA option is available.
- Optional cash purchases allowed.
- Direct debits are available.

Industrie Natuzzi S.p.A.
Italy: Housewares
NYSE: NTZ
c/o Bank of New York
48 Wall Street
New York, NY 10286
www.natuzzi.com

Industrie Natuzzi is one of the world's largest producers of leather furniture.

Phone to enroll:
Bank of New York
888-BNY-ADRS or 888-269-2377

EasyStock Investment Plan:
- Initial minimum investment: $250
- Minimum per month (optional): $50
- Maximum per transaction: $250,000
- Cash dividends are offered.
- Partial dividend reinvestment.
- No discount is available.
- No IRA option is available.
- Optional cash purchases allowed.
- Direct debits are available.

ING Groep N.V.
Netherlands: Banking/Insurance
NYSE: ING
c/o Morgan Guaranty Trust Company
PO Box 9073
Boston, MA 02205-9948
www.inggroup.com

ING Groep is the world's second-largest publicly held life and health insurer and its banking operations are also quite substantial.

Phone to enroll:
Morgan Guaranty Trust Company
800-997-8970

EasyStock Investment Plan:
- Initial minimum investment: $250
- Minimum per month (optional): $50
- Maximum annual investment: $100,000
- No cash dividends paid.
- Partial dividend reinvestment.
- No discount is available.
- No IRA option is available.
- Optional cash purchases allowed.
- Direct debits are available.

Interchange Financial Services Corp.
United States: Banking
AMEX: ISB

Park 80 West
Plaza Two
Saddle Brook, NJ 07662
201-703-2265

Interchange Financial Services Corporation is a bank holding company with one principal subsidiary, Interchange State Bank.

Phone to enroll:
Morgan Guaranty Trust Company
201-703-2265

EasyStock Investment Plan:
- Initial minimum investment: $100
- Minimum per month (optional): $25
- Maximum annual investment: -
- Cash dividends are offered.
- No partial dividend reinvestment.
- No discount is available.
- No IRA option is available.
- Optional cash purchases allowed.
- No direct debit option.

International Business Machines Corp. (IBM)
United States: Computer Systems
NYSE: IBM
One Old Orchard Road
Armonk, NY 10504
www.ibm.com
914-499-1900

International Business Machines or IBM is the world's top provider of computer hardware, software, and services. The company makes a broad range of computers, including desktop, mid-range, and mainframe computers and servers.

Phone to enroll:
Continental Stock Transfer & Trust
888-IBM-6700 or 888-426-6700

EasyStock Investment Plan:
- Initial minimum investment: $500
- Minimum per month (optional): $50
- Maximum quarterly investment: $25,000
- Maximum annual investment: $100,000
- Cash dividends are offered.
- Partial dividend reinvestment.
- No discount is available.
- No IRA option is available.
- Optional cash purchases allowed.
- Direct debits are available.
- View materials and enroll online at www.netstockdirect.com.

Interstate Energy Corp.
United States: Electric Utilities
NYSE: LNT
222 West Washington Avenue
Madison, WI 53703
www.alliant-energy.com
608-252-3311

Interstate Energy, formed from the merger of WPL Holdings, IES Industries, and Interstate Power Company, is a public-utility holding company serving more than 850,000 electric customers and 360,000 natural-gas customers.

Phone to enroll:
First Chicago Trust Company
319-582-5421

EasyStock Investment Plan:
- Initial minimum investment: $50
- Minimum per month (optional): $25
- Maximum monthly investment: $2,000
- Cash dividends are offered.
- Partial dividend reinvestment.
- No discount is available.
- No IRA option is available.
- Optional cash purchases allowed.
- No direct debit option.

Investors Financial Services Corp.
United States: Financial Services
NASDAQ: IFIN
89 South Street
Boston, MA 02205-1537
www.investorsbnk.com
617-330-6700

Investors Financial Services provides asset administration services for fund managers, investment advisors, insurance companies, and banks.

Phone company to enroll:
888-333-5336

EasyStock Investment Plan:
- Initial minimum investment: $250
- Minimum per month (optional): $100
- Maximum annual investment: -
- Cash dividends are offered.
- No partial dividend reinvestment.
- No discount is available.
- No IRA option is available.
- Optional cash purchases allowed.
- Direct debits are available.
- View materials and enroll online at www.netstockdirect.com.

IPALCO Enterprises, Inc.
United States: Electric Services
NYSE: IPL
One Monument Circle
PO Box 798
Indianapolis, IN 46206-0798
www.ipalco.com
317-261-8261

Ipalco Enterprises is the holding company for Indianapolis Power & Light, which generates, transmits, distributes, and sells electricity to more than 420,000 customers in the Indianapolis area.

Phone to enroll:
First Chicago Trust Company
800-877-0153

EasyStock Investment Plan:
- Initial minimum investment: $250
- Minimum per month (optional): $25
- Maximum annual investment: $100,000
- Cash dividends are offered.
- Partial dividend reinvestment.
- No discount is available.
- No IRA option is available.
- Optional cash purchases allowed.
- Direct debits are available.

IRSA Inversiones y Representaciones S.A.
Argentina: Real Estate
NYSE: IRS
c/o Bank of New York
48 Wall Street
New York, NY 10286
www.irsa.com.ar

IRSA develops and operates a rapidly expanding portfolio of commercial rental properties—mainly office and retail space—and develops residential properties in Argentina.

Phone to enroll:
Bank of New York
888-BNY-ADRS or 888-269-2377

EasyStock Investment Plan:
- Initial minimum investment: $200
- Minimum per month (optional): $50
- Maximum per transaction: $250,000
- Cash dividends are offered.
- Partial dividend reinvestment.
- No discount is available.
- No IRA option is available.
- Optional cash purchases allowed.
- Direct debits are available.

Ispat International N.V.
Netherlands: Steel
NYSE: IST
c/o Bank of New York
48 Wall Street
New York, NY 10286
www.ispatinternational.com

After acquiring failing state-owned steel mills around the world, Ispat now operates Imexsa (Mexico), CIL (Trinidad), Sibdec-Dosco (Canada), IHSW (Germany), and Irish Ispat.

Phone to enroll:
Bank of New York
888-BNY-ADRS or 888-269-2377

EasyStock Investment Plan:
- Initial minimum investment: $250
- Minimum per month (optional): $50
- Maximum per transaction: $250,000
- No cash dividends paid.
- Partial dividend reinvestment.
- No discount is available.
- No IRA option is available.
- Optional cash purchases allowed.
- Direct debits are available.

Israel Land Development Corp.
Israel: Real Estate
NASDAQ: ILDCY
c/o Bank of New York
48 Wall Street
New York, NY 10286
www.ild.co.il

The Israel Land Development Company has bought and sold land for urban and agricultural settlement in Israel since before Israel's independence. The firm also has publishing, insurance, hotel, medical-services, and leisure divisions.

Phone to enroll:
Bank of New York
888-BNY-ADRS or 888-269-2377

EasyStock Investment Plan:
- Initial minimum investment: $250
- Minimum per month (optional): $50
- Maximum per transaction: $250,000
- No cash dividends paid.
- Partial dividend reinvestment.
- No discount is available.
- No IRA option is available.
- Optional cash purchases allowed.
- Direct debits are available.

Istituto Mobiliare Italiano S.p.A.
Italy: Financial Services
NYSE: IMI
c/o Morgan Guaranty Trust Company
PO Box 9073
Boston, MA 02205-9948
www.imisigeco.it

Istituto Mobiliare Italiano is an Italian banking group whose lending activities include loans and leases to clients in the telecommunications, energy, transportation, manufacturing, and construction industries.

Phone to enroll:
Morgan Guaranty Trust Company
800-997-8970

EasyStock Investment Plan:
- Initial minimum investment: $250
- Minimum per month (optional): $50
- Maximum annual investment: $100,000
- Cash dividends are offered.
- Partial dividend reinvestment.
- No discount is available.
- No IRA option is available.
- Optional cash purchases allowed.
- Direct debits are available.

Istituto Nazionale delle Assicurazioni S.p.A.
Italy: Insurance Carriers
NYSE: INZ
c/o Bank of New York
48 Wall Street
New York, NY 10286
www.ina.it

Istituto Nazionale delle Assicurazioni S.p.A. is an Italian insurance company that offers life, property and casualty insurance. The company sells individual and group life policies and encourages policy retention by granting loans to policyholders.

Phone to enroll:
Morgan Guaranty Trust Company
800-997-8970

EasyStock Investment Plan:
- Initial minimum investment: $250
- Minimum per month (optional): $50
- Maximum per transaction: $250,000
- Cash dividends are offered.
- Partial dividend reinvestment.
- No discount is available.
- No IRA option is available.
- Optional cash purchases allowed.
- Direct debits are available.

IWC Resources Corp.
United States
NASDAQ: IWCR
1220 Waterway Blvd
Indianapolis, IN 46206
www.iwcr.com
317-639-1501

IWC Resources provides water to 235,000 customers through its principal subsidiary, the Indianapolis Water Company.

Phone to enroll:
Bank of New York
317-639-1501

EasyStock Investment Plan:
- Initial minimum investment: $100
- Minimum per month (optional): $100
- Maximum annual investment: $100,000
- Cash dividends are offered.
- Partial dividend reinvestment.
- Discounts on share purchases.
- No IRA option is available.
- Optional cash purchases allowed.
- No direct debit option.

J.C. Penney Co., Inc.
United States: Department Stores
NYSE: JCP
6501 Legacy Drive
Plano, TX 75024
www.jcpenney.com
972-431-1000

J.C. Penney is America's number four retailer, with more than 1,100 J.C. Penney stores located nationwide and in Mexico, Puerto Rico, and Chile, selling apparel, accessories, and home furnishings.

Phone to enroll:
Fifth Third Bank
800-565-2576

EasyStock Investment Plan:
- Initial minimum investment: $250
- Minimum per month (optional): $20
- Maximum monthly investment: $10,000
- Cash dividends are offered.
- Partial dividend reinvestment.
- No discount is available.
- No IRA option is available.
- Optional cash purchases allowed.
- Direct debits are available.

Jilin Chemical Industrial Co. Ltd.
China: Chemicals
NYSE: JCC
c/o Bank of New York
48 Wall Street
New York, NY 10286
www.jcic.com

Jilin Chemical Co. makes petroleum products, organic chemical and petrochemical products, dye products, chemical fertilizers, and synthetic rubber products.

Phone to enroll:
Bank of New York
888-BNY-ADRS or 888-269-2377

EasyStock Investment Plan:
- Initial minimum investment: $250
- Minimum per month (optional): $50
- Maximum per transaction: $250,000
- Cash dividends are offered.
- Partial dividend reinvestment.
- No discount is available.
- No IRA option is available.
- Optional cash purchases allowed.
- Direct debits are available.

John H. Harland Company Ltd.
United States: Printing/Supplies
NYSE: JH
PO Box 105250
Atlanta, GA 30348
www.harland.net
770-981-9460

John H. Harland is the number two check printer in the nation, after Deluxe. Through its Financial Services segment, it offers check and form printing, which comprises about 75% of sales. Subsidiaries provide database marketing and consulting through Marketing Profiles, Inc.

Phone to enroll:
Bank of New York
800-649-2202

EasyStock Investment Plan:
- Initial minimum investment: $500
- Minimum per month (optional): $25
- Maximum quarterly investment: $3,000
- No cash dividends paid.
- No partial dividend reinvestment.
- No discount is available.
- No IRA option is available.
- Optional cash purchases allowed.
- Direct debits are available.
- View materials and enroll online at www.netstockdirect.com.

Johnson Controls, Inc.
United States: Building Materials
NYSE: JCI
5757 North Green Bay Avenue
Milwaukee, WI 53201-0591
www.jci.com
414-228-1200

Johnson Controls makes automobile seating, interior systems, and batteries; control systems for commercial buildings; and plastics machinery.

Phone to enroll:
First Chicago Trust Company
414-228-2363

EasyStock Investment Plan:
- Initial minimum investment: $50
- Minimum per month (optional): $50
- Maximum quarterly investment: $15,000
- Cash dividends are offered.
- Partial dividend reinvestment.
- No discount is available.
- No IRA option is available.
- Optional cash purchases allowed.
- Direct debits are available.

Justin Industries, Inc.
United States: Manufacturing
NASDAQ: JSTN
2821 West Seventh Street
Fort Worth, TX 76107
www.justinind.com
817-336-5125

Justin Industries' building material subsidiaries include Acme Brick, makers of face brick; Featherlite Building Products, which makes concrete building products; and American Tile Supply, which distributes ceramic and marble flooring.

Phone to enroll:
Firstar Trust Company

EasyStock Investment Plan:
- Initial minimum investment: $500
- Minimum per month (optional): $25
- Maximum per transaction: $5,000
- Maximum annual investment: $100,000
- Cash dividends are offered.
- Partial dividend reinvestment.
- No discount is available.
- No IRA option is available.
- Optional cash purchases allowed.
- Direct debits are available.

K

Kaman Corp.
United States: Defense/Industrial
NASDAQ: KAMNA
Blue Hills Avenue
Bloomfield, CT 06002
www.kaman.com
860-243-7100

Kaman brings on both the sound and the fury, manufacturing both guitars and military helicopters. Its Kaman Music subsidiary makes and sells Ovation and Hamer guitars, along with other musical instruments and accessories.

Phone to enroll:
Bank of New York
800-842-7629

EasyStock Investment Plan:
- Initial minimum investment: $250
- Minimum per month (optional): $50
- Maximum annual investment: -
- No cash dividends paid.
- No partial dividend reinvestment.
- No discount is available.
- No IRA option is available.
- Optional cash purchases allowed.
- No direct debit option.

Kellwood Company Ltd.
United States: Clothing
NYSE: KWD
600 Kellwood Parkway
St. Louis MO 63178
www.kwdco.com
314-576-3100

Kellwood and its fifteen subsidiaries make and sell branded apparel and camping gear. Its subsidiaries that produce clothing include Cape Cod-Cricket Lane, E Z Sportswear, and Smart Shirts Limited of Hong Kong.

Phone to enroll:
Chase Mellon
314-576-3100

EasyStock Investment Plan:
- Initial minimum investment: $100
- Minimum per month (optional): $25
- Maximum monthly investment: $3,000
- No cash dividends paid.
- Partial dividend reinvestment.
- No discount is available.

- No IRA option is available.
- Optional cash purchases allowed.
- No direct debit option.

Kerr-McGee Corp.
United States: Domestic Refiners
NYSE: KMG
123 Robert South Kerr Avenue
Oklahoma City, OK 73102
www.kerr-mcgee.com
405-270-1313

Kerr-McGee explores for and produces oil and natural gas in China, the Gulf of Mexico, Indonesia, the North Sea, and Thailand. Kerr-McGee also produces industrial and specialty chemicals.

Phone to enroll:
Liberty National Bank & Trust Co.
800-395-2662

EasyStock Investment Plan:
- Initial minimum investment: $750
- Minimum per month (optional): $10
- Maximum monthly investment: $1,000
- Maximum quarterly investment: $3,000
- Cash dividends are offered.
- Partial dividend reinvestment.
- No discount is available.
- No IRA option is available.
- Optional cash purchases allowed.
- No direct debit option.

Kerr Group, Inc.
United States: Plastics
NYSE: KGM
500 New Holland Avenue
Lancaster, PA 17602-2104
717-299-6511

Kerr Group makes plastic and consumer products.

Phone to enroll:
Harris Bank
800-395-2662

EasyStock Investment Plan:
- Initial minimum investment: $750
- Minimum per month (optional): $10
- Maximum quarterly investment: $3,000
- No cash dividends paid.
- No partial dividend reinvestment.
- No discount is available.
- No IRA option is available.
- Optional cash purchases allowed.
- No direct debit option.

KeySpan Energy Corporation
United States:
NYSE: KSE
One MetroTech Center
Brooklyn, NY 11201
www.keyspanenergy.com
718-403-1000

KeySpan Energy owns natural gas distributor Brooklyn Union Gas, serving 1.6 million New Yorkers in Brooklyn, Long Island, Queens, and Staten Island.

Phone to enroll:
Liberty National Bank & Trust Co.
800-328-5090

EasyStock Investment Plan:
- Initial minimum investment: $250
- Minimum per month (optional): $25
- Maximum annual investment: $100,000
- No cash dividends paid.
- Partial dividend reinvestment.
- No discount is available.
- No IRA option is available.
- Optional cash purchases allowed.
- Direct debits are available.

Koor Industries Ltd.
Israel: Conglomerates
NYSE: KOR
c/o Bank of New York
48 Wall Street
New York, NY 10286
www.koor.co.il

Koor Industries is Israel's largest holding company. Its core interests include telecommunications and electronics, building materials, and agrochemicals.

Phone to enroll:
Bank of New York
888-BNY-ADRS or 888-269-2377

EasyStock Investment Plan:
- Initial minimum investment: $250
- Minimum per month (optional): $50
- Maximum per transaction: $250,000
- Cash dividends are offered.
- Partial dividend reinvestment.
- No discount is available.
- No IRA option is available.
- Optional cash purchases allowed.
- Direct debits are available.

Korea Electric Power Corp.
South Korea: Electric Services
NYSE: KEP
c/o Bank of New York
48 Wall Street
New York, NY 10286
www.kepco.co.kr

Korea Electric Power is an electric utility 75% owned by the government of South Korea. It provides electricity to more than 13 million homes, as well as industrial and commercial customers throughout South Korea.

Phone to enroll:
Bank of New York
888-BNY-ADRS or 888-269-2377

EasyStock Investment Plan:
- Initial minimum investment: $250
- Minimum per month (optional): $50
- Maximum per transaction: $250,000
- Cash dividends are offered.
- Partial dividend reinvestment.
- No discount is available.
- No IRA option is available.
- Optional cash purchases allowed.
- Direct debits are available.

L

Lear Corporation
United States: Automotive Parts
NYSE: LEA
21557 Telegraph Road
Southfield, MI 48034
www.lear.com
248-746-1500

Lear is a leading supplier of automotive interior components and it leads the North American car seat systems market, with more than a 35% share.

Phone to enroll:
Bank of New York
800-432-0140

EasyStock Investment Plan:
- Initial minimum investment: $250
- Minimum per month (optional): $50
- Maximum annual investment: $150,000
- No cash dividends paid.
- No partial dividend reinvestment.
- No discount is available.
- No IRA option is available.
- Optional cash purchases allowed.
- No direct debit option.

Libbey Inc.
United States: Housewares
NYSE: LBY
c/o Bank of New York
48 Wall Street
New York, NY 10286
www.libbey.com
419-325-2100

Libbey designs, manufactures, and markets glass tableware worldwide, primarily beverage ware such as tumblers, stemware, and mugs. In total, the company markets over 2,000 products.

Phone to enroll:
Bank of New York
888-BNY-ADRS or 888-269-2377

EasyStock Investment Plan:
- Initial minimum investment: $250
- Minimum per month (optional): $50
- Maximum per transaction: $250,000
- No cash dividends paid.
- Partial dividend reinvestment.
- No discount is available.
- No IRA option is available.
- Optional cash purchases allowed.
- Direct debits are available.

Liberty Property Trust
United States: Real Estate Investment Trust
NYSE: LRY
65 Valley Stream Parkway
Suite 100
Malvern, PA 19355
www.libertyproperty.com
610-648-1700

Liberty Property Trust owns and leases suburban industrial properties and office real estate, primarily in the U.S. The trust acquires, designs, develops, and constructs properties, providing leasing and property management.

Phone to enroll:
Bank of New York
800-944-2214

EasyStock Investment Plan:
- Initial minimum investment: $1,000
- Minimum per month (optional): $250
- Maximum monthly investment: $7,500
- Cash dividends are offered.
- Partial dividend reinvestment.
- Discounts on share purchases.
- No IRA option is available.
- Optional cash purchases allowed.
- No direct debit option.

Lihir Gold Limited
Papua New Guinea: Minerals/Mining
NASDAQ: LIHRY
c/o Bank of New York
48 Wall Street
New York, NY 10286
www.lihir.com.pg

Lihir Gold is the owner and developer of a gold mine in the New Ireland province of Papua New Guinea. Planned since the late 1970s, the mine may be one of the world's largest, with an estimated 40 million ounces of gold that it should take thirty-six years to extract.

Phone to enroll:
Bank of New York
888-BNY-ADRS or 888-269-2377

EasyStock Investment Plan:
- Initial minimum investment: $250
- Minimum per month (optional): $50
- Maximum per transaction: $250,000

- No cash dividends paid.
- Partial dividend reinvestment.
- No discount is available.
- No IRA option is available.
- Optional cash purchases allowed.
- Direct debits are available.

London International Group PLC
United Kingdom: Contraceptives
NASDAQ: LONDY
c/o Bank of New York
48 Wall Street
New York, NY 10286
www.lig.com

London International Group makes the world a safer place by manufacturing condoms and latex gloves. Its contraceptive products, accounting for 40% of sales, include Sheik, Ramses, and Kingtex brand latex condoms.

Phone to enroll:
Bank of New York
888-BNY-ADRS or 888-269-2377

EasyStock Investment Plan:
- Initial minimum investment: $250
- Minimum per month (optional): $50
- Maximum per transaction: $250,000
- Cash dividends are offered.
- Partial dividend reinvestment.
- No discount is available.
- No IRA option is available.
- Optional cash purchases allowed.
- Direct debits are available.

Long Island Lighting Co. Ltd.
United States: Electric Utilities
NYSE: LIL
175 East Old Country Road
Hicksville, NY 11801
www.lilco.com

Phone to enroll:
Bank of New York
800-432-0140

EasyStock Investment Plan:
- Initial minimum investment: $250
- Minimum per month (optional): $50
- Maximum quarterly investment: $5,000
- Cash dividends are offered.
- No partial dividend reinvestment.
- No discount is available.
- No IRA option is available.
- Optional cash purchases allowed.
- No direct debit option.

Longs Drug Stores Corp.
United States: Drug Stores
NYSE: LDG
141 North Civic Drive
Walnut Creek, CA 94596
www.longs.com
925-937-1170

Longs is a leading U.S. drugstore chain, with more than 330 stores in California, Colorado, Hawaii, and Nevada. The company prides itself on its decentralized management style, which gives managers considerable independence in running their stores.

Phone to enroll:
Bank of New York
800-842-7629

EasyStock Investment Plan:
- Initial minimum investment: $500
- Minimum per month (optional): $25

- Maximum quarterly investment: $5,000
- No cash dividends paid.
- Partial dividend reinvestment.
- No discount is available.
- No IRA option is available.
- Optional cash purchases allowed.
- Direct debits are available.

Lucas Varity PLC
United Kingdom: Automotive Parts
NYSE: LVA
c/o Morgan Guaranty Trust Company
PO Box 9073
Boston, MA 02205-9948
www.lucasvarity.co.uk

Lucas Varity can really bring things to a halt, like certain Mercedes and Ford cars. Braking systems for light and heavy vehicles make up about 40% of sales.

Phone to enroll:
Morgan Guaranty Trust Company
800-997-8970

EasyStock Investment Plan:
- Initial minimum investment: $250
- Minimum per month (optional): $50
- Maximum annual investment: $100,000
- Cash dividends are offered.
- Partial dividend reinvestment.
- No discount is available.
- No IRA option is available.
- Optional cash purchases allowed.
- Direct debits are available.

Lucent Technologies Inc.
United States: Telecommunications Equipment
NYSE: LU
600 Mountain Avenue
Murray Hill, NJ 07974
www.lucent.com
908-582-8500

Lucent Technologies is the leading U.S. maker of telecommunications equipment and software, from telephones to business communications systems, as well as switching and transmission equipment, and wireless networks.

Phone to enroll:
Morgan Guaranty Trust Company
800-997-8970

EasyStock Investment Plan:
- Initial minimum investment: $1,000
- Minimum per month (optional): $100
- Maximum annual investment: $50,000
- Cash dividends are offered.
- Partial dividend reinvestment.
- No discount is available.
- An IRA option is available.
- Optional cash purchases allowed.
- Direct debits are available.

Luxottica Group S.p.A.
Italy: Eyewear
NYSE: LUX
c/o Bank of New York
48 Wall Street
New York, NY 10286
www.luxottica.it

The Luxottica Group sells its Italian-made eyewear through its subsidiary LensCrafters' 650 stores, making it the world's largest optical retailer. The company makes high-quality eyeglass frames and sunglasses in the mid- and premium-price market segments.

Phone to enroll:
Bank of New York
888-BNY-ADRS or 888-269-2377

EasyStock Investment Plan:
- Initial minimum investment: $250
- Minimum per month (optional): $50
- Maximum per transaction: $250,000
- Cash dividends are offered.
- Partial dividend reinvestment.
- No discount is available.
- No IRA option is available.
- Optional cash purchases allowed.
- Direct debits are available.

M

Macerich Co.
United States: Real Estate Investment Trust
NYSE: MAC
233 Wilshire Blvd, Suite 700
Santa Monica, CA 90401
www.macerich.com
310-394-6911

The Macerich Company acquires, redevelops, leases, and manages regional shopping malls and community shopping centers.

Phone to enroll:
Bank of New York
800-567-0169

EasyStock Investment Plan:
- Initial minimum investment: $250
- Minimum per month (optional): $50
- Maximum annual investment: $250,000
- Cash dividends are offered.
- No partial dividend reinvestment.
- No discount is available.
- No IRA option is available.
- Optional cash purchases allowed.
- Direct debits are available.

Macronix International Co., Ltd.
Taiwan: Integrated Circuits
NASDAQ: MXICY
c/o Bank of New York
48 Wall Street
New York, NY 10286
www.mxic.com.tw

Macronix makes high-performance non-volatile memory integrated circuits (ICs), microcontroller ICs, and "system-on-a-chip" ICs. Macronix has an alliance with Philips Electronics N.V. and a manufacturing agreement with Matsushita.

Phone to enroll:
Bank of New York
888-BNY-ADRS or 888-269-2377

EasyStock Investment Plan:
- Initial minimum investment: $250
- Minimum per month (optional): $50
- Maximum per transaction: $250,000
- Cash dividends are offered.
- Partial dividend reinvestment.
- No discount is available.
- No IRA option is available.
- Optional cash purchases allowed.
- Direct debits are available.

Maderas y Sinteticos S.A. (Masisa)
Chile: Building Materials
NYSE: MYS
c/o Bank of New York
48 Wall Street
New York, NY 10286
www.masisa.com

MASISA is one of South America's top producers of particleboard and medium-density fiberboard (MDF).

Phone to enroll:
Bank of New York
888-BNY-ADRS or 888-269-2377

EasyStock Investment Plan:
- Initial minimum investment: $200
- Minimum per month (optional): $50
- Maximum annual investment: $250,000
- Cash dividends are offered.
- Partial dividend reinvestment.
- No discount is available.
- No IRA option is available.
- Optional cash purchases allowed.
- Direct debits are available.

Madison Gas & Electric Co.
United States: Utilities
NASDAQ: MDSN
133 South Blair Street
PO Box 1231
Madison, WI 53701-1231
www.mge.com
608-252-7000

Madison Gas and Electric generates and transmits electricity and purchases, transports, and distributes natural gas in southern Wisconsin, supplying electricity to more than 118,000 customers.

Phone to enroll:
Bank of New York
800-356-6423

EasyStock Investment Plan:
- Initial minimum investment: $50
- Minimum per month (optional): $25
- Maximum quarterly investment: $25,000
- Cash dividends are offered.
- Partial dividend reinvestment.
- No discount is available.
- No IRA option is available.
- Optional cash purchases allowed.
- No direct debit option.

Magyar Tavozlesi Rt. (Matav)
Hungary: Telecommunications
NYSE: MTA
c/o Morgan Guaranty Trust Company
PO Box 9073
Boston, MA 02205-9948
www.matav.hu

Magyar Tevkozlesi Rt., or Matav, is Hungary's largest phone utility, enjoying a monopoly on 75% of the Hungarian local phone-services market and a similar monopoly on long-distance services until 2001.

Phone to enroll:
Morgan Guaranty Trust Company
800-997-8970

EasyStock Investment Plan:
- Initial minimum investment: $250
- Minimum per month (optional): $50
- Maximum annual investment: $100,000
- Cash dividends are offered.
- Partial dividend reinvestment.
- No discount is available.
- No IRA option is available.
- Optional cash purchases allowed.
- Direct debits are available.

Makita Corp.
Japan: Electrical Equipment
NASDAQ: MKTAY
c/o Bank of New York
48 Wall Street
New York, NY 10286
www.makita.co.jp

Makita is a leading global producer of electric power tools.

Phone to enroll:
Bank of New York
888-BNY-ADRS or 888-269-2377

EasyStock Investment Plan:
- Initial minimum investment: $250
- Minimum per month (optional): $50
- Maximum per transaction: $250,000
- Cash dividends are offered.
- Partial dividend reinvestment.
- No discount is available.
- No IRA option is available.
- Optional cash purchases allowed.
- Direct debits are available.

MAS Technology Inc.
New Zealand:
NASDAQ: MASSY
c/o Bank of New York
48 Wall Street
New York, NY 10286
www.mas.co.nz

MAS Technology manufactures and services digital microwave radio technology, which is used to link rural areas to public telephone networks, connect cellular and digital phone networks, and create private communications networks used by utility systems, businesses, and government agencies.

Phone to enroll:
Bank of New York
888-BNY-ADRS or 888-269-2377

EasyStock Investment Plan:
- Initial minimum investment: $250
- Minimum per month (optional): $50
- Maximum per transaction: $250,000
- No cash dividends paid.
- Partial dividend reinvestment.
- No discount is available.
- No IRA option is available.
- Optional cash purchases allowed.
- Direct debits are available.

Matav-Cable Systems Media Ltd.
Israel: Telecommunications
NASDAQ: MATVY
c/o Bank of New York
48 Wall Street
New York, NY 10286
www.matav.co.il

Matav-Cable Systems Media has the exclusive service rights to about 25% of households in Israel, including Haifa and other northern cities. The company broadcasts approximately forty channels to more than 250,000 subscribers.

Phone to enroll:
Bank of New York
888-BNY-ADRS or 888-269-2377

EasyStock Investment Plan:
- Initial minimum investment: $250
- Minimum per month (optional): $50
- Maximum per transaction: $250,000
- No cash dividends paid.
- Partial dividend reinvestment.
- No discount is available.
- No IRA option is available.
- Optional cash purchases allowed.
- Direct debits are available.

Matsushita Electric Industrial
Japan: Consumer Electronics
NYSE: MC
c/o Morgan Guaranty Trust Company
PO Box 9073
Boston, MA 02205-9948
www.panasonic.co.jp

Matsushita Electric Works makes about 220,000 products, including lighting, wiring, home appliances, personal-care products, building materials, electronics, and automation-control products.

Phone to enroll:
Morgan Guaranty Trust Company
800-997-8970

EasyStock Investment Plan:
- Initial minimum investment: $250
- Minimum per month (optional): $50
- Maximum annual investment: $100,000
- Cash dividends are offered.
- Partial dividend reinvestment.
- No discount is available.
- No IRA option is available.
- Optional cash purchases allowed.
- Direct debits are available.

Mattel, Inc.
United States: Toys
NYSE: MAT
333 Continental Blvd
El Segundo, CA 90245-5012
www.mattel.com
310-252-2000

Mattel is the number one American toy maker, whose major toy and games brands include Barbie, Fisher-Price, Disney entertainment lines, Hot Wheels, Matchbox, Cabbage Patch Kids, Skip-Bo, and UNO.

Phone to enroll:
Morgan Guaranty Trust Company
888-909-9922

EasyStock Investment Plan:
- Initial minimum investment: $500
- Minimum per month (optional): $100
- Maximum annual investment: $100,000
- Cash dividends are offered.
- No partial dividend reinvestment.
- No discount is available.
- No IRA option is available.
- Optional cash purchases allowed.
- Direct debits are available.

Mavesa S.A.
Venezuela: Food Products
NASDAQ: MAV
c/o Bank of New York
48 Wall Street
New York, NY 10286
www.mavesa.com.ve

Mavesa is one of Venezuela's largest food processors. The company manufactures, markets, and distributes a variety of food and household items, including margarine, mayonnaise, cheese, milk substitutes, vegetables, vinegar, and other processed foods.

Phone to enroll:
Bank of New York
888-BNY-ADRS or 888-269-2377

EasyStock Investment Plan:
- Initial minimum investment: $250
- Minimum per month (optional): $50
- Maximum per transaction: $250,000
- Cash dividends are offered.
- Partial dividend reinvestment.
- No discount is available.
- No IRA option is available.
- Optional cash purchases allowed.
- Direct debits are available.

McCormick & Co. Ltd.
United States: Food Products
NYSE: MCCRK
18 Loveton Circle
Sparks, MD 21152
www.mccormick.com
410-771-7301

The world's largest spice maker, McCormick & Co. manufactures an assortment of spices and seasonings in addition to specialty food products such as sauces, mixes, and salad products.

Phone company to enroll:
800-424-5855

EasyStock Investment Plan:
- Initial minimum investment: $250
- Minimum per month (optional): $50
- Maximum per transaction: $50,000
- Cash dividends are offered.
- Partial dividend reinvestment.
- No discount is available.
- No IRA option is available.
- Optional cash purchases allowed.
- Direct debits are available.

McDonald's Corp.
United States: Restaurants
NYSE: MCD
McDonalds Plaza
One Kroc Drive
Oak Brook, IL 60521
www.mcdonalds.com
630-623-3000

McDonald's, which boasts one of the world's most valuable brand names, is the world's number one fast-food chain. It operates more than 25,000 restaurants worldwide, and its more than 12,300 U.S. outlets have given it more than a 40% share of the domestic fast-food market.

Phone to enroll:
Bank of New York
800-228-9623

EasyStock Investment Plan:
- Initial minimum investment: $1,000
- Minimum per month (optional): $100
- Maximum annual investment: $250,000
- Cash dividends are offered.
- Partial dividend reinvestment.
- No discount is available.
- An IRA option is available.
- Optional cash purchases allowed.
- Direct debits are available.

MCN Energy Group, Inc.
United States: Natural Gas
NYSE: MCN
500 Griswold Street
Detroit, MI 48226
www.mcnenergy.com
313-256-5500

MCN Energy Group is a diversified energy holding company. Its Michigan Consolidated Gas subsidiary distributes natural gas to 1.2 million customers in more than five hundred communities throughout Michigan.

Phone to enroll:
First Chicago Trust Company
800-955-4793

EasyStock Investment Plan:
- Initial minimum investment: $250
- Minimum per month (optional): $25
- Maximum annual investment: $150,000
- Cash dividends are offered.
- Partial dividend reinvestment.
- No discount is available.
- An IRA option is available.
- Optional cash purchases allowed.

- Direct debits are available.
- View materials and enroll online at www.netstockdirect.com.

Meadowbrook Insurance Group
United States: Insurance
NYSE: MIG
26600 Telegraph Road
Southfield, MI 48034
www.meadowbrookinsgrp.com
248-358-1100

Meadowbrook Insurance develops and operates alternative-market risk management programs, including captives, risk retention, and risk purchasing groups, governmental pools and trusts, and self-insurance plans.

Phone to enroll:
Norwest Bank
800-649-2579

EasyStock Investment Plan:
- Initial minimum investment: $250
- Minimum per month (optional): $25
- Maximum annual investment: $50,000
- No cash dividends paid.
- No partial dividend reinvestment.
- No discount is available.
- No IRA option is available.
- Optional cash purchases allowed.
- Direct debits are available.

Medeva PLC
United Kingdom: Pharmaceuticals
NYSE: MDV
c/o Bank of New York
48 Wall Street
New York, NY 10286
www.medeva.co.uk

Medeva is a U.K.-based company that manufactures prescription pharmaceuticals. The company manufactures and distributes respiratory, attention-deficit disorder, appetite suppressant, pain management, and anesthetic products.

Phone to enroll:
Bank of New York
888-BNY-ADRS or 888-269-2377

EasyStock Investment Plan:
- Initial minimum investment: $250
- Minimum per month (optional): $50
- Maximum per transaction: $250,000
- Cash dividends are offered.
- Partial dividend reinvestment.
- No discount is available.
- No IRA option is available.
- Optional cash purchases allowed.
- Direct debits are available.

MediaOne Group Inc.
United States: Telecommunications
NYSE: UMG
7800 East Orchard Road
Englewood, CO 80111
www.mediaone.com
303-858-3000

MediaOne Group is the third largest cable operator in the U.S. and is the subject of various takeover bids.

Phone to enroll:
Boston Equiserve LP
800-537-0222

EasyStock Investment Plan:
- Initial minimum investment: $300
- Minimum per month (optional): $25
- Maximum annual investment: $100,000
- No cash dividends paid.
- Partial dividend reinvestment.
- No discount is available.
- No IRA option is available.
- Optional cash purchases allowed.
- Direct debits are available.

Mellon Bank Corporation
United States: Banking
NYSE: MEL
One Mellon Bank Center
Pittsburgh, PA 15258
www.mellon.com
412-234-5000

Mellon is a multibank holding company whose subsidiaries provide full-service banking in Delaware, Florida, Maryland, Massachusetts, New Jersey, and Pennsylvania. Consumer banking and investment services are available at 420 locations.

Phone to enroll:
Bank of New York
800-842-7629

EasyStock Investment Plan:
- Initial minimum investment: $500
- Minimum per month (optional): $100
- Maximum monthly investment: $100,000
- Cash dividends are offered.
- Partial dividend reinvestment.
- No discount is available.
- No IRA option is available.
- Optional cash purchases allowed.
- Direct debits are available.

Mercantile Bank Corporation
United States: Banking
NYSE: MTL
PO Box 524
St. Louis, MO 63166
www.mercantile.com
616-242-9000

Mercantile Bank Corporation was formed as the holding company for a new commercial bank, Mercantile Bank, which has branches in Kent County, Michigan, including Grand Rapids and its suburbs.

Phone to enroll:
Chase Mellon
800-286-9178

EasyStock Investment Plan:
- Initial minimum investment: $500
- Minimum per month (optional): $100
- Maximum per transaction: $10,000
- Maximum monthly investment: $10,000
- Maximum quarterly investment: $30,000
- Maximum annual investment: $120,000
- Cash dividends are offered.
- Partial dividend reinvestment.
- No discount is available.
- No IRA option is available.
- Optional cash purchases allowed.
- Direct debits are available.

Merck & Co., Inc.
United States: Pharmaceuticals
NYSE: MRK
One Merck Drive
Whitehouse Station, NJ 08889
www.merck.com
908-423-1000

Merck is the number one drugmaker in America and is tied for first in the

world with Glaxo Wellcome in prescription drugs. The company develops products for both humans and animals.

Phone to enroll:
Harris Bank
800-286-9178

EasyStock Investment Plan:
- Initial minimum investment: $350
- Minimum per month (optional): $50
- Maximum annual investment: $50,000
- Cash dividends are offered.
- Partial dividend reinvestment.
- No discount is available.
- No IRA option is available.
- Optional cash purchases allowed.
- Direct debits are available.
- View materials and enroll online at www.netstockdirect.com.

Meritor Automotive, Inc.
United States: Automotive
NYSE: MRA
2135 West Maple Road
Troy, MI 48084-7186
www.meritorauto.com
248-435-1000

Meritor Automotive, a spinoff of Rockwell International, is a leading global supplier of automotive components and systems. Operating forty-six plants worldwide, including in Brazil, Canada, China, and the U.S., it generates about 40% of its sales outside North America.

Phone to enroll:
Norwest Bank
800-483-2277

EasyStock Investment Plan:
- Initial minimum investment: $500
- Minimum per month (optional): $50
- Maximum annual investment: $100,000
- Cash dividends are offered.
- Partial dividend reinvestment.
- No discount is available.
- No IRA option is available.
- Optional cash purchases allowed.
- Direct debits are available.

Michaels Stores, Inc.
United States: Craft Stores
NASDAQ: MIKE
5931 Campus Circle Drive
Irving, TX 75063
www.michaels.com
972-409-1300

Michaels is the nation's largest specialty retailer of arts, crafts, and decorative items, operating about 450 stores in forty-five states, Puerto Rico, and Canada.

Phone to enroll:
First Chicago Trust Company
800-577-4676

EasyStock Investment Plan:
- Initial minimum investment: $500
- Minimum per month (optional): $100
- Maximum annual investment:
- Cash dividends are offered.
- Partial dividend reinvestment.
- No discount is available.
- No IRA option is available.
- Optional cash purchases allowed.
- No direct debit option.

Micro Focus Group PLC
United Kingdom: Technology
NASDAQ: MIFGY
c/o Bank of New York
48 Wall Street
New York, NY 10286
www.mfltd.co.uk

Micro Focus is a U.K.-based technology company.

Phone to enroll:
Bank of New York
888-BNY-ADRS or 888-269-2377

EasyStock Investment Plan:
- Initial minimum investment: $250
- Minimum per month (optional): $50
- Maximum per transaction: $250,000
- No cash dividends paid.
- Partial dividend reinvestment.
- No discount is available.
- No IRA option is available.
- Optional cash purchases allowed.
- Direct debits are available.

MidAmerican Energy Co.
United States: Utilities
NYSE: MEC
666 Grand Avenue
PO Box 9244
Des Moines, IA 50306-9244
www.midamerican.com
515-252-6400

MidAmerican Energy Holdings is a holding company whose subsidiaries supply gas and electricity to customers in the upper Midwest.

Phone to enroll:
Bank of New York
800-247-5211

EasyStock Investment Plan:
- Initial minimum investment: $250
- Minimum per month (optional): $25
- Maximum monthly investment: $10,000
- Cash dividends are offered.
- Partial dividend reinvestment.
- No discount is available.
- No IRA option is available.
- Optional cash purchases allowed.
- No direct debit option.

MidSouth Bancorp, Inc.
United States: Banking
AMEX: MSL
102 Versailles Blvd
Lafayette, LA 70501
www.midsouthbank.com
318-237-8343

A bank holding company, MidSouth owns MidSouth National Bank, which serves customers in southern Louisiana. MidSouth offers banking services from more than a dozen locations, catering primarily to commercial and industrial customers.

Phone company to enroll:
800-842-7629

EasyStock Investment Plan:
- Initial minimum investment: $1,000
- Minimum per month (optional): $100
- Maximum monthly investment: $10,000
- Cash dividends are offered.
- Partial dividend reinvestment.
- No discount is available.
- An IRA option is available.
- Optional cash purchases allowed.
- Direct debits are available.

Minnesota Power & Light Co.
United States: Utilities
NYSE: MPL
30 West Superior Street

Duluth, MN 55802-2093
www.mnpower.com
218-722-2641

Minnesota Power operates electric, water, and gas utilities in four states, as well as auto auctions, an automotive finance company, and real estate interests.

Phone to enroll:
Chase Mellon
800-535-3056

EasyStock Investment Plan:
- Initial minimum investment: $250
- Minimum per month (optional): $10
- Maximum annual investment: $100,000
- Cash dividends are offered.
- Partial dividend reinvestment.
- No discount is available.
- No IRA option is available.
- Optional cash purchases allowed.
- Direct debits are available.

Modern Times Group AB
Sweden: Publishers
NASDAQ: MTGNY
c/o Bank of New York
48 Wall Street
New York, NY 10286
www.mtg.se

Modern Times Group (MTG) is a Swedish media company operating in the areas of broadcasting, publishing, radio, electronic retailing, and media services. MTG owns eight television channels including Scandinavia's first commercial channel, TV3.

Phone to enroll:
Bank of New York
888-BNY-ADRS or 888-269-2377

EasyStock Investment Plan:
- Initial minimum investment: $250
- Minimum per month (optional): $50
- Maximum per transaction: $250,000
- No cash dividends paid.
- Partial dividend reinvestment.
- No discount is available.
- No IRA option is available.
- Optional cash purchases allowed.
- Direct debits are available.

Montana Power Co.
United States: Utilities
NYSE: MTP
40 East Broadway
Butte, MT 59701-9394
www.mtpower.com
406-723-5421

Montana Power supplies electricity and natural gas and related services. The company's Utility Division provides approximately 600,000 customers in nearly two hundred Montana communities with electricity and gas. The company also sells discounted power to Californians.

Phone to enroll:
Bank of New York
800-245-6767

EasyStock Investment Plan:
- Initial minimum investment: $100
- Minimum per month (optional): $10
- Maximum annual investment: $60,000
- Cash dividends are offered.
- Partial dividend reinvestment.
- No discount is available.
- No IRA option is available.
- Optional cash purchases allowed.
- Direct debits are available.

Morgan Stanley, Dean Witter & Co. Ltd.
United States: Financial Services
NYSE: MWD
Two World Trade Center
New York, NY 10048
www.deanwitterdiscover.com
212-761-4000

Morgan Stanley Dean Witter & Co. is the result of the 1997 merger between investment bank Morgan Stanley and retail financial service firm Dean Witter, Discover. The company is one of the largest financial services firms in the world.

Phone to enroll:
First Chicago Trust Company
800-228-0829

EasyStock Investment Plan:
- Initial minimum investment: $1,000
- Minimum per month (optional): $100
- Maximum per transaction: $40,000
- Maximum annual investment: $40,000
- Cash dividends are offered.
- Partial dividend reinvestment.
- No discount is available.
- No IRA option is available.
- Optional cash purchases allowed.
- Direct debits are available.

Morton International, Inc.
United States: Specialized Chemicals
NYSE: MII
100 North Riverside Plaza
Chicago, IL 60606-1596
www.mortonintl.com
312-807-2000

Morton International, the salt processor with the umbrella girl logo, makes specialty chemicals for a variety of applications. The company's other products include adhesives for food packaging, liquid plastic coatings for automobiles, and electronic materials.

Phone company to enroll:
800-990-1010

EasyStock Investment Plan:
- Initial minimum investment: $1,000
- Minimum per month (optional): $50
- Maximum annual investment: $60,000
- Cash dividends are offered.
- Partial dividend reinvestment.
- No discount is available.
- An IRA option is available.
- Optional cash purchases allowed.
- Direct debits are available.
- View materials and enroll online at www.netstockdirect.com.

Mycogen Corp.
United States: Chemicals
NASDAQ: MYCO
5501 Oberlin Drive
San Diego, CA 92121
www.mycogen.com
619-453-8030

Mycogen develops technology-based seed and biopesticide products. Its products control agricultural pests and improve crop yields.

Phone to enroll:
First Chicago Trust Company
800-477-6506

EasyStock Investment Plan:
- Initial minimum investment: $250
- Minimum per month (optional): $100

- Maximum annual investment: $100,000
- No cash dividends paid.
- Partial dividend reinvestment.
- No discount is available.
- No IRA option is available.
- Optional cash purchases allowed.
- Direct debits are available.

N

National Fuel Gas Company
United States: Natural Gas
NYSE: NFG
30 Rockefeller Plaza
New York, NY 10112
www.natfuel.com
716-857-6980

National Fuel Gas explores for, transports, and sells natural gas. Its distribution subsidiary sells or transports natural gas to more than 700,000 users in western New York and northwestern Pennsylvania.

Phone to enroll:
Boston Equiserve LP
716-857-7706

EasyStock Investment Plan:
- Initial minimum investment: $200
- Minimum per month (optional): $25
- Maximum monthly investment: $5,000
- Cash dividends are offered.
- No partial dividend reinvestment.
- No discount is available.
- No IRA option is available.
- Optional cash purchases allowed.
- No direct debit option.

National Westminister Bank PLC
United Kingdom: Banking
NYSE: NW
c/o Morgan Guaranty Trust Company
PO Box 9073
Boston, MA 02205-9948
www.natwest.com

National Westminster Bank is the leader of NatWest Group, one of the leading banking companies operating in the U.K. The bank offers consumer and commercial banking at more than 2,200 locations.

Phone to enroll:
Morgan Guaranty Trust Company
800-997-8970

EasyStock Investment Plan:
- Initial minimum investment: $250
- Minimum per month (optional): $50
- Maximum annual investment: $100,000
- No cash dividends paid.
- Partial dividend reinvestment.
- No discount is available.
- No IRA option is available.
- Optional cash purchases allowed.
- Direct debits are available.

Nationwide Financial Services, Inc.
United States: Financial Services
NYSE: NFS
One Nationwide Plaza
Columbus, OH 43215
www.boafuture.com
614-249-7111

Nationwide Financial Services is a holding company for Nationwide Life Insurance Company and other units of Nationwide Insurance Enterprise that offer savings and retirement products.

Phone to enroll:
Chase Mellon
800-409-7514

EasyStock Investment Plan:
- Initial minimum investment: $500
- Minimum per month (optional): $100
- Maximum annual investment: $120,000
- Cash dividends are offered.
- Partial dividend reinvestment.
- No discount is available.
- No IRA option is available.
- Optional cash purchases allowed.
- Direct debits are available.

NEC Corporation
Japan: Office Equipment
NASDAQ: NIPNY
c/o Bank of New York
48 Wall Street
New York, NY 10286
www.nec.co.jp

NEC is Japan's number one PC-maker, with about 40% of the market. The company is also the world's second-largest maker of semiconductors, behind Intel, and is a global supplier of computers and telecommunications equipment.

Phone to enroll:
Bank of New York
888-BNY-ADRS or 888-269-2377

EasyStock Investment Plan:
- Initial minimum investment: $250
- Minimum per month (optional): $50
- Maximum per transaction: $250,000
- Cash dividends are offered.
- Partial dividend reinvestment.
- No discount is available.
- No IRA option is available.
- Optional cash purchases allowed.
- Direct debits are available.

Nera A.S.
Norway: Telecommunications
NYSE: NERAY
c/o Bank of New York
48 Wall Street
New York, NY 10286
www.nera.no

Nera is an electronics supplier of telecommunications systems and equipment to customers in more than 100 countries and is the world's largest supplier of mobile satellite communications equipment.

Phone to enroll:
Bank of New York
888-BNY-ADRS or 888-269-2377

EasyStock Investment Plan:
- Initial minimum investment: $250
- Minimum per month (optional): $50
- Maximum per transaction: $250,000
- Cash dividends are offered.
- Partial dividend reinvestment.
- No discount is available.
- No IRA option is available.
- Optional cash purchases allowed.
- Direct debits are available.

NetCom Systems AB
Sweden: Telecommunications
NASDAQ: NECSY
c/o Bank of New York
48 Wall Street
New York, NY 10286
www.netcom-systems.se

NetCom Systems provides telecommunications services in Scandinavia. NetCom System's Danmark and Tele2 Norge both provide telephone services in their respective markets.

Phone to enroll:
Bank of New York
888-BNY-ADRS or 888-269-2377

EasyStock Investment Plan:
- Initial minimum investment: $250
- Minimum per month (optional): $50
- Maximum per transaction: $250,000
- Cash dividends are offered.
- Partial dividend reinvestment.
- No discount is available.
- No IRA option is available.
- Optional cash purchases allowed.
- Direct debits are available.

New Holland N.V.
Netherlands: Machinery
NYSE: NH
c/o Morgan Guaranty Trust Company
PO Box 9073
Boston, MA 02205-9948
www.newholland.com

New Holland is one of the world's leading manufacturers of agricultural and construction equipment. New Holland machinery sales generate about 85% of the company's sales.

Phone to enroll:
Morgan Guaranty Trust Company
800-997-8970

EasyStock Investment Plan:
- Initial minimum investment: $250
- Minimum per month (optional): $50
- Maximum annual investment: $100,000
- No cash dividends paid.
- Partial dividend reinvestment.
- No discount is available.
- No IRA option is available.
- Optional cash purchases allowed.
- Direct debits are available.

New York Broker Deutschland AG
Germany: Financial Services
OTC: NYBDY
c/o Bank of New York
48 Wall Street
New York, NY 10286

Phone to enroll:
Bank of New York
888-BNY-ADRS or 888-269-2377

EasyStock Investment Plan:
- Initial minimum investment: $250
- Minimum per month (optional): $50
- Maximum per transaction: $250,000
- No cash dividends paid.
- Partial dividend reinvestment.
- No discount is available.
- No IRA option is available.
- Optional cash purchases allowed.
- Direct debits are available.

Newport Corp.
United States: Electronics
NASDAQ: NEWP
1791 Deere Avenue
Irvine, CA 92714
www.newport.com
714-863-3144

Newport Corporation designs, produces, and markets instruments and electronic devices used by scientists, researchers, and precision manufacturers.

Phone to enroll:
Bank of New York
888-200-3169

EasyStock Investment Plan:
- Initial minimum investment: $100
- Minimum per month (optional): $50
- Maximum per transaction: $10,000
- Maximum annual investment: $100,000

- Cash dividends are offered.
- Partial dividend reinvestment.
- No discount is available.
- No IRA option is available.
- Optional cash purchases allowed.
- Direct debits are available.

Newport News Shipbuilding Corp.
United States: Shipbuilding
NYSE: NNS
4101 Washington Avenue
Newport News, VA 23607
www.nns.com
757-380-2000

Newport News Shipbuilding is the largest shipbuilder in the U.S. Its business consists primarily of building, maintaining, and refitting U.S. Navy vessels, particularly nuclear submarines and aircraft carriers.

Phone to enroll:
American Stock Transfer & Trust
800-649-1861

EasyStock Investment Plan:
- Initial minimum investment: $500
- Minimum per month (optional): $50
- Maximum annual investment: $250,000
- Cash dividends are offered.
- Partial dividend reinvestment.
- No discount is available.
- No IRA option is available.
- Optional cash purchases allowed.
- Direct debits are available.

NFC, PLC
United Kingdom: Transportation
AMEX: NFC
c/o Bank of New York
48 Wall Street
New York, NY 10286
www.nfc.co.uk

NFC is a logistics and moving services company operating worldwide through subsidiaries, including Allied Van Lines.

Phone to enroll:
Bank of New York
888-BNY-ADRS or 888-269-2377

EasyStock Investment Plan:
- Initial minimum investment: $250
- Minimum per month (optional): $50
- Maximum per transaction: $250,000
- Cash dividends are offered.
- Partial dividend reinvestment.
- No discount is available.
- No IRA option is available.
- Optional cash purchases allowed.
- Direct debits are available.

NICE Systems Ltd.
Israel: Technology
NASDAQ: NICEY
c/o Bank of New York
48 Wall Street
New York, NY 10286
www.nice.com

Nice Systems designs, develops, manufactures, and markets digital recording and retrieval systems. The company makes NiceLog voice logging systems that simultaneously record and monitor communications from multiple channels.

Phone to enroll:
Bank of New York
888-BNY-ADRS or 888-269-2377

EasyStock Investment Plan:
- Initial minimum investment: $250
- Minimum per month (optional): $50
- Maximum per transaction: $250,000
- No cash dividends paid.
- Partial dividend reinvestment.
- No discount is available.
- No IRA option is available.
- Optional cash purchases allowed.
- Direct debits are available.

Nippon Telephone and Telegraph
Japan: Telecommunications
NYSE: NTT
c/o Morgan Guaranty Trust Company
PO Box 9073
Boston, MA 02205-9948
www.ntt.co.jp

NTT is the world's largest telecommunications company. It has a virtual monopoly on Japan's local phone service but shares the long-distance market with several smaller carriers. NTT will soon be split into three companies.

Phone to enroll:
Morgan Guaranty Trust Company
800-997-8970

EasyStock Investment Plan:
- Initial minimum investment: $250
- Minimum per month (optional): $50
- Maximum annual investment: $100,000
- Cash dividends are offered.
- Partial dividend reinvestment.
- No discount is available.
- No IRA option is available.
- Optional cash purchases allowed.
- Direct debits are available.

Nokia Corporation
Finland: Telecommunications Equipment
NYSE: NOKA
PO Box 226
Fin-00045 Nokia Group
www.nokia.com

Nokia ranks second in global cellular-telephone sales, after Motorola and ahead of Ericsson. However, Nokia is number one in the fast-growing market for digital cell phones.

Phone to enroll:
Citibank
800-483-9010

EasyStock Investment Plan:
- Initial minimum investment: $250
- Minimum per month (optional): $50
- Maximum annual investment: $100,000
- Cash dividends are offered.
- Partial dividend reinvestment.
- No discount is available.
- No IRA option is available.
- Optional cash purchases allowed.
- Direct debits are available.

Norsk Hydro A.S.
Norway: Oil and Gas
NYSE: NHY
c/o Morgan Guaranty Trust Company
PO Box 9073
Boston, MA 02205-9948
www.hydro.com

Norsk Hydro is Norway's largest public industrial company, with interests in fertilizer, oil and gas, petrochemicals, and light metals companies.

Phone to enroll:
Morgan Guaranty Trust Company
800-997-8970

EasyStock Investment Plan:
- Initial minimum investment: $250
- Minimum per month (optional): $50
- Maximum annual investment: $100,000
- Cash dividends are offered.
- Partial dividend reinvestment.
- No discount is available.
- No IRA option is available.
- Optional cash purchases allowed.
- Direct debits are available.

Nortel Inversora S.A.
Argentina: Telecommunications
NYSE: NTL
c/o Morgan Guaranty Trust Company
PO Box 9073
Boston, MA 02205-9948

Nortel Inversora has a 60% controlling stake in Telecom Argentina, the monopoly telephone company serving northern Argentina. Telecom Argentina's monopoly is set to expire in November 1999.

Phone to enroll:
Morgan Guaranty Trust Company
800-997-8970

EasyStock Investment Plan:
- Initial minimum investment: $250
- Minimum per month (optional): $50
- Maximum annual investment: $100,000
- Cash dividends are offered.
- Partial dividend reinvestment.
- No discount is available.
- No IRA option is available.
- Optional cash purchases allowed.
- Direct debits are available.

Northern States Power Co.
United States: Electric Services
NYSE: NSP
414 Nicollet Mall
Minneapolis, MN 55401
www.nspco.com
612-330-5500

Northern States Power (NSP), a utility holding company, generates, transmits, and distributes electricity to about 1.4 million customers throughout a 49,000 square mile area that primarily includes the Dakotas, Michigan, Minnesota, and Wisconsin.

Phone to enroll:
Morgan Guaranty Trust Company
800-527-4677

EasyStock Investment Plan:
- Initial minimum investment: $100
- Minimum per month (optional): $25
- Maximum quarterly investment: $10,000
- Cash dividends are offered.
- Partial dividend reinvestment.
- No discount is available.
- No IRA option is available.
- Optional cash purchases allowed.
- No direct debit option.

Northwestern Public Service Co. Ltd.
United States: Electric Services
NYSE: NPS
33 Third Street SE
Huron, SD 57350
www.northwestern.com
605-352-8411

Northwestern Public Service is a South Dakota-based electric utility.

Phone company to enroll:
605-352-8411

EasyStock Investment Plan:
- Initial minimum investment: $10
- Minimum per month (optional): $10
- Maximum monthly investment: $2,000
- Cash dividends are offered.
- Partial dividend reinvestment.
- No discount is available.
- No IRA option is available.
- Optional cash purchases allowed.
- No direct debit option.

Novo Nordisk A.S.
Denmark: Pharmaceuticals
NYSE: NVO
c/o Morgan Guaranty Trust Company
PO Box 9073
Boston, MA 02205-9948
www.novo.dk

Novo Nordisk is the world's leading producer of insulin and industrial enzymes. Its health care products account for 75% of sales and include insulin injection and monitoring systems and women's hormone-replacement products.

Phone to enroll:
Morgan Guaranty Trust Company
800-997-8970

EasyStock Investment Plan:
- Initial minimum investment: $250
- Minimum per month (optional): $50
- Maximum annual investment: $100,000
- Cash dividends are offered.
- Partial dividend reinvestment.
- No discount is available.
- No IRA option is available.
- Optional cash purchases allowed.
- Direct debits are available.

NUI Corporation
United States: Natural Gas
NYSE: NUI
550 Route 202-206, PO Box 760
Bedminster, NJ 07921-0760
www.nui.com
908-781-0500

NUI provides natural gas to about 360,000 residential and commercial customers. Its northern division's Elizabethtown Gas Company serves customers in New Jersey and accounts for more than half of revenues.

Phone to enroll:
Morgan Guaranty Trust Company
800-649-9893

EasyStock Investment Plan:
- Initial minimum investment: $125
- Minimum per month (optional): $25
- Maximum annual investment: $60,000
- Cash dividends are offered.
- Partial dividend reinvestment.
- No discount is available.
- No IRA option is available.
- Optional cash purchases allowed.
- Direct debits are available.
- View materials and enroll online at www.netstockdirect.com.

Oce N.V.
Netherlands: Office Equipment
NASDAQ: OCENY
c/o Morgan Guaranty Trust Company
PO Box 9073
Boston, MA 02205-9948
www.oce.com

OCE N.V. based in the Netherlands, designs, manufactures, markets, and services copying equipment, laser printers, plotter systems, and related supplies for the office systems and design engineering markets.

Phone to enroll:
Morgan Guaranty Trust Company
800-997-8970

EasyStock Investment Plan:
- Initial minimum investment: $250
- Minimum per month (optional): $50
- Maximum annual investment:
- Cash dividends are offered.
- Partial dividend reinvestment.
- No discount is available.
- No IRA option is available.
- Optional cash purchases allowed.
- Direct debits are available.

OGE Energy Corp.
United States: Electric Services
NYSE: OGE
321 North Robinson
PO Box 321
Oklahoma City, OK 73101-0321
www.oge.com
405-553-3000

OGE Energy is the holding company for Oklahoma Gas and Electric, a public utility serving about 685,000 customers in a 30,000-square-mile territory in Oklahoma and western Arkansas. Its electric sales come primarily from commercial and industrial accounts.

Phone to enroll:
Morgan Guaranty Trust Company
800-842-7629

EasyStock Investment Plan:
- Initial minimum investment: $250
- Minimum per month (optional): $25
- Maximum annual investment: $100,000
- No cash dividends paid.
- Partial dividend reinvestment.
- No discount is available.
- No IRA option is available.
- Optional cash purchases allowed.
- Direct debits are available.

Old National Bancorp
United States: Banking
NASDAQ: OLDB
420 Main Street
Evansville, IN 47705-0718
www.oldnational.com
812-464-1200

Old National Bancorp is a multibank holding company with thirteen Indiana banking subsidiaries, four Kentucky banking subsidiaries, and four Illinois banking subsidiaries.

Phone to enroll:
Chase Mellon
800-677-1749

EasyStock Investment Plan:
- Initial minimum investment: $500
- Minimum per month (optional): $50
- Maximum quarterly investment: $3,500
- Maximum annual investment: $50,000
- Cash dividends are offered.

- Partial dividend reinvestment.
- Discounts on share purchases.
- No IRA option is available.
- Optional cash purchases allowed.
- No direct debit option.

OLS Asia Holdings Ltd.
Hong Kong: Construction
NASDAQ: OLSAY
c/o Bank of New York
48 Wall Street
New York, NY 10286
www.olsasia.com

OLS Asia is a specialty construction contractor that tackles large-scale renovations in Hong Kong and China. The company's construction services are offered through its controlled subsidiary, OLS Group.

Phone to enroll:
Bank of New York
888-BNY-ADRS or 888-269-2377

EasyStock Investment Plan:
- Initial minimum investment: $250
- Minimum per month (optional): $50
- Maximum per transaction: $250,000
- Cash dividends are offered.
- Partial dividend reinvestment.
- No discount is available.
- No IRA option is available.
- Optional cash purchases allowed.
- Direct debits are available.

Oneok Inc.
United States: Natural Gas
NYSE: OKE
100 West Fifth Street
Tulsa, OK 74103
www.oneok.com
918-588-7000

Through its divisions, Oklahoma Natural Gas and Kansas Gas Service, Oneok provides natural gas to 1.4 million customers in Oklahoma and Kansas, grabbing 88% and 65% of those respective markets.

Phone to enroll:
Bank of New York
800-395-2662

EasyStock Investment Plan:
- Initial minimum investment: $100
- Minimum per month (optional): $25
- Maximum annual investment: $100,000
- Cash dividends are offered.
- Partial dividend reinvestment.
- Discounts on share purchases.
- No IRA option is available.
- Optional cash purchases allowed.
- Direct debits are available.

Owens-Corning Ltd.
United States: Building Materials
NYSE: OWC
One Owens-Corning Parkway
Tolego, OH 43659
www.owens-corning.com
419-248-8000

Owens-Corning is the world's number one maker of glass fiber and composite materials. Using the Pink Panther cartoon character as its pitchman, it sells fiberglass insulation and other products under the Fiberglas and Miraflex PinkPlus brand names.

Phone to enroll:
Liberty National Bank & Trust Company
800-GET-PINK or 800-438-7465

EasyStock Investment Plan:
- Initial minimum investment: $100
- Minimum per month (optional): $100

- Maximum annual investment: $120,000
- Cash dividends are offered.
- No partial dividend reinvestment.
- No discount is available.
- No IRA option is available.
- Optional cash purchases allowed.
- Direct debits are available.

OzEMail Limited
Australia: Computer Software
NASDAQ: OZEMY
c/o Bank of New York
48 Wall Street
New York, NY 10286
www.ozemail.com

OzEmail Limited is the leading provider of comprehensive Internet services in Australia and New Zealand, with more than 125,000 customers. Its network covers more than 90% of Australia's population with forty points of presence.

Phone to enroll:
Bank of New York
888-BNY-ADRS or 888-269-2377

EasyStock Investment Plan:
- Initial minimum investment: $250
- Minimum per month (optional): $50
- Maximum per transaction: $250,000
- No cash dividends paid.
- Partial dividend reinvestment.
- No discount is available.
- No IRA option is available.
- Optional cash purchases allowed.
- Direct debits are available.

P

Pacific Century Financial Corp.
United States: Multi-Service
NYSE: BOH
130 Merchant Street
Honolulu, HI 96813
www.boh.com
888-643-3888

Formerly Bancorp Hawaii, this regional financial services holding company operates more than 160 locations from Hawaii to New York.

Phone to enroll:
Bank of New York
808-537-8239

EasyStock Investment Plan:
- Initial minimum investment: $250
- Minimum per month (optional): $50
- Maximum annual investment: $100,000
- Cash dividends are offered.
- Partial dividend reinvestment.
- No discount is available.
- No IRA option is available.
- Optional cash purchases allowed.
- Direct debits are available.

Pacific Dunlop Limited
Australia: Multi-Industry
NASDAQ: PDLPY
c/o Morgan Guaranty Trust Company
PO Box 9073
Boston, MA 02205-9948
www.pacdun.com

Pacific Dunlop has more than 150 manufacturing plants for its six core businesses, which include manufacturing batteries and condoms.

Phone to enroll:
Morgan Guaranty Trust Company
800-997-8970

EasyStock Investment Plan:
- Initial minimum investment: $250
- Minimum per month (optional): $50
- Maximum per transaction: $250,000
- Cash dividends are offered.
- Partial dividend reinvestment.
- No discount is available.
- No IRA option is available.
- Optional cash purchases allowed.
- Direct debits are available.

Peoples Energy Corp.
United States: Natural Gas
NYSE: PGL
122 South Michigan Avenue
Chicago, IL 60603
www.pecorp.com
312-240-4000

People's Energy is a holding company for two public utilities and five energy-related subsidiaries that serve Chicago and northeastern Illinois.

Phone to enroll:
Bank of New York
800-901-8878

EasyStock Investment Plan:
- Initial minimum investment: $250
- Minimum per month (optional): $25
- Maximum monthly investment: $3,000
- Maximum annual investment: $10,000
- Cash dividends are offered.
- No partial dividend reinvestment.
- No discount is available.
- No IRA option is available.
- Optional cash purchases allowed.
- Direct debits are available.

Petsec Energy Limited
Indonesia: Oil and Gas
NASDAQ: PSALY
c/o Bank of New York
48 Wall Street
New York, NY 10286

PETSEC is an Indonesian oil and gas company.

Phone to enroll:
Bank of New York
888-BNY-ADRS or 888-269-2377

EasyStock Investment Plan:
- Initial minimum investment: $250
- Minimum per month (optional): $50
- Maximum per transaction: $250,000
- No cash dividends paid.
- Partial dividend reinvestment.
- No discount is available.
- No IRA option is available.
- Optional cash purchases allowed.
- Direct debits are available.

Pfeiffer Vacuum Technology AG
Germany: Machinery
NYSE: PV
c/o Bank of New York
48 Wall Street
New York, NY 10286
www.pfeiffer-vacuum.com

Pfeiffer Vacuum is a German maker of vacuum pumps. The company's turbomolecular pumps create vacuum environments for special processing in manufacturing applications. The pumps are used for freeze-drying by food processors.

Phone to enroll:
Bank of New York
888-BNY-ADRS or 888-269-2377

EasyStock Investment Plan:
- Initial minimum investment: $250
- Minimum per month (optional): $50
- Maximum annual investment: $100,000
- No cash dividends paid.
- Partial dividend reinvestment.
- No discount is available.
- No IRA option is available.
- Optional cash purchases allowed.
- Maximum per transaction: $250,000
- Direct debits are available.

Pharmacia & Upjohn, Inc.
United States: Pharmaceuticals
NYSE: PNU
7000 Portage Road
Kalamazoo, MO 49001
www.pnu.com
908-306-4400

Pharmacia & Upjohn, one of the world's largest pharmaceutical companies, makes prescription drugs, over-the-counter health products, diagnostics, and biotechnology equipment.

Phone to enroll:
Bank of New York
800-286-9178

EasyStock Investment Plan:
- Initial minimum investment: $250
- Minimum per month (optional): $50
- Maximum monthly investment: $10,000
- Maximum annual investment: $100,000
- Cash dividends are offered.
- No partial dividend reinvestment.
- No discount is available.
- No IRA option is available.
- Optional cash purchases allowed.
- Direct debits are available.

Philadelphia Suburban Corp.
United States: Water Services
NYSE: PSC
762 Lancaster Avenue
Bryn Mawr, PA 19010-3489
www.suburbanwater.com
610-527-8000

Philadelphia Suburban is a holding company for a regulated public utility and a small data-processing company. The company's primary subsidiary, Philadelphia Suburban Water, supplies water to some 900,000 residential, commercial, and industrial customers.

Phone to enroll:
Harris Bank
800-205-8314

EasyStock Investment Plan:
- Initial minimum investment: $500
- Minimum per month (optional): $50
- Maximum annual investment: $30,000
- Cash dividends are offered.
- Partial dividend reinvestment.
- Discounts on share purchases.
- An IRA option is available.
- Optional cash purchases allowed.
- Direct debits are available.

Phillips Petroleum Co.
United States: International Oils
NYSE: P
Phillips Building
Bartlesville, OK 74004
www.phillips66.com
918-661-6600

Phillips produces, refines, transports, and markets oil products and natural gas. It has oil and gas properties in twenty countries and conducts exploration and production activities worldwide.

Phone to enroll:
Chase Mellon
888-887-2968

EasyStock Investment Plan:
- Initial minimum investment: $500
- Minimum per month (optional): $50
- Cash dividends are offered.
- Maximum monthly investment: $10,000
- Partial dividend reinvestment.
- No discount is available.
- No IRA option is available.
- Optional cash purchases allowed.
- Direct debits are available.

Piedmont Natural Gas Co., Inc.
United States: Natural Gas
NYSE: PNY
1915 Rexford Road
Charlotte, NC 28211
www.piedmontng.com
704-364-3120

Piedmont Natural Gas transports and sells natural gas and propane to customers in the Carolinas and Tennessee. The company's regulated utility business provides natural gas to about 600,000 residential, commercial, and industrial customers.

Phone to enroll:
Chase Mellon
800-693-9917

EasyStock Investment Plan:
- Initial minimum investment: $250
- Minimum per month (optional): $25
- Maximum monthly investment: $3,000
- Cash dividends are offered.
- Partial dividend reinvestment.
- Discounts on share purchases.
- No IRA option is available.
- Optional cash purchases allowed.
- Direct debits are available.

Pinnacle West Capital Corp.
United States: Electric Services
NYSE: PNW
400 East Van Buren Street
Suite 700
Phoenix, AZ 85004
www.pinnaclewest.com
602-379-2500

Pinnacle West Capital is a holding company for a diverse range of subsidiaries. It owns Arizona Public Service, Arizona's largest electric utility, which provides service to nearly 740,000 customers. Another subsidiary, SunCor, is a real estate development company.

Phone to enroll:
Wachovia Bank of North Carolina
602-379-2500

EasyStock Investment Plan:
- Initial minimum investment: $50
- Minimum per month (optional): -
- Maximum annual investment: $60,000
- Cash dividends are offered.
- Partial dividend reinvestment.
- No discount is available.
- No IRA option is available.
- Optional cash purchases allowed.
- Direct debits are available.

Pohang Iron & Steel Co. Ltd.
South Korea: Iron/Steel
NYSE: PKX
c/o Bank of New York
48 Wall Street
New York, NY 10286
www.posco.co.kr

Pohang Iron and Steel Co. is one of the world's top steel producers and has interests in a number of other industries, including engineering, construction, and telecommunications.

Phone to enroll:
Bank of New York
888-BNY-ADRS or 888-269-2377

EasyStock Investment Plan:
- Initial minimum investment: $250
- Minimum per month (optional): $50
- Maximum per transaction: $250,000
- Cash dividends are offered.
- Partial dividend reinvestment.
- No discount is available.
- No IRA option is available.
- Optional cash purchases allowed.
- Direct debits are available.

Portugal Telecom
Portugal: Telecommunications
NYSE: PT
c/o Bank of New York
48 Wall Street
New York, NY 10286
www.telecom.pt
415-543-0404

Portugal Telecom provides local telephone and international long-distance services throughout Portugal. Through its subsidiaries, the company also provides mobile telephone services, paging, and data communications/Internet services.

Phone to enroll:
Bank of New York
888-BNY-ADRS or 888-269-2377

EasyStock Investment Plan:
- Initial minimum investment: $250
- Minimum per month (optional): $50
- Maximum per transaction: $250,000
- Cash dividends are offered.
- Partial dividend reinvestment.
- No discount is available.
- No IRA option is available.
- Optional cash purchases allowed.
- Direct debits are available.

Providian Financial Corp.
United States: Financial Services
NYSE: PSE
201 Mission Street
San Francisco, CA 94105
www.providian.com

Providian Financial is the largest U.S. issuer of secured credit cards, which allow consumers with poor credit to borrow money from savings accounts they set up with the company. It also issues traditional credit cards and offers revolving lines of credit.

Phone company to enroll:
First Chicago Trust Company
800-482-8690

EasyStock Investment Plan:
- Initial minimum investment: $500
- Minimum per month (optional): $50
- Maximum annual investment: $250,000
- Cash dividends are offered.
- Partial dividend reinvestment.
- No discount is available.
- No IRA option is available.
- Optional cash purchases allowed.
- Direct debits are available.
- View materials and enroll online at www.netstockdirect.com.

P.T. IndoSat
Indonesia: Telecommunications
NYSE: IIT
c/o Bank of New York
48 Wall Street
New York, NY 10286

P.T. Indonesian Satellite uses a network of satellites, submarine cables, and microwave links to deliver telecommunications services to its Indonesian customers. Indosat also

has joint ventures and consortia for developing multimedia, cellular, and digital communications services throughout Southeast Asia.

Phone to enroll:
Bank of New York
888-BNY-ADRS or 888-269-2377

EasyStock Investment Plan:
- Initial minimum investment: $250
- Minimum per month (optional): $50
- Maximum per transaction: $250,000
- Cash dividends are offered.
- Partial dividend reinvestment.
- No discount is available.
- No IRA option is available.
- Optional cash purchases allowed.
- Direct debits are available.

P.T. Inti Indorayon Utama
Indonesia: Paper
NYSE: PTIDY
c/o Bank of New York
48 Wall Street
New York, NY 10286

Inti Indorayon is a large Indonesian paper company.

Phone to enroll:
Bank of New York
888-BNY-ADRS or 888-269-2377

EasyStock Investment Plan:
- Initial minimum investment: $250
- Minimum per month (optional): $50
- Maximum per transaction: $250,000
- Cash dividends are offered.
- Partial dividend reinvestment.
- No discount is available.
- No IRA option is available.
- Optional cash purchases allowed.
- Direct debits are available.

P.T. Pasifik Satelit Nusantara
Indonesia: Telecommunications
NASDAQ: PSNRY
c/o Bank of New York
48 Wall Street
New York, NY 10286
www.psn.co.id

P.T. Pasifik Satelit Nusantara was the first to provide satellite telecommunications service to Indonesia. The company is one of two in the country delivering long-distance and local phone access through a satellite network, focusing on becoming a fully integrated provider of satellite telecommunications.

Phone to enroll:
Bank of New York
888-BNY-ADRS or 888-269-2377

EasyStock Investment Plan:
- Initial minimum investment: $250
- Minimum per month (optional): $50
- Maximum per transaction: $250,000
- No cash dividends paid.
- Partial dividend reinvestment.
- No discount is available.
- No IRA option is available.
- Optional cash purchases allowed.
- Direct debits are available.

P.T. Telkom
Indonesia: Telecommunications
NYSE: TLK
c/o Bank of New York
48 Wall Street
New York, NY 10286
www.telekom.co.id

P.T. Telekomunikasi Indonesia (Telkom) is Indonesia's main provider of local and long-distance telecommunications services, operating nearly five million lines. The company retains its exclusive right to local

fixed line and fixed wireless service until 2011, but faces competition from cellular operators.

Phone to enroll:
Bank of New York
888-BNY-ADRS or 888-269-2377

EasyStock Investment Plan:
- Initial minimum investment: $250
- Minimum per month (optional): $25
- Maximum quarterly investment: $5,000
- Cash dividends are offered.
- Partial dividend reinvestment.
- No discount is available.
- No IRA option is available.
- Optional cash purchases allowed.
- Direct debits are available.

Public Service Company of New Mexico, Inc.
United States: Natural Gas
NYSE: PNM
Alvarado Square
Albuquerque, NM 87158
www.pnm.com
505-241-2700

Public Service Company of New Mexico is a utility and energy services firm providing natural gas and electricity service to customers in New Mexico. Its service areas have a population of more than 1.3 million.

Phone company to enroll:
800-545-4425

EasyStock Investment Plan:
- Initial minimum investment: $50
- Minimum per month (optional): $50
- Maximum annual investment: $60,000
- Cash dividends are offered.
- Partial dividend reinvestment.
- No discount is available.
- No IRA option is available.
- Optional cash purchases allowed.
- Direct debits are available.

Public Service Company of North Carolina, Inc.
United States: Natural Gas
NYSE: PGS
400 Cox Road, PO Box 1398
Gastonia, NC 28053-1398
www.psnc.com
704-864-6731

Public Service Company of North Carolina provides natural gas and related services to more than 300,000 customers in North Carolina.

Phone to enroll:
First Union National Bank of North Carolina
800-774-4117

EasyStock Investment Plan:
- Initial minimum investment: $250
- Minimum per month (optional): $25
- Maximum quarterly investment: $15,000
- Cash dividends are offered.
- Partial dividend reinvestment.
- Discounts on share purchases.
- No IRA option is available.
- Optional cash purchases allowed.
- Direct debits are available.

Public Service Enterprise Group Ltd.
United States: Utilities
NYSE: PEG
80 Park Plaza, PO Box 1171
Newark, NJ 07101
www.pseg.com
973-430-7000

Public Service Enterprise Group is a utility holding company whose principal subsidiary, Public Service Electric and Gas, accounts for almost all of its sales, delivering electricity to about 1.9 million customers in three hundred New Jersey cities.

Phone to enroll:
First Chicago Trust Company
800-242-0813

EasyStock Investment Plan:
- Initial minimum investment: $250
- Minimum per month (optional): $50
- Maximum annual investment: -
- Cash dividends are offered.
- Partial dividend reinvestment.
- No discount is available.
- No IRA option is available.
- Optional cash purchases allowed.
- Direct debits are available.

Puget Sound Energy, Inc.
United States: Electric Services
NYSE: PSD
10608 NE Fourth Street
Bellevue, WA 98004-5028
www.psechoice.com
425-454-6363

Puget Sound Energy is the largest gas utility in the Pacific Northwest, providing electricity in the Puget Sound region and operating storage facilities in Jackson Prairie, Washington.

Phone to enroll:
Chase Mellon
800-997-8438

EasyStock Investment Plan:
- Initial minimum investment: $25
- Minimum per month (optional): $25
- Maximum annual investment: $100,000
- Cash dividends are offered.
- No partial dividend reinvestment.
- No discount is available.
- No IRA option is available.
- Optional cash purchases allowed.
- No direct debit option.

Q

Quaker Oats Co.
United States: Food Products
NYSE: OAT
321 North Clark Street
Chicago, IL 60610
www.quakeroats.com
312-222-7111

The Quaker Oats Company is an international marketer and manufacturer of foods and beverages, with annual sales from ongoing businesses of nearly $5 billion. Its major brands include Quaker Oaks, Gatorade, and Snapple.

Phone to enroll:
Chase Mellon
800-286-9178

EasyStock Investment Plan:
- Initial minimum investment: $500
- Minimum per month (optional): $50
- Maximum annual investment: $120,000
- Cash dividends are offered.
- Partial dividend reinvestment.

- No discount is available.
- No IRA option is available.
- Optional cash purchases allowed.
- Direct debits are available.

Questar Corporation
United States: Natural Gas
NYSE: STR
180 East First South
Salt Lake City, UT 84145
www.questarcorp.com
801-324-5000

Questar, a holding company, oversees businesses that explore, produce, transport, store, and market natural gas, oil, electricity, and related services. Subsidiaries Celsius Energy, Universal Resources, and Wexpro explore for and produce gas and oil.

Phone to enroll:
Harris Bank
800-729-6788

EasyStock Investment Plan:
- Initial minimum investment: $250
- Minimum per month (optional): $50
- Maximum annual investment: $100,000
- Cash dividends are offered.
- Partial dividend reinvestment.
- No discount is available.
- No IRA option is available.
- Optional cash purchases allowed.
- No direct debit option.

R

Rangold & Exploration Company
South Africa: Minerals/Mining
NASDAQ: RANGY
c/o Bank of New York
48 Wall Street
New York, NY 10286
Phone to enroll:
Bank of New York
888-BNY-ADRS or 888-269-2377

EasyStock Investment Plan:
- Initial minimum investment: $250
- Minimum per month (optional): $50
- Maximum per transaction: $250,000
- Cash dividends are offered.
- Partial dividend reinvestment.
- No discount is available.
- No IRA option is available.
- Optional cash purchases allowed.
- Direct debits are available.

Rank Group PLC
United Kingdom: Entertainment
NASDAQ: RANKY
c/o Morgan Guaranty Trust Company
PO Box 9073
Boston, MA 02205-9948
www.rank.com

The Rank Group owns the Hard Rock Café chain of restaurants, which has about eighty-five locations worldwide and is one of the U.K.'s leading entertainment and leisure companies. Rank has a range of businesses in the film, vacation, and leisure industries.

Phone to enroll:
Morgan Guaranty Trust Company
800-997-8970

EasyStock Investment Plan:
- Initial minimum investment: $250
- Minimum per month (optional): $50
- Maximum annual investment: $100,000
- Cash dividends are offered.
- Partial dividend reinvestment.
- No discount is available.
- No IRA option is available.
- Optional cash purchases allowed.
- Direct debits are available.

Rauma Oy
Finland: Heavy Machinery
NYSE: RMA
c/o Bank of New York
48 Wall Street
New York, NY 10286
www.rauma.com

Delimbing and slashing equipment is among Rauma Oy's metal and engineering products. One of the Finnish company's four units, Timberjack, is the world's number one maker of forest machines, with a 30% share.

Phone to enroll:
Bank of New York
888-BNY-ADRS or 888-269-2377

EasyStock Investment Plan:
- Initial minimum investment: $250
- Minimum per month (optional): $50
- Maximum per transaction: $250,000
- Cash dividends are offered.
- Partial dividend reinvestment.
- No discount is available.
- No IRA option is available.
- Optional cash purchases allowed.
- Direct debits are available.

Reader's Digest Association, Inc.
United States: Publishing
NYSE: RDA
Reader's Digest Road
Pleasantville, NY 10570-7000
www.readersdigest.com
914-238-1000

The Reader's Digest Association publishes the world's most widely read magazine. Flagship publication *Readers Digest* is published in nineteen languages and has a circulation of more than 25 million. The company also produces a range of books.

Phone to enroll:
Bank of New York
800-242-4653

EasyStock Investment Plan:
- Initial minimum investment: $1,000
- Minimum per month (optional): $100
- Maximum monthly investment: $10,000
- Cash dividends are offered.
- Partial dividend reinvestment.
- No discount is available.
- No IRA option is available.
- Optional cash purchases allowed.
- Direct debits are available.

Redwood Trust, Inc.
United States: Mortgage Finance
NASDAQ: RWTI
591 Redwood Highway
Suite 3100
Mill Valley, CA 94941
www.redwoodtrust.com
415-389-7373

Redwood Trust acquires and manages real estate mortgage assets, which it acquires as mortgage loans or mortgage securities.

Phone to enroll:
Chase Mellon
800-962-4293

EasyStock Investment Plan:
- Initial minimum investment: $500
- Minimum per month (optional): $500
- Maximum per transaction: $5,000
- Cash dividends are offered.
- Partial dividend reinvestment.
- Discounts on share purchases.
- No IRA option is available.
- Optional cash purchases allowed.
- No direct debit option.

Regions Financial Corp.
United States: Banking
NASDAQ: RGBK
417 North 20th Street
PO Box 10247
Birmingham, AL 35202
www.regionsbank.com
205-832-8450

Regions Financial is a bank holding company that operates more than 490 banking offices in Alabama, Florida, Georgia, Louisiana, South Carolina, and Tennessee. Its purchase of First Commercial will make it the number one bank in Arkansas.

Phone to enroll:
Chase Mellon
800-922-3468

EasyStock Investment Plan:
- Initial minimum investment: $500
- Minimum per month (optional): $25
- Maximum monthly investment: $10,000
- Maximum annual investment: $120,000
- Cash dividends are offered.
- No partial dividend reinvestment.
- No discount is available.
- No IRA option is available.
- Optional cash purchases allowed.
- Direct debits are available.
- View materials and enroll online at www.netstockdirect.com.

Reliant Energy Inc.
United States: Electric Services
NYSE: REI
111 Louisiana Street
Houston, TX 77002
www.reliantenergy.com

Reliant Energy has 3.6 million electric and gas customers in the U.S. It also has investments in electric utilities in Argentina, Brazil, and Columbia that serve 3.3 million customers.

Phone company to enroll:
800-231-6406

EasyStock Investment Plan:
- Initial minimum investment: $250
- Minimum per month (optional): $50
- Maximum annual investment: $120,000
- Cash dividends are offered.
- Partial dividend reinvestment.
- No discount is available.
- No IRA option is available.
- Optional cash purchases allowed.
- Direct debits are available.
- View materials and enroll online at www.netstockdirect.com.

Reliv International, Inc.
United States: Nutritional Products
NASDAQ: RELV
136 Chesterfield Industrial Blvd.
Chesterfield, MO 63005
www.reliv.com
314-537-9715

Reliv International is a network marketing firm that sells nutritional supplements, weight-management products, skin-care products, nutritional bars, sport drink mixes, and dietary fiber products.

Phone to enroll:
First Chicago Trust Company
888-333-0203

EasyStock Investment Plan:
- Initial minimum investment: $100
- Minimum per month (optional): $50
- Maximum annual investment: $100,000
- Cash dividends are offered.
- Partial dividend reinvestment.
- No discount is available.
- No IRA option is available.
- Optional cash purchases allowed.
- Direct debits are available.

Repsol S.A.
Spain: Oil and Gas
NYSE: REP
c/o Bank of New York
48 Wall Street
New York, NY 10286
www.repsol.com

Spain's largest industrial company, Repsol is a fully integrated oil and gas enterprise and the dominant domestic player in the markets for oil and liquefied petroleum gas, a major source of fuel for Spanish households.

Phone to enroll:
Bank of New York
888-BNY-ADRS or 888-269-2377

EasyStock Investment Plan:
- Initial minimum investment: $250
- Minimum per month (optional): $50
- Maximum per transaction: $250,000
- Cash dividends are offered.
- Partial dividend reinvestment.
- No discount is available.
- No IRA option is available.
- Optional cash purchases allowed.
- Direct debits are available.

Reuters Holdings PLC
United Kingdom: Publishing
NASDAQ: RTRSY
c/o Morgan Guaranty Trust Company
PO Box 9073
Boston, MA 02205-9948
www.reuters.com

Reuters is a general news agency and a financial information distributor, providing real-time financial data, transaction systems, access to numerical and textual historical databases, news, graphics, and still photographs.

Phone to enroll:
Morgan Guaranty Trust Company
800-997-8970

EasyStock Investment Plan:
- Initial minimum investment: $250
- Minimum per month (optional): $50
- Maximum annual investment: 100,000
- Cash dividends are offered.
- Partial dividend reinvestment.
- No discount is available.
- No IRA option is available.
- Optional cash purchases allowed.
- Direct debits are available.

Ricoh Company Ltd.
Japan: Office Equipment
OTC: RICOY
c/o Bank of New York
48 Wall Street
New York, NY 10286
www.ricoh.co.jp

Ricoh has over 350 subsidiaries and affiliates worldwide and is one of the world's leading manufacturers of copiers and fax machines. The company also makes cameras, scanners, computers, printers, and software, among other products.

Phone to enroll:
Bank of New York
888-BNY-ADRS or 888-269-2377

EasyStock Investment Plan:
- Initial minimum investment: $250
- Minimum per month (optional): $50
- Maximum per transaction: $250,000
- Cash dividends are offered.
- Partial dividend reinvestment.
- No discount is available.
- No IRA option is available.
- Optional cash purchases allowed.
- Direct debits are available.

Rio Tinto Limited
Australia: Mining
NYSE: RTOLY
c/o Bank of New York
48 Wall Street
New York, NY 10286
www.riotinto.com

The mines of Rio Tinto Limited (formerly CRA Limited) dot every continent except Antarctica, producing primarily aluminum, copper, coal, uranium, gold, and iron ore.

Phone to enroll:
Bank of New York
888-BNY-ADRS or 888-269-2377

EasyStock Investment Plan:
- Initial minimum investment: $250
- Minimum per month (optional): $50
- Maximum per transaction: $250,000
- Cash dividends are offered.
- Partial dividend reinvestment.
- No discount is available.
- No IRA option is available.
- Optional cash purchases allowed.
- Direct debits are available.

Roadway Express, Inc.
United States: Trucking
NASDAQ: ROAD
1077 Gorge Blvd
Akron, OH 44310
www.roadway.com/rexmain.cgi
330-384-1717

Roadway Express is the number two less-than-truckload (under 10,000 pounds) motor freight carrier in the U.S. (behind Yellow Corp). It provides service within the U.S., Canada, Mexico, and sixty-six other countries. The company operates about 30,000 trailers and 10,000 tractors.

Phone to enroll:
Harris Trust Co.
800-286-9178

EasyStock Investment Plan:
- Initial minimum investment: $250
- Minimum per month (optional): $50
- Maximum annual investment: $100,000
- Cash dividends are offered.
- Partial dividend reinvestment.
- No discount is available.
- No IRA option is available.

- Optional cash purchases allowed.
- Direct debits are available.

Robbins & Myers, Inc.
United States: Fluids Management
NASDAQ: ROBN
1400 Kettering Tower
Dayton, OH 45423
www.robn.com
937-222-2610

Robbins & Myers makes vessels, pumps, and mixers for different processing industries.

Phone to enroll:
Harris Bank
800-622-6757

EasyStock Investment Plan:
- Initial minimum investment: $500
- Minimum per month (optional): $50
- Maximum quarterly investment: $5,000
- Cash dividends are offered.
- Partial dividend reinvestment.
- No discount is available.
- No IRA option is available.
- Optional cash purchases allowed.
- Direct debits are available.

Rockwell International Corp.
United States: Aircraft
NYSE: ROK
2201 Seal Beach Blvd
Seal Beach, CA 90740
www.rockwell.com
714-424-4200

Former defense industry giant Rockwell International is now one of the world's largest industrial automation companies. Its automation unit makes programmable controllers, worker-machine interface devices, industrial motors, and power transmission products.

Phone to enroll:
National City Bank
800-842-7629

EasyStock Investment Plan:
- Initial minimum investment: $1,000
- Minimum per month (optional): $100
- Maximum annual investment: $100,000
- No cash dividends paid.
- Partial dividend reinvestment.
- No discount is available.
- No IRA option is available.
- Optional cash purchases allowed.
- No direct debit option.

Royal Ahold N.V.
Netherlands: Retail/Restaurants
NYSE: AHO
c/o Bank of New York
48 Wall Street
New York, NY 10286
www.ahold.nl

Royal Ahold controls about 3,600 supermarkets, hypermarkets, discount and specialty stores in seventeen countries.

Phone to enroll:
Bank of New York
888-BNY-ADRS or 888-269-2377

EasyStock Investment Plan:
- Initial minimum investment: $250
- Minimum per month (optional): $50
- Maximum per transaction: $250,000
- Cash dividends are offered.
- Partial dividend reinvestment.
- No discount is available.
- No IRA option is available.

- Optional cash purchases allowed.
- Maximum annual investment: $250,000
- Direct debits are available.

Royal Bank of Scotland PLC
United Kingdom: Banking
NYSE: RBSB
c/o Bank of New York
48 Wall Street
New York, NY 10286

If you have overdraft protection for your checking account, you can thank the Royal Bank of Scotland, which invented the service in 1728. With seven hundred branches in the U.K., banking is the largest part of the company's business.

Phone to enroll:
Bank of New York
888-BNY-ADRS or 888-269-2377

EasyStock Investment Plan:
- Initial minimum investment: $250
- Minimum per month (optional): $50
- Maximum per transaction: $250,000
- Cash dividends are offered.
- Partial dividend reinvestment.
- No discount is available.
- No IRA option is available.
- Optional cash purchases allowed.
- Direct debits are available.

Royal Dutch Petroleum Co.
Netherlands: International Oils
NYSE: RD
c/o Morgan Guaranty Trust Company
PO Box 9073
Boston, MA 02205-9948
www.shell.com

Royal Dutch Petroleum is the majority partner in the Royal Dutch/Shell Group, the world's largest oil and gas conglomerate, with a 60% interest.

Phone to enroll:
Morgan Guaranty Trust Company
800-997-8970

EasyStock Investment Plan:
- Initial minimum investment: $250
- Minimum per month (optional): $50
- Maximum annual investment: $100,000
- No cash dividends paid.
- Partial dividend reinvestment.
- No discount is available.
- No IRA option is available.
- Optional cash purchases allowed.
- Direct debits are available.

Ryanair Holdings PLC
Ireland: Airlines
NASDAQ: RYAAY
c/o Bank of New York
48 Wall Street
New York, NY 10286
www.ryanair.ie

Ryanair Holdings offers no-frills air transportation throughout Europe, with more than one hundred scheduled flights each day.

Phone to enroll:
Bank of New York
888-BNY-ADRS or 888-269-2377

EasyStock Investment Plan:
- Initial minimum investment: $250
- Minimum per month (optional): $50
- Maximum per transaction: $250,000
- No cash dividends paid.
- Partial dividend reinvestment.
- No discount is available.
- No IRA option is available.
- Optional cash purchases allowed.
- Direct debits are available.

Sanderson Farms, Inc.
United States: Food Products
NASDAQ: SAFM
225 North 13th Avenue
PO Box 988
Laurel MS 39441
601-649-4030

Sanderson Farms sells ice-pack, chill-pack, and frozen chicken in whole, cut-up, and boneless forms.

Phone to enroll:
Bank of New York
800-842-7629

EasyStock Investment Plan:
- Initial minimum investment: $500
- Minimum per month (optional): $50
- Maximum per transaction: $10,000
- Maximum monthly investment: $10,000
- Cash dividends are offered.
- Partial dividend reinvestment.
- No discount is available.
- No IRA option is available.
- Optional cash purchases allowed.
- No direct debit option.

Santos Ltd.
Australia: Oil and Gas
NASDAQ: STOSY
c/o Morgan Guaranty Trust Company
PO Box 9073
Boston, MA 02205-9948

Santos is an independent company involved in the exploration and production of petroleum products in and around Australia, the U.S., and the U.K. It produces and supplies gas, gas liquids, and oil, predominately to Australian customers.

Phone to enroll:
Morgan Guaranty Trust Company
800-997-8970

EasyStock Investment Plan:
- Initial minimum investment: $250
- Minimum per month (optional): $50
- Maximum annual investment: $100,000
- No cash dividends paid.
- Partial dividend reinvestment.
- No discount is available.
- No IRA option is available.
- Optional cash purchases allowed.
- Direct debits are available.

Saville Systems PLC
Ireland: Technology
NASDAQ: SAVLY
c/o Bank of New York
48 Wall Street
New York, NY 10286
www.savillesys.com

Phone to enroll:
Bank of New York
888-BNY-ADRS or 888-269-2377

EasyStock Investment Plan:
- Initial minimum investment: $250
- Minimum per month (optional): $50

- Maximum per transaction: $250,000
- No cash dividends paid.
- Partial dividend reinvestment.
- No discount is available.
- No IRA option is available.
- Optional cash purchases allowed.
- Direct debits are available.

SBC Communications Inc.
United States
NYSE: SBC
175 East Houston
Houston, TX 78205-2233
www.sbc.com
210-821-4105

SBC provides local telephone service in seven of the top ten metropolitan areas in the U.S. and cellular phone service to 5.5 million people in 78 markets. The company has agreed to buy Ameritech in a deal that would create America's largest local telephone company.

Phone to enroll:
First Chicago Trust Company
800-351-7221

EasyStock Investment Plan:
- Initial minimum investment: $500
- Minimum per month (optional): $50
- Maximum annual investment: $120,000
- No cash dividends paid.
- No partial dividend reinvestment.
- No discount is available.
- No IRA option is available.
- No Optional cash purchases.
- No direct debit option.

SCANA Corporation
United States: Utilities
NYSE: SCG
1426 Main Street
Columbia, SC 29201
www.scana.com
803-748-3000

SCANA is a holding company for a public utility and other subsidiaries. South Carolina Electric & Gas provides electricity to approximately 475,000 customers in South Carolina. It also provides natural gas to about 240,000 customers.

Phone to enroll:
Bank of New York
800-763-5891

EasyStock Investment Plan:
- Initial minimum investment: $250
- Minimum per month (optional): $25
- Maximum annual investment: $100,000
- Cash dividends are offered.
- Partial dividend reinvestment.
- No discount is available.
- No IRA option is available.
- Optional cash purchases allowed.
- Direct debits are available.

Schnitzer Steel Industries, Inc.
United States: Steel
NASDAQ: SCHN
3200 NW Yeon Avenue
Portland, OR 97210
www.schn.com
503-224-9900

Schnitzer Steel Industries is an integrated recycler of finished steel products. It collects, processes, and recycles steel scrap in plants on the

East Coast and West Coast and ships it to flourishing steel mini-mill markets across Asia.

Phone to enroll:
Bank of New York
800-524-4458

EasyStock Investment Plan:
- Initial minimum investment: $500
- Minimum per month (optional): $50
- Maximum per transaction: $10,000
- Maximum annual investment: $100,000
- Cash dividends are offered.
- Partial dividend reinvestment.
- No discount is available.
- No IRA option is available.
- Optional cash purchases allowed.
- Direct debits are available.

Scoot.com PLC
United Kingdom: Services
NASDAQ: SCOP
c/o Bank of New York
48 Wall Street
New York, NY 10286
www.scoot.com

Scoot.com (once Freepages Group) is a business listings and information company operating on the Internet, by phone, and through CD-ROM distribution. Scoot.com has alliances with Yahoo! and MSN.

Phone to enroll:
Bank of New York
888-BNY-ADRS or 888-269-2377

EasyStock Investment Plan:
- Initial minimum investment: $250
- Minimum per month (optional): $50
- Maximum per transaction: $250,000
- Cash dividends are offered.
- Partial dividend reinvestment.
- No discount is available.
- No IRA option is available.
- Optional cash purchases allowed.
- Direct debits are available.

SCOR
France: Insurance
NYSE: SCO
c/o Bank of New York
48 Wall Street
New York, NY 10286
www.scor.fr

SCOR provides insurance worldwide through offices in Europe, the Americas, and Asia. The company provides treaty and facultative insurance through branch offices.

Phone to enroll:
Bank of New York
888-BNY-ADRS or 888-269-2377

EasyStock Investment Plan:
- Initial minimum investment: $250
- Minimum per month (optional): $50
- Maximum per transaction: $250,000
- Cash dividends are offered.
- Partial dividend reinvestment.
- No discount is available.
- No IRA option is available.
- Optional cash purchases allowed.
- Direct debits are available.

Scottish Power PLC
United Kingdom: Utilities
NYSE: SPYAY
c/o Bank of New York
48 Wall Street
New York, NY 10286
www.scottishpower.plc.uk

Scottish Power transmits and distributes electricity to about 1.8 million customers in Scotland, and owns Manweb, a regional electricity company serving 1.3 million customers in England and Wales. Its Scottish Telecom unit is the U.K.'s second largest Internet service provider.

Phone to enroll:
Bank of New York
888-BNY-ADRS or 888-269-2377

EasyStock Investment Plan:
- Initial minimum investment: $250
- Maximum annual investment: $250,000
- Minimum per month (optional): $50
- Cash dividends are offered.
- Partial dividend reinvestment.
- No discount is available.
- No IRA option is available.
- Optional cash purchases allowed.
- Direct debits are available.

Sears, Roebuck and Co.
United States: Department Stores
NYSE: S
Sears Tower
Chicago, IL 60684
www.sears.com
847-286-2500

Sears, the United States' number two retailer after Wal-Mart, is trying to attract female customers to its upgraded, mainly mall-based department stores by offering more women's apparel.

Phone to enroll:
First Chicago Trust Company
888-SEARS-88 or 888-732-7788

EasyStock Investment Plan:
- Initial minimum investment: $500
- Minimum per month (optional): $50
- Maximum annual investment: $150,000
- Cash dividends are offered.
- No partial dividend reinvestment.
- No discount is available.
- An IRA option is available.
- Optional cash purchases allowed.
- Direct debits are available.

Sedgwick Group PLC
United Kingdom: Insurance
NYSE: SGWKY
c/o Bank of New York
48 Wall Street
New York, NY 10286

Sedgwick Group offers insurance, reinsurance, employee benefits services, risk consulting, and financial services through more than 270 offices in more than sixty-five countries in North America, Europe, and Asia.

Phone to enroll:
Bank of New York
888-BNY-ADRS or 888-269-2377

EasyStock Investment Plan:
- Initial minimum investment: $250
- Minimum per month (optional): $50
- Maximum annual investment: $250,000
- Cash dividends are offered.
- Partial dividend reinvestment.
- No discount is available.
- No IRA option is available.

- Optional cash purchases allowed.
- Direct debits are available.

Select Appointments Holdings PLC
United Kingdom: Staffing Services
NASDAQ: SELAY
c/o Bank of New York
48 Wall Street
New York, NY 10286
www.selectgroup.com

Select Appointments Holdings provides temporary staffing services through more than 450 offices in twenty-one countries worldwide. The company's services include information technology staffing, which comprises 25% of sales.

Phone to enroll:
Bank of New York
888-BNY-ADRS or 888-269-2377

EasyStock Investment Plan:
- Initial minimum investment: $250
- Minimum per month (optional): $50
- Maximum per transaction: $250,000
- Cash dividends are offered.
- Partial dividend reinvestment.
- No discount is available.
- No IRA option is available.
- Optional cash purchases allowed.
- Direct debits are available.

Select Software Tools PLC
United Kingdom: Technology
NASDAQ: SLCTY
c/o Bank of New York
48 Wall Street
New York, NY 10286
www.selectst.com

Select Software Tools makes products for designing customized soft ware. The products combine a client's current applications with newer component-based technology that integrates seemingly incompatible software functions.

Phone to enroll:
Bank of New York
888-BNY-ADRS or 888-269-2377

EasyStock Investment Plan:
- Initial minimum investment: $250
- Minimum per month (optional): $50
- Maximum per transaction: $250,000
- No cash dividends paid.
- Partial dividend reinvestment.
- No discount is available.
- No IRA option is available.
- Optional cash purchases allowed.
- Direct debits are available.

SEMCO Energy Corp.
United States: Utilities
NASDAQ: SMGS
405 Water Street
PO Box 5026
Port Huron, MI 48061
810-987-2200

SEMCO Energy, formerly Southeastern Michigan Gas Enterprises, sells natural gas in regulated and unregulated markets. Subsidiary SEMCO Energy Gas distributes natural gas to approximately 240,000 customers.

Phone company to enroll:
800-649-1856

EasyStock Investment Plan:
- Initial minimum investment: $250
- Minimum per month (optional): $25
- Maximum monthly investment: $5,000
- Maximum annual investment: $100,000

- Cash dividends are offered.
- Partial dividend reinvestment.
- No discount is available.
- No IRA option is available.
- Optional cash purchases allowed.
- No direct debit option.

Sempra Energy Corp.
United States: Utilities
NYSE: SRE
101 Ash Street
San Diego, CA 92101
www.sempra.com

Sempra Energy, formerly Enova, is a Fortune 500 energy services holding company whose subsidiaries provide electricity, natural gas and value-added products and services.

Phone to enroll:
First Chicago Trust Company
877-773-6772

EasyStock Investment Plan:
- Initial minimum investment: $250
- Minimum per month (optional): $25
- Maximum annual investment: $150,000
- Cash dividends are offered.
- Partial dividend reinvestment.
- No discount is available.
- No IRA option is available.
- Optional cash purchases allowed.
- Direct debits are available.
- Get a loan secured by your shares.
- View materials and enroll online at www.netstockdirect.com.

Senetek PLC
United Kingdom: Pharmaceuticals
NASDAQ: SNTKY
c/o Bank of New York
48 Wall Street
New York, NY 10286
www.senetekPlc.com

Pharmaceutical research and development company Senetek focuses on treatments for erectile dysfunction and skin conditions.

Phone to enroll:
Bank of New York
888-BNY-ADRS or 888-269-2377

EasyStock Investment Plan:
- Initial minimum investment: $200
- Minimum per month (optional): $50
- Maximum per transaction: $250,000
- No cash dividends paid.
- Partial dividend reinvestment.
- No discount is available.
- No IRA option is available.
- Optional cash purchases allowed.
- Direct debits are available.

Shandong Huaneng Power
China: Utilities
NYSE: SH
c/o Bank of New York
48 Wall Street
New York, NY 10286
www.spc.com.cn/english

Shandong Huaneng Power Development delivers coal-generated power to the people, with a total generating capacity of 2.1 MW.

Phone to enroll:
Bank of New York
888-BNY-ADRS or 888-269-2377

EasyStock Investment Plan:
- Initial minimum investment: $200
- Minimum per month (optional): $50
- Maximum per transaction: $250,000
- Cash dividends are offered.
- Partial dividend reinvestment.
- No discount is available.
- No IRA option is available.
- Optional cash purchases allowed.
- Direct debits are available.

Shanghai Petrochemical Co.
China: Specialty Chemicals
NYSE: SHI
c/o Bank of New York
48 Wall Street
New York, NY 10286

Shanghai Petrochemical Company produces ethylene, resins, and plastics.

Phone to enroll:
Bank of New York
888-BNY-ADRS or 888-269-2377

EasyStock Investment Plan:
- Initial minimum investment: $250
- Minimum per month (optional): $50
- Maximum per transaction: $250,000
- Cash dividends are offered.
- Partial dividend reinvestment.
- No discount is available.
- No IRA option is available.
- Optional cash purchases allowed.
- Direct debits are available.

Signet Group PLC
United Kingdom: Merchandising
OTC: SIGYY
c/o Bank of New York
48 Wall Street
New York, NY 10286

Signet Group hired Cindy Crawford to endorse its Kay Jewelers stores and is now one of the largest jewelry retailers in the U.S. The group also owns a U.K.-based chain.

Phone to enroll:
Bank of New York
888-BNY-ADRS or 888-269-2377

EasyStock Investment Plan:
- Initial minimum investment: $250
- Minimum per month (optional): $50
- Maximum per transaction: $250,000
- No cash dividends paid.
- Partial dividend reinvestment.
- No discount is available.
- No IRA option is available.
- Optional cash purchases allowed.
- Direct debits are available.

SIS Bancorp, Inc.
United States: Banking
NASDAQ: SISB
1441 Main Street
Springfield, MA 01102
413-748-8000

SIS Bancorp, the holding company for Springfield Institution for Savings Bank, has twenty-two branches in Hampden and Hampshire Counties in western Massachusetts.

Phone to enroll:
Chase Mellon
800-842-7629

EasyStock Investment Plan:
- Initial minimum investment: $1,000
- Minimum per month (optional): $100
- Maximum monthly investment: $10,000
- Cash dividends are offered.
- Partial dividend reinvestment.
- No discount is available.
- No IRA option is available.
- Optional cash purchases allowed.
- Direct debits are available.

Small World PLC
United Kingdom: Computer Software
NASDAQ: SWLDY
c/o Bank of New York
48 Wall Street
New York, NY 10286

Small World is a U.K.-based software company.

Phone to enroll:
Bank of New York
888-BNY-ADRS or 888-269-2377

EasyStock Investment Plan:
- Initial minimum investment: $200
- Minimum per month (optional): $50
- Maximum per transaction: $250,000
- No cash dividends paid.
- Partial dividend reinvestment.
- No discount is available.
- No IRA option is available.
- Optional cash purchases allowed.
- Direct debits are available.

SmithKline Beecham PLC
United Kingdom: Pharmaceuticals
NYSE: SBH
c/o Bank of New York
48 Wall Street
New York, NY 10286
www.sb.com

SmithKline Beecham is one of the world's largest drug companies and is the maker of such familiar over-the-counter products as Geritol vitamin supplements, Nicorette gum, Contac cold and flu medication, Tums antacids, Tagamet heartburn control, and Aquafresh toothpaste.

Phone to enroll:
Bank of New York
888-BNY-ADRS or 888-269-2377
800-882-3359

EasyStock Investment Plan:
- Initial minimum investment: $250
- Minimum per month (optional): $50
- Maximum per transaction: $250,000
- Cash dividends are offered.
- Partial dividend reinvestment.
- No discount is available.
- No IRA option is available.
- Optional cash purchases allowed.
- Direct debits are available.

Snap-on, Incorporated
United States: Manufacturing
NYSE: SNA
2801 - 80th Street
Kenosha, WI 53141
www.snapon.com
414-656-5200

Snap-on is a leading manufacturer and distributor of high-quality mechanics' hand tools, auto-diagnostic equipment, and shop equipment.

Phone to enroll:
First Chicago Trust Company
800-446-2617

EasyStock Investment Plan:
- Initial minimum investment: $500
- Minimum per month (optional): $100
- Maximum annual investment: $150,000
- Cash dividends are offered.
- Partial dividend reinvestment.
- No discount is available.
- No IRA option is available.
- Optional cash purchases allowed.
- Direct debits are available.

Sonoma Valley Bank Corp.
United States: Banking
NASDAQ: SOVY
202 West Napa Street
PO Box 2260
Sonoma, CA 95476

Phone to enroll:
American Stock Transfer & Trust
888-200-3163

EasyStock Investment Plan:
- Initial minimum investment: $100
- Minimum per month (optional): $50
- Cash dividends are offered.
- Maximum per transaction: $10,000
- Maximum annual investment: $100,000
- No partial dividend reinvestment.
- No discount is available.
- No IRA option is available.
- Optional cash purchases allowed.
- Direct debits are available.

Sony Corporation
Japan: Consumer Electronics
NYSE: SNE
c/o Morgan Guaranty Trust Company
PO Box 9073
Boston, MA 02205-9948
www.sony.com

Sony is a consumer electronics and multimedia entertainment giant. Its electronic products, which include TVs, VCRs, stereos, and the PlayStation home video game system, account for more than 75% of its total revenues.

Phone to enroll:
Morgan Guaranty Trust Company
800-997-8970

EasyStock Investment Plan:
- Initial minimum investment: $250
- Minimum per month (optional): $50
- Maximum annual investment: $100,000
- No cash dividends paid.
- Partial dividend reinvestment.
- No discount is available.
- No IRA option is available.
- Optional cash purchases allowed.
- Direct debits are available.

Southern Company Ltd.
United States: Electric Services
NYSE: SO
270 Peachtree Street
Atlanta, GA 30303
www.southernco.com
404-506-5000

Southern Company, the largest publicly traded utility in the U.S., provides service to more than 3.6 million customers in four southeastern states. Its five operating companies are Alabama Power, Georgia Power,

Gulf Power, Mississippi Power, and Savannah Electric.

Phone company to enroll:
800-565-2577

EasyStock Investment Plan:
- Initial minimum investment: $250
- Minimum per month (optional): $25
- Maximum quarterly investment: $6,000
- Maximum annual investment: $150,000
- Cash dividends are offered.
- Partial dividend reinvestment.
- No discount is available.
- No IRA option is available.
- Optional cash purchases allowed.
- Direct debits are available.

Southern Union Co. Ltd.
United States: Natural Gas
NYSE: SUG
504 Lavaca Street, Suite 800
Austin, TX 78701
www.southernunco.com
512-477-5852

Southern Union Company is a holding company for public utilities and other energy industry businesses. Its Southern Union Gas division distributes natural gas to 497,000 customers.

Phone to enroll:
Boston Equiserve LP
800-793-8938

EasyStock Investment Plan:
- Initial minimum investment: $250
- Minimum per month (optional): $50
- Maximum annual investment: $100,000
- Cash dividends are offered.
- No partial dividend reinvestment.
- No discount is available.
- No IRA option is available.
- Optional cash purchases allowed.
- Direct debits are available.

Southwest Gas Corp.
United States: Natural Gas
NYSE: SWX
5241 Spring Mountain Road
Las Vegas, NV 89193
www.swgas.com
702-876-7237

Southwest is a regulated utility providing natural gas to residential, commercial, and industrial users. With about one million customers, the company serves portions of Arizona, Nevada, and California.

Phone company to enroll:
702-876-7280
EasyStock Investment Plan:
- Initial minimum investment: $100
- Minimum per month (optional): $25
- Maximum annual investment: $50,000
- Cash dividends are offered.
- Partial dividend reinvestment.
- No discount is available.
- No IRA option is available.
- Optional cash purchases allowed.
- Direct debits are available.

STMicroelectronics
France: Semiconductors
NYSE: STM
c/o Bank of New York
48 Wall Street
New York, NY 10286
www.st.com

STMicroelectronics (ST), formerly SGS-THOMSON, is Europe's second largest chip maker and a leading supplier of analog and mixed-signal

(analog/digital) integrated circuits (ICs), video decoder chips, and smart cards.

Phone to enroll:
Bank of New York
888-BNY-ADRS or 888-269-2377

EasyStock Investment Plan:
- Initial minimum investment: $200
- Minimum per month (optional): $50
- Maximum annual investment: $250,000
- Cash dividends are offered.
- Partial dividend reinvestment.
- No discount is available.
- No IRA option is available.
- Optional cash purchases allowed.
- Direct debits are available.

Storage Trust Realty Corp.
United States: Real Estate
NYSE: SEA
2407 Rangeline
Columbia, MO 65202

Storage Trust Realty owns or operates ninety-one public self-storage facilities in fourteen midwestern, southern, and mid-Atlantic states.

Phone to enroll:
Chase Mellon
800-842-7629

EasyStock Investment Plan:
- Initial minimum investment: $250
- Minimum per month (optional): $100
- Maximum per transaction: $5,000
- Maximum monthly investment: $5,000
- Cash dividends are offered.
- Partial dividend reinvestment.
- No discount is available.
- No IRA option is available.
- Optional cash purchases allowed.
- No direct debit option.

Sunstone Hotel Investors, Inc.
United States: Real Estate Investment Trust
NYSE: SSI
115 Calle De Industrias, Suite 201
San Clemente, CA 92672
www.sunstonehotels.com
949-361-3900

Sunstone Hotel Investors buys and renovates mid-price, full-service hotels in the western U.S. The company owns or has an interest in sixty hotels with nearly 11,000 rooms in twelve western states.

Phone to enroll:
Chase Mellon
800-922-9542

EasyStock Investment Plan:
- Initial minimum investment: $1,000
- Minimum per month (optional): $100
- Maximum monthly investment: $3,000
- No cash dividends paid.
- No partial dividend reinvestment.
- No discount is available.
- No IRA option is available.
- Optional cash purchases allowed.
- No direct debit option.

Super-Sol Ltd.
Israel: Supermarkets
NYSE: SAE
c/o Morgan Guaranty Trust Company
PO Box 9073
Boston, MA 02205-9948
www.supersol.co.il

Super-Sol Limited is the top supermarket chain in Israel. The company

has about 120 grocery stores and also owns an office equipment and supply chain.

Phone to enroll:
Morgan Guaranty Trust Company
800-997-8970

EasyStock Investment Plan:
- Initial minimum investment: $250
- Minimum per month (optional): $50
- Maximum annual investment: $100,000
- Cash dividends are offered.
- Partial dividend reinvestment.
- No discount is available.
- No IRA option is available.
- Optional cash purchases allowed.
- Direct debits are available.

Supermercados Unimarc S.A.
Chile: Supermarkets
NYSE: UNR
c/o Bank of New York
48 Wall Street
New York, NY 10286
www.unimarc.cl

One of Chile's largest supermarket operators, Supermercados Unimarc controls a chain of about thirty-five stores in Chile, and another five in Argentina.

Phone to enroll:
Bank of New York
888-BNY-ADRS or 888-269-2377

EasyStock Investment Plan:
- Initial minimum investment: $200
- Minimum per month (optional): $50
- Maximum per transaction: $250,000
- Cash dividends are offered.
- Partial dividend reinvestment.
- No discount is available.
- No IRA option is available.
- Optional cash purchases allowed.
- Direct debits are available.

Synovus Financial Corp.
United States: Financial Services
NYSE: SNV
901 Front Avenue, Suite 301
Columbus, GA 31901
www.snv.com
706-649-2387

Synovus Financial is a holding company for thirty-five banks in Alabama, Florida, Georgia, and South Carolina that offer deposit accounts and personal, consumer, and commercial loans. Total System Services' customers, including AT&T Universal Card Services and BankAmerica, represent almost 93 million cardholder accounts

Phone to enroll:
Boston Equiserve LP
800-337-0896

EasyStock Investment Plan:
- Initial minimum investment: $250
- Minimum per month (optional): $50
- Maximum annual investment: $250,000
- Cash dividends are offered.
- Partial dividend reinvestment.
- No discount is available.
- No IRA option is available.
- Optional cash purchases allowed.
- Direct debits are available.

TAG Heuer International S.A.
Switzerland: Consumer Products
NYSE: THW
c/o Morgan Guaranty Trust Company
PO Box 9073
Boston, MA 02205-9948
www.tag-heuer.ch

TAG Heuer International makes watches and chronographs and markets them in over one hundred countries.

Phone to enroll:
Morgan Guaranty Trust Company
800-997-8970

EasyStock Investment Plan:
- Initial minimum investment: $250
- Minimum per month (optional): $50
- Maximum annual investment: $100,000
- Cash dividends are offered.
- Partial dividend reinvestment.
- No discount is available.
- No IRA option is available.
- Optional cash purchases allowed.
- Direct debits are available.

Tandy Corp.
United States: Electronics Stores
NYSE: TAN
1800 One Tandy Center
Fort Worth, TX 76102
www.tandy.com
817-415-3700

Tandy, one of the America's leading electronics retailers, operates the RadioShack and Computer City chains. The company's flagship, RadioShack, sells private-label electronic parts, PCs, and telephone and audio and video equipment at about 6,900 locations.

Phone to enroll:
Boston Equiserve LP
888-218-4374

EasyStock Investment Plan:
- Initial minimum investment: $250
- Minimum per month (optional): $50
- Maximum annual investment: $150,000
- Cash dividends are offered.
- Partial dividend reinvestment.
- No discount is available.
- No IRA option is available.
- Optional cash purchases allowed.
- No direct debit option.

Taubman Centers, Inc.
United States: Real Estate
NYSE: TCO
200 East Long Lake Road
Bloomfield Hills, MI 48304
www.taubman.com
248-258-6800

Taubman Centers is a real estate investment trust that owns, manages, and develops large, regional shopping centers and malls. The company owns twenty-seven shopping centers in twelve states, primarily in Michigan and California.

Phone to enroll:
Chase Mellon
800-437-1329

EasyStock Investment Plan:
- Initial minimum investment: $250
- Minimum per month (optional): $25
- Maximum monthly investment: $25,000
- Cash dividends are offered.
- Partial dividend reinvestment.
- No discount is available.

- No IRA option is available.
- Optional cash purchases allowed.
- Direct debits are available.

TDK Corporation
Japan: Consumer Electronics
NYSE: TDK
c/o Morgan Guaranty Trust Company
PO Box 9073
Boston, MA 02205-9948
www.tdk.com

Although its name is synonymous with blank audio and video tapes, TDK generates about 75% of sales from electronic materials and components sold to original equipment manufacturers.

Phone to enroll:
Morgan Guaranty Trust Company
800-997-8970

EasyStock Investment Plan:
- Initial minimum investment: $250
- Minimum per month (optional): $50
- Maximum annual investment: $100,000
- Cash dividends are offered.
- Partial dividend reinvestment.
- No discount is available.
- No IRA option is available.
- Optional cash purchases allowed.
- Direct debits are available.

Tektronix, Inc.
United States: Computer Systems
NYSE: TEK
26600 SW Parkway
Wilsonville, OR 97070
www.tek.com
503-327-7111

Tektronix has three major product lines: oscilloscopes and other measurement devices, video and networking products, and color printers and related products.

Phone to enroll:
Chase Mellon
800-842-7629

EasyStock Investment Plan:
- Initial minimum investment: $500
- Minimum per month (optional): $100
- Maximum per transaction: $10,000
- Maximum monthly investment: $10,000
- Cash dividends are offered.
- Partial dividend reinvestment.
- No discount is available.
- No IRA option is available.
- Optional cash purchases allowed.
- Direct debits are available.

Telebras HOLDR
Brazil: Telecommunications
NYSE: TBH
c/o Bank of New York
48 Wall Street
New York, NY 10286
www.telebras.com.br

Telebras HOLDR holds shares in all the former companies that were part of the Telebras phone monopoly.

Phone to enroll:
Bank of New York
888-BNY-ADRS or 888-269-2377

EasyStock Investment Plan:
- Initial minimum investment: $250
- Minimum per month (optional): $50
- Maximum per transaction: $250,000
- No cash dividends paid.
- Partial dividend reinvestment.
- No discount is available.
- No IRA option is available.

- Optional cash purchases allowed.
- Direct debits are available.

Telecom Argentina STET-France Telecom S.A.
Argentina: Telecommunications
NYSE: TEO
c/o Morgan Guaranty Trust Company
PO Box 9073
Boston, MA 02205-9948
www.telecom.com

One of Argentina's largest telecommunications companies, Telecom Argentina STET-France Telecom S.A. holds an exclusive license to provide phone service to the northern part of Argentina. The company operates more than three million telephone lines.

Phone to enroll:
Morgan Guaranty Trust Company
800-997-8970

EasyStock Investment Plan:
- Initial minimum investment: $250
- Minimum per month (optional): $50
- Maximum annual investment: $100,000
- Cash dividends are offered.
- Partial dividend reinvestment.
- No discount is available.
- No IRA option is available.
- Optional cash purchases allowed.
- Direct debits are available.

Telecom Italia S.p.A.
Italy: Telecommunications
NYSE: TI
c/o Morgan Guaranty Trust Company
PO Box 9073
Boston, MA 02205-9948
www.telecomitalia.it

Telecom Italia (formerly known as STET) provides telecommunications services, products, and installation, primarily in Italy. The company is currently the subject of a takeover battle between Olivetti and Deutsche Telekom.

Phone to enroll:
Morgan Guaranty Trust Company
800-997-8970

EasyStock Investment Plan:
- Initial minimum investment: $250
- Minimum per month (optional): $50
- Maximum annual investment: $100,000
- Cash dividends are offered.
- Partial dividend reinvestment.
- No discount is available.
- No IRA option is available.
- Optional cash purchases allowed.
- Direct debits are available.

Telefonica del Perú S.A.
Peru: Telecommunications
NYSE: TDP
c/o Morgan Guaranty Trust Company
PO Box 9073
Boston, MA 02205-9948
www.telefonica.com.pe

Telefonica del Perú offers fixed local, domestic, and international long-distance services exclusively throughout the country. The

company, which loses its monopoly this year, also provides cellular telephone, paging, business communications, cable television, and other telecommunications services.

Phone to enroll:
Morgan Guaranty Trust Company
800-997-8970

EasyStock Investment Plan:
- Initial minimum investment: $250
- Minimum per month (optional): $50
- Maximum annual investment: $100,000
- No cash dividends paid.
- Partial dividend reinvestment.
- No discount is available.
- No IRA option is available.
- Optional cash purchases allowed.
- Direct debits are available.

Telefonos de Mexico S.A. de C.V.
Mexico: Telecommunications
NYSE: TMX
c/o Morgan Guaranty Trust Company
PO Box 9073 Boston, MA 02205-9948
www.telmex.com.mx

Telefonos de Mexico (Telmex) has more than 9 million phone lines, including about 240,000 public phones. The company's TelCel subsidiary provides cellular phone service to more than 650,000 customers.

Phone to enroll:
Morgan Guaranty Trust Company
800-997-8970

EasyStock Investment Plan:
- Initial minimum investment: $250
- Minimum per month (optional): $50
- Maximum annual investment: $100,000
- Cash dividends are offered.
- Partial dividend reinvestment.
- No discount is available.
- No IRA option is available.
- Optional cash purchases allowed.
- Direct debits are available.

Tenneco Inc.
United States: Automotive Equipment and Parts
NYSE: TEN
1275 King Street
Greenwich, CT 06831
www.tenneco.com
203-863-1000

Tenneco has moved away from diversity to focus on automotive parts and packaging products. Tenneco Automotive makes Walker exhaust systems and Monroe shocks and struts for vehicle manufacturers and the replacement market.

Phone to enroll:
First Chicago Trust Company
800-519-3111

EasyStock Investment Plan:
- Initial minimum investment: $500
- Minimum per month (optional): $50
- Maximum annual investment: $250,000
- Cash dividends are offered.
- Partial dividend reinvestment.
- Discounts on share purchases.
- No IRA option is available.
- Optional cash purchases allowed.
- Direct debits are available.

Texaco Inc.
United States: International Oils
NYSE: TX
2000 Westchester Avenue
White Plains, NY 10650
www.texaco.com
914-253-4000

Texaco is America's third largest oil and gas enterprise, producing crude oil and natural gas and operating twenty-five refineries worldwide. The company also markets fuel and lubricants at 22,000 gas stations, and operates transportation, trading, and distribution facilities.

Phone company to enroll:
800-283-9785

EasyStock Investment Plan:
- Initial minimum investment: $250
- Minimum per month (optional): $50
- Maximum annual investment: $120,000
- Cash dividends are offered.
- No partial dividend reinvestment.
- No discount is available.
- No IRA option is available.
- Optional cash purchases allowed.
- Direct debits are available.
- View materials and enroll online at www.netstockdirect.com.

Thorn PLC
United Kingdom: Retail
NASDAQ: THRNY
c/o Morgan Guaranty Trust Company
PO Box 9073
Boston, MA 02205-9948

Thorn rents home appliances, electronics, furniture, jewelry, and personal computers to customers with poor credit.

Phone to enroll:
Morgan Guaranty Trust Company
800-997-8970

EasyStock Investment Plan:
- Initial minimum investment: $250
- Minimum per month (optional): $50
- Maximum annual investment: $100,000
- No cash dividends paid.
- Partial dividend reinvestment.
- No discount is available.
- No IRA option is available.
- Optional cash purchases allowed.
- Direct debits are available.

Thornburg Mortgage Asset Corp.
United States: Real Estate Investment Trust
NYSE: TMA
119 East Marcy Street
Suite 201
Santa Fe, NM 87501
www.thornburgmortgage.com
505-989-1900

Thornburg Mortgage Asset Corporation specializes in investing in adjustable rate mortgages, profiting from the spread between what it pays for the mortgages and what it can earn in the market.

Phone to enroll:
Continental Stock Transfer & Trust
800-509-5586

EasyStock Investment Plan:
- Initial minimum investment: $500
- Minimum per month (optional): $100
- Maximum per transaction: $5,000
- Maximum monthly investment: $5,000
- Cash dividends are offered.
- Partial dividend reinvestment.
- Discounts on share purchases.

- No IRA option is available.
- Optional cash purchases allowed.
- No direct debit option.

Timken Company
United States: Industrial Products
NYSE: TKR
1835 Dueber Avenue SW
Canton, OH 44706
www.timken.com
330-438-3000

Timken's antifriction bearings are used in vehicles, machine tools, and railcars. Subsidiary MPB Corp. makes precision bearings for computer peripherals, medical instruments, and missile guidance systems.

Phone to enroll:
First Chicago Trust Company
888-347-2453

EasyStock Investment Plan:
- Initial minimum investment: $1,000
- Minimum per month (optional): $100
- Maximum annual investment: $250,000
- Cash dividends are offered.
- Partial dividend reinvestment.
- No discount is available.
- No IRA option is available.
- Optional cash purchases allowed.
- Direct debits are available.

TNP Enterprises, Inc.
United States: Electric Services
NYSE: TNP
4100 International Plaza
Fort Worth, TX 76109
www.tnpe.com
817-731-0099

TNP Enterprises is a holding company for an operating utility and other energy industry businesses that generate, purchase, transmit, distribute, and sell electricity to approximately 217,000 customers.

Phone to enroll:
Bank of New York
800-649-0929

EasyStock Investment Plan:
- Initial minimum investment: $100
- Minimum per month (optional): $25
- Maximum annual investment: $100,000
- Cash dividends are offered.
- Partial dividend reinvestment.
- No discount is available.
- No IRA option is available.
- Optional cash purchases allowed.
- Direct debits are available.
- View materials and enroll online at www.netstockdirect.com.

Transocean Offshore Drilling Inc.
United States
NYSE: RIG
4 Greenway Plaza
Houston, TX 77046
www.deepwater.com
713-871-7500

Transocean Offshore engages in contract drilling of oil and gas wells in offshore areas throughout the world. The company operates twenty-one offshore drilling units.

Phone to enroll:
Bank of New York
800-524-4458

EasyStock Investment Plan:
- Initial minimum investment: -
- Minimum per month (optional): -
- Maximum annual investment: -
- No cash dividends paid.
- No partial dividend reinvestment.
- No discount is available.
- No IRA option is available.
- No Optional cash purchases.
- No direct debit option.

Tribune Company Ltd.
United States: Newspapers
NYSE: TRB
435 North Michigan Avenue
Chicago, IL 60611
www.tribune.com
312-222-9100

Tribune Company is a newspaper and entertainment company. It publishes four major daily newspapers including the *Chicago Tribune*; owns TV stations in Chicago, Los Angeles, and New York; and holds an interest in America Online.

Phone to enroll:
First Chicago Trust Company
800-446-2617

EasyStock Investment Plan:
- Initial minimum investment: $500
- Minimum per month (optional): $50
- Maximum monthly investment: $2,000
- Maximum annual investment: $120,000
- Cash dividends are offered.
- Partial dividend reinvestment.
- No discount is available.
- No IRA option is available.
- Optional cash purchases allowed.
- No direct debit option.

Tubos de Acero de Mexico, S.A. de C.V.
Mexico: Steel
AMEX: TAM
c/o Morgan Guaranty Trust Company
PO Box 9073
Boston, MA 02205-9948
www.tamsa.com.mx

Tubos de Acero de Mexico, S.A. (TAMSA) is that country's only maker of seamless steel tubes.

Phone to enroll:
Morgan Guaranty Trust Company
800-997-8970

EasyStock Investment Plan:
- Initial minimum investment: $250
- Minimum per month (optional): $50
- Maximum annual investment: $100,000
- Cash dividends are offered.
- Partial dividend reinvestment.
- No discount is available.
- No IRA option is available.
- Optional cash purchases allowed.
- Direct debits are available.

TV Azteca S.A. de C.V.
Mexico: Media
NYSE: TZA
c/o Bank of New York
48 Wall Street
New York, NY 10286
www.tvazteca.com.mx

TV Azteca is one of Mexico's largest broadcasters.

Phone to enroll:
Bank of New York
888-BNY-ADRS or 888-269-2377

EasyStock Investment Plan:
- Initial minimum investment: $250
- Minimum per month (optional): $50
- Maximum per transaction: $250,000
- No cash dividends paid.
- Partial dividend reinvestment.
- No discount is available.
- No IRA option is available.
- Optional cash purchases allowed.
- Direct debits are available.

Tyson Foods, Inc.
United States: Food Products
NASDAQ: TSN
2210 West Oaklawn Drive
Springdale, AR 72762
www.tyson.com
501-290-4000

The nation's number one poultry processor, Tyson Foods operates more than fifty food production facilities in twenty-two U.S. states and seventeen other countries. The company breeds and markets chickens and Cornish game hens.

Phone to enroll:
First Chicago Trust Company
800-317-4445

EasyStock Investment Plan:
- Initial minimum investment: $250
- Minimum per month (optional): $50
- Maximum annual investment: $100,000
- Cash dividends are offered.
- No partial dividend reinvestment.
- No discount is available.
- No IRA option is available.
- Optional cash purchases allowed.
- Direct debits are available.
- View materials and enroll online at www.netstockdirect.com.

U

U.S. WEST, Inc.
United States: Telecommunications
NYSE: USW
7800 East Orchard Road
Englewood, CO 80111
www.uswest.com
800-879-4357

U.S. West provides local phone service to over 25 million customers in fourteen western and midwestern U.S. states. There has been mounting speculation that the company will merge with Global Crossing.

Phone to enroll:
Boston Equiserve LP
800-537-0222

EasyStock Investment Plan:
- Initial minimum investment: $300
- Minimum per month (optional): $25
- Maximum annual investment: $100,000
- Cash dividends are offered.
- Partial dividend reinvestment.
- No discount is available.
- No IRA option is available.
- Optional cash purchases allowed.
- Direct debits are available.

Unilever N.V.
Netherlands: Consumer Products
NYSE: UN
c/o Morgan Guaranty Trust Company
PO Box 9073
Boston, MA 02205-9948
www.unilever.com

Unilever N.V. owns half of Unilever, the world's second-largest packaged consumer goods company, behind Procter & Gamble. The companies share a board of directors and essentially operate as a single company.

Phone to enroll:
Morgan Guaranty Trust Company
800-997-8970

EasyStock Investment Plan:
- Initial minimum investment: $250
- Minimum per month (optional): $50
- Maximum annual investment: $100,000
- Cash dividends are offered.
- Partial dividend reinvestment.
- No discount is available.
- No IRA option is available.
- Optional cash purchases allowed.
- Direct debits are available.

Unilever PLC
United Kingdom: Consumer Products
NYSE: UL
c/o Morgan Guaranty Trust Company
PO Box 9073
Boston, MA 02205-9948
www.unilever.com

U.K.-based Unilever PLC owns half of Unilever, the world's second-largest packaged consumer goods company, behind Procter & Gamble. The companies share a board of directors and essentially operate as a single company.

Phone to enroll:
Morgan Guaranty Trust Company
800-997-8970

EasyStock Investment Plan:
- Initial minimum investment: $250
- Minimum per month (optional): $50
- Maximum annual investment: 100,000
- Cash dividends are offered.
- Partial dividend reinvestment.
- Discounts on share purchases.
- No IRA option is available.
- Optional cash purchases allowed.
- Direct debits are available.

Unionamerica Holdings PLC
United Kingdom: Insurance
NYSE: UA
c/o Morgan Guaranty Trust Company
PO Box 9073
Boston, MA 02205-9948
www.unionamerica.com

Unionamerica is a U.K.-based liability insurance company that derives over 80% of its business in the U.S.

Phone to enroll:
Morgan Guaranty Trust Company
800-997-8970

EasyStock Investment Plan:
- Initial minimum investment: $250
- Minimum per month (optional): $50
- Maximum annual investment: $100,000
- No cash dividends paid.
- Partial dividend reinvestment.
- No discount is available.
- No IRA option is available.
- Optional cash purchases allowed.
- Direct debits are available.

United National Bancorp
United States: Banking
NASDAQ: UNBJ
65 Readington Rd.
Branchburg, NJ 08876
www.united-national.com
908-429-2200

United National Bancorp is the bank holding company for United National Bank, which operates thirty-five branches in New Jersey.

Phone to enroll:
Bank of New York
800-524-4458

EasyStock Investment Plan:
- Initial minimum investment: -
- Minimum per month (optional): -
- Maximum annual investment: -
- No cash dividends paid.
- No partial dividend reinvestment.
- No discount is available.
- No IRA option is available.
- No Optional cash purchases.
- No direct debit option.

United Water Resources Inc.
United States: Water Services
NYSE: UWR
200 Old Hook Road
Harrington Park, NJ 07640
www.unitedwater.com
201-784-9434

United Water Resources provides water and wastewater services to government-owned systems used by about 5 million people in nineteen states.

Phone to enroll:
First Interstate Bank
201-767-2811

EasyStock Investment Plan:
- Initial minimum investment: $25
- Minimum per month (optional): $25
- Maximum quarterly investment: $3,000
- Cash dividends are offered.
- Partial dividend reinvestment.
- No discount is available.
- No IRA option is available.
- Optional cash purchases allowed.
- No direct debit option.

Urban Shopping Centers, Inc.
United States: Real Estate Investment Trust
NYSE: URB
900 North Michigan Avenue
Chicago, IL 60611
312-915-2000

Urban Shopping Centers is a real estate investment trust that owns and operates a portfolio of super-regional and regional malls located throughout the U.S. The firm owns approximately 16 million square feet of retail space.

Phone to enroll:
First Chicago Trust Company
800-446-2617

EasyStock Investment Plan:
- Initial minimum investment: $500
- Minimum per month (optional): $50
- Maximum quarterly investment: $3,000
- Cash dividends are offered.
- Partial dividend reinvestment.
- No discount is available.
- No IRA option is available.
- Optional cash purchases allowed.
- Direct debits are available.
- View materials and enroll online at www.netstockdirect.com.

UtiliCorp United Inc.
United States: Electric Services
NYSE: UCU
20 West Ninth Street
Kansas City, MO 64105
www.utilicorp.com
816-421-6600

UtiliCorp United is a holding company whose UtiliCorp Energy Delivery subsidiary sells electricity and natural gas to customers in eight U.S. states (Colorado, Iowa, Kansas, Michigan, Minnesota, Missouri, Nebraska, and West Virginia) and British Columbia.

Phone to enroll:
First Chicago Trust Company
800-647-2789

EasyStock Investment Plan:
- Initial minimum investment: $250
- Minimum per month (optional): $50
- Maximum monthly investment: $10,000
- Cash dividends are offered.
- Partial dividend reinvestment.
- Discounts on share purchases.
- An IRA option is available.
- Optional cash purchases allowed.
- Direct debits are available.
- View materials and enroll online at www.netstockdirect.com.

V

Valmet Corporation
Finland: Automotive
NYSE: VA
c/o Bank of New York
48 Wall Street
New York, NY 10286
www.valmet.com

Valmet is a leading supplier of paper- and board-producing machines, and a manufacturer of specialty cars.

Phone to enroll:
Bank of New York
888-BNY-ADRS or 888-269-2377

EasyStock Investment Plan:
- Initial minimum investment: $200
- Minimum per month (optional): $50
- Maximum per transaction: $250,000
- Cash dividends are offered.
- Partial dividend reinvestment.
- No discount is available.
- No IRA option is available.
- Optional cash purchases allowed.
- Direct debits are available.

Valspar Corp.
United States: Chemicals
NYSE: VAL
1101 Third Street South
Minneapolis, MN 55415
www.valspar.com
612-332-7371

Valspar makes paints, coatings, mirror-backing metals, resins, and emulsions. Its consumer brands include Valspar, Laura Ashley, Magicolor, and Masury latex and oil-based paints, stains, and varnishes for the do-it-yourself market.

Phone to enroll:
Chase Mellon
800-842-7629

EasyStock Investment Plan:
- Initial minimum investment: $1,000
- Minimum per month (optional): $100
- Maximum per transaction: -
- No cash dividends paid.
- No partial dividend reinvestment.
- No discount is available.
- No IRA option is available.
- Optional cash purchases allowed.
- No direct debit option.

VEBA AG
Germany: Multi-Industry
NYSE: VEB
c/o Morgan Guaranty Trust Company
PO Box 9073
Boston, MA 02205-9948
www.veba.de

VEBA is Germany's third largest cable company; it supplies 20% of Germany's electricity; owns an oil company that operates Germany's largest chain of gas stations, and also has interests in real estate and transportation.

Phone to enroll:
Morgan Guaranty Trust Company
800-997-8970

EasyStock Investment Plan:
- Initial minimum investment: $250
- Minimum per month (optional): $50
- Maximum annual investment: $100,000
- Cash dividends are offered.
- Partial dividend reinvestment.
- No discount is available.
- No IRA option is available.
- Optional cash purchases allowed.
- Direct debits are available.

Vimpel-Communications
Russia: Telecommunications
NYSE: VIP
c/o Bank of New York
48 Wall Street
New York, NY 10286
www.vimpelcom.ru

Vimpel is Russia's largest cellular telephone company, with over 95,000 subscribers.

Phone to enroll:
Bank of New York
888-BNY-ADRS or 888-269-2377

EasyStock Investment Plan:
- Initial minimum investment: $250
- Minimum per month (optional): $50
- Maximum per transaction: $250,000
- No cash dividends paid.
- Partial dividend reinvestment.
- No discount is available.
- No IRA option is available.
- Optional cash purchases allowed.
- Direct debits are available.

Vina Concha y Toro, S.A.
Chile: Food Products
NYSE: VCO
c/o Bank of New York
48 Wall Street
New York, NY 10286
www.reuna.cl/cyt/home.htm

Vina Concha y Toro is a leading Chilean winery with numerous vineyards in that country and several elsewhere in South America. A significant portion of the winery's production is exported to the U.S. where it is the second largest wine import.

Phone to enroll:
Bank of New York
888-BNY-ADRS or 888-269-2377

EasyStock Investment Plan:
- Initial minimum investment: $250
- Minimum per month (optional): $50
- Maximum per transaction: $250,000
- Cash dividends are offered.
- Partial dividend reinvestment.
- No discount is available.
- No IRA option is available.
- Optional cash purchases allowed.
- Direct debits are available.

Vodafone Group PLC
United Kingdom: Telecommunications
NYSE: VOD
c/o Bank of New York
48 Wall Street
New York, NY 10286
www.vodafone.co.uk

Vodafone Group is the U.K.'s number one mobile telecommunications company. It operates analog and digital cellular networks offering voice communication, voice and data messaging, paging, and a radio-based data network.

Phone to enroll:
Bank of New York
888-BNY-ADRS or 888-269-2377

EasyStock Investment Plan:
- Initial minimum investment: $250
- Minimum per month (optional): $50
- Maximum per transaction: $250,000
- Cash dividends are offered.
- Partial dividend reinvestment.
- No discount is available.
- No IRA option is available.
- Optional cash purchases allowed.
- Direct debits are available.

W

Wal-Mart Stores, Inc.
United States: Discount Stores
NYSE: WMT
702 SW 8th Street
Bentonville, AR 72716
www.wal-mart.com
501-273-4000

Wal-Mart is the world's largest retailer, operating more than 3,400 Wal-Marts, Sam's Clubs, and Wal-Mart Supercenters around the world.

Phone to enroll:
First Chicago Trust Company
800-438-6278

EasyStock Investment Plan:
- Initial minimum investment: $250
- Minimum per month (optional): $50
- Maximum annual investment: $150,000
- Cash dividends are offered.
- Partial dividend reinvestment.
- No discount is available.
- No IRA option is available.
- Optional cash purchases allowed.
- Direct debits are available.
- View materials and enroll online at www.netstockdirect.com.

Walgreen Co.
United States: Drug Stores
NYSE: WAG
200 Wilmot Road
Deerfield, IL 60015
www.walgreens.com
847-940-2500

Walgreen is the number one drugstore chain in the U.S. in terms of sales, although it has fewer locations than several of its rivals. The

company's 2,400-plus stores are located in 34 states and Puerto Rico.

Phone to enroll:
Harris Bank
800-286-9178

EasyStock Investment Plan:
- Initial minimum investment: $50
- Minimum per month (optional): $50
- Maximum quarterly investment: $5,000
- Cash dividends are offered.
- No partial dividend reinvestment.
- No discount is available.
- No IRA option is available.
- Optional cash purchases allowed.
- No direct debit option.

Walt Disney Co.
United States: Entertainment
NYSE: DIS
PO Box 7773
Burbank, CA 91510-7773
www.disney.com
818-560-1000

The Walt Disney Company is the world's second-largest media conglomerate, after Time Warner. The company has interests in TV and movie production, theme parks, publishing companies, professional sports franchises, and owns television network ABC.

Phone to enroll:
SunGard Shareholder Systems, Inc.
800-948-2222

EasyStock Investment Plan:
- Initial minimum investment: $1,000
- Minimum per month (optional): $100
- Maximum annual investment: $250,000
- Cash dividends are offered.
- No partial dividend reinvestment.
- No discount is available.
- No IRA option is available.
- Optional cash purchases allowed.
- Direct debits are available.

Warner-Lambert Co.
United States: Pharmaceuticals
NYSE: WLA
201 Tabor Road
Morris Plains, NJ 07950
www.warner-lambert.com
973-540-2000

Warner-Lambert manufactures and markets drugs, consumer health care products, and confectionery products.

Phone to enroll:
First Chicago Trust Company
888-767-7166

EasyStock Investment Plan:
- Initial minimum investment: $250
- Minimum per month (optional): $50
- Maximum annual investment: $60,000
- Cash dividends are offered.
- Partial dividend reinvestment.
- No discount is available.
- No IRA option is available.
- Optional cash purchases allowed.
- No direct debit option.

Warner Chilcott PLC
Ireland:
NYSE: WCRX
c/o Bank of New York
48 Wall Street
New York, NY 10286
www.wclabs.com

Warner Chilcott develops and markets pharmaceuticals for the

cardiology and women's health care markets.

Phone to enroll:
Bank of New York
888-BNY-ADRS or 888-269-2377

EasyStock Investment Plan:
- Initial minimum investment: $250
- Minimum per month (optional): $50
- Maximum annual investment: $250,000
- Cash dividends are offered.
- Partial dividend reinvestment.
- No discount is available.
- No IRA option is available.
- Optional cash purchases allowed.
- Direct debits are available.

Waterford Wedgwood PLC
Ireland: Housewares
NASDAQ: WATFZ
c/o Bank of New York
48 Wall Street
New York, MA 10286
www.fitzwilton.ie/ww.htm

For more than two centuries, Waterford Wedgwood has been making America's number one luxury crystal and the U.K.'s best selling fine china.

Phone to enroll:
Bank of New York
888-BNY-ADRS or 888-269-2377

EasyStock Investment Plan:
- Initial minimum investment: $250
- Minimum per month (optional): $50
- Maximum per transaction: $250,000
- Cash dividends are offered.
- Partial dividend reinvestment.
- No discount is available.
- No IRA option is available.
- Optional cash purchases allowed.
- Direct debits are available.

Weingarten Realty Investors
United States: Real Estate Investment Trust
NYSE: WRI
2600 Citadel Plaza Drive
Houston, TX 77008
www.weingarten.com
713-866-6000

Weingarten Realty owns over 170 shopping centers, primarily in Texas, but also in eleven other states.

Phone to enroll:
Chase Mellon
888-887-2966

EasyStock Investment Plan:
- Initial minimum investment: $500
- Minimum per month (optional): $100
- Maximum monthly investment: $25,000
- Maximum quarterly investment: $15,000
- Cash dividends are offered.
- Partial dividend reinvestment.
- No discount is available.
- No IRA option is available.
- Optional cash purchases allowed.
- Direct debits are available.

Western Resources, Inc.
United States: Utilities
NYSE: WR
818 Kansas Avenue
Topeka, KS 66612
www.wstnres.com
785-575-6300

Western Resources' subsidiaries KPL and Kansas Gas and Electric supply electrical energy to about 600,000 customers.

Phone company to enroll:
800-527-2495

EasyStock Investment Plan:
- Initial minimum investment: $250
- Minimum per month (optional): $50
- Maximum annual investment: $120,000
- Cash dividends are offered.
- Partial dividend reinvestment.
- No discount is available.
- No IRA option is available.
- Optional cash purchases allowed.
- Direct debits are available.

Westernbank Puerto Rico
Puerto Rico: Banking
NASDAQ: WBPR
c/o Bank of New York
48 Wall Street
New York, NY 10286
www.wbpr.com/index.html
787-834-8000

Phone to enroll:
Bank of New York
888-BNY-ADRS or 888-269-2377

EasyStock Investment Plan:
- Initial minimum investment: $250
- Minimum per month (optional): $50
- Maximum annual investment: $250,000
- Cash dividends are offered.
- Partial dividend reinvestment.
- No discount is available.
- No IRA option is available.
- Optional cash purchases allowed.
- Direct debits are available.

Westpac Banking Corporation
Ireland: Banking
NYSE: WBK
c/o Morgan Guaranty Trust Company
PO Box 9073
Boston, MA 02205-9948
www.westpac.com/au

Westpac Banking provides a broad range of banking and financial services to individual and corporate customers, primarily in Australia, New Zealand, and the Pacific Islands. The bank operates a network of 1,500 branches and service centers.

Phone to enroll:
Morgan Guaranty Trust Company
800-997-8970

EasyStock Investment Plan:
- Initial minimum investment: $250
- Minimum per month (optional): $50
- Maximum annual investment: $100,000
- Cash dividends are offered.
- Partial dividend reinvestment.
- No discount is available.
- No IRA option is available.
- Optional cash purchases allowed.
- Direct debits are available.

Wharf Holdings Limited
Australia: Multi-Industry
OTC: WARFY
c/o Bank of New York
48 Wall Street
New York, NY 10286

Wharf Holdings is a conglomerate built on real estate ownership and property management, with recent expansion into telecommunications and cable television.

Phone to enroll:
Bank of New York
888-BNY-ADRS or 888-269-2377

EasyStock Investment Plan:
- Initial minimum investment: $250
- Minimum per month (optional): $50
- Maximum per transaction: $250,000
- Cash dividends are offered.

- Partial dividend reinvestment.
- No discount is available.
- No IRA option is available.
- Optional cash purchases allowed.
- Direct debits are available.

Whitman Corp.
United States: Consumer Products
NYSE: WH
3501 Algonquin Road
Rolling Meadows, IL 60008
www.whitmancorp.com
847-818-5000

Whitman Corporation, through its Pepsi-Cola General Bottlers subsidiary, is the largest independent Pepsi distributor in the world. In addition to Pepsi brands, the company distributes such non-cola beverages as Mug Root Beer, All Sport isotonic drinks, and Ocean Spray.

Phone to enroll:
First Chicago Trust Company
800-660-4187

EasyStock Investment Plan:
- Initial minimum investment: $250
- Minimum per month (optional): $10
- Maximum annual investment: $60,000
- Cash dividends are offered.
- Partial dividend reinvestment.
- No discount is available.
- No IRA option is available.
- Optional cash purchases allowed.
- Direct debits are available.
- View materials and enroll online at www.netstockdirect.com.

Wicor, Inc.
United States: Natural Gas
NYSE: WIC
Overpeck Center
85 Challenger Road
Ridgefield Park, NJ 07880
www.wicor.com
414-291-7026

Wicor is a holding company for three energy-services companies and three pump-manufacturing companies. Energy operations account for almost 60% of revenues. Its primary energy operation is Wisconsin Gas, a gas-distribution public utility.

Phone to enroll:
Chase Mellon
800-842-7629

EasyStock Investment Plan:
- Initial minimum investment: $500
- Minimum per month (optional): $100
- Maximum per transaction: $10,000
- Maximum monthly investment: $10,000
- Maximum quarterly investment: $30,000
- Maximum annual investment: $120,000
- Cash dividends are offered.
- Partial dividend reinvestment.
- No discount is available.
- No IRA option is available.
- Optional cash purchases allowed.
- Direct debits are available.

Wisconsin Energy Corp.
United States: Utilities
NYSE: WEC
231 West Michigan Street
Milwaukee, WI 53201
www.wisenergy.com
414-221-2345

Wisconsin Energy is a holding company that provides electricity, natural gas, and steam. Its Wisconsin Electric subsidiary generates, transmits, and sells electricity in Wisconsin and Michigan's Upper Peninsula.

Phone to enroll:
Boston Equiserve LP
800-558-9663

EasyStock Investment Plan:
- Initial minimum investment: $50
- Minimum per month (optional): $25
- Maximum quarterly investment: $50,000
- Cash dividends are offered.
- Partial dividend reinvestment.
- No discount is available.
- No IRA option is available.
- Optional cash purchases allowed.
- Direct debits are available.

WLR Foods, Inc.
United States: Food Products
NASDAQ: WLRF
PO Box 228
Hinton, VA 22831
www.wlrfoods.com
540-896-7001

WLR Foods is a poultry-processing company that produces, processes, and sells turkey and chicken products and distributes poultry and meat products. It also manufactures ice for retail distribution and provides public refrigerated-warehousing services.

Phone company to enroll:
540-896-7001

EasyStock Investment Plan:
- Initial minimum investment: $250
- Minimum per month (optional): $100
- Maximum monthly investment: $2,000
- Maximum annual investment: $20,000
- Cash dividends are offered.
- Partial dividend reinvestment.
- No discount is available.
- No IRA option is available.
- Optional cash purchases allowed.
- No direct debit option.

WMC Holdings Limited
Australia: Mining
NYSE: WMC
c/o Bank of New York
48 Wall Street
New York, NY 10286
www.wmc.com.au

Australian mining giant WMC is one of the world's largest nickel miners, producing about 10% of the world's supply. In mineral-rich Australia, WMC ranks number one in nickel, number two in gold, and number two in copper.

Phone to enroll:
Bank of New York
888-BNY-ADRS or 888-269-2377

EasyStock Investment Plan:
- Initial minimum investment: $250
- Minimum per month (optional): $50
- Maximum per transaction: $250,000
- Cash dividends are offered.

- Partial dividend reinvestment.
- No discount is available.
- No IRA option is available.
- Optional cash purchases allowed.
- Direct debits are available.

WPS Resources Corp.
United States: Electric Services
NYSE: WPS
700 North Adams Street
PO Box 19001
Green Bay, WI 54307
www.wpsr.com
920-433-1466

WPS Resources is the holding company for Wisconsin Public Service, a regulated electric and gas utility. The utility, with a generating capacity of 1.8 million kilowatts, supplies electricity to some 375,000 customers, mainly in northeastern and central Wisconsin.

Phone company to enroll:
920-433-1050

EasyStock Investment Plan:
- Initial minimum investment: $100
- Minimum per month (optional): $25
- Maximum annual investment: $100,000
- Cash dividends are offered.
- Partial dividend reinvestment.
- No discount is available.
- No IRA option is available.
- Optional cash purchases allowed.
- No direct debit option.

X

Xeikon N.V.
Belgium: Packaging/Printing
NYSE: XEIKY
c/o Bank of New York
48 Wall Street
New York, NY 10286
www.xeikon.be

Xeikon makes large-sized digital color printing systems.

Phone to enroll:
Bank of New York
888-BNY-ADRS or 888-269-2377

EasyStock Investment Plan:
- Initial minimum investment: $250
- Minimum per month (optional): $50
- Maximum per transaction: $250,000
- No cash dividends paid.
- Partial dividend reinvestment.
- No discount is available.
- No IRA option is available.
- Optional cash purchases allowed.
- Direct debits are available.

Xenova Group PLC
United Kingdom: Pharmaceuticals
NASDAQ: XNVAY
c/o Bank of New York
48 Wall Street
New York, NY 10286
www.xenova.co.uk

A pharmaceutical development company, Xenova Group explores the use of natural compounds such as plant extracts to develop cancer treatment and anti-clotting drugs.

Phone to enroll:
Bank of New York
888-BNY-ADRS or 888-269-2377

EasyStock Investment Plan:
- Initial minimum investment: $250
- Minimum per month (optional): $50
- Maximum per transaction: $250,000
- No cash dividends paid.
- Partial dividend reinvestment.
- No discount is available.
- No IRA option is available.
- Optional cash purchases allowed.
- Direct debits are available.

XXsys Technologies, Inc.
United States: Biological Research
NASDAQ: XSYS
4619 Viewridge Avenue
San Diego, CA 92123
www.xxsys.com
619-974-8200

XXsys Technologies repairs and reinforces bridge and building columns. The company's Robo-Wrapper uses carbon fiber to produce a composite jacket that surrounds the column and helps prevent collapse caused by seismic activity or decay.

Phone to enroll:
American Stock Transfer & Trust
800-278-4353

EasyStock Investment Plan:
- Initial minimum investment: $100
- Minimum per month (optional): $50
- Maximum per transaction: $10,000
- Maximum annual investment: $100,000
- No cash dividends paid.
- No partial dividend reinvestment.
- No discount is available.
- No IRA option is available.
- Optional cash purchases allowed.
- Direct debits are available.

York International Corp.
United States
NYSE: YRK
631 South Richland Avenue
York, PA 17403
www.york.com
717-771-7890

York is the fourth largest U.S. manufacturer of heating, ventilating, air-conditioning, and refrigeration equipment after United Technologies, Carrier, and Trane.

Phone to enroll:
Chase Mellon
800-437-6726

EasyStock Investment Plan:
- Initial minimum investment: $1,000
- Minimum per month (optional): $100
- Maximum monthly investment: $10,000
- Cash dividends are offered.
- Partial dividend reinvestment.
- No discount is available.
- No IRA option is available.
- Optional cash purchases allowed.
- Direct debits are available.

YPF S.A.
Argentina: Oil and Gas
NYSE: YPF
c/o Bank of New York
48 Wall Street
New York, NY 10286
www.ypf.com

YPF is an integrated oil and gas firm, operating a retail network of more than 2,400 gas stations in Latin America.

Phone to enroll:
Bank of New York
888-BNY-ADRS or 888-269-2377

EasyStock Investment Plan:
- Initial minimum investment: $250
- Minimum per month (optional): $50
- Maximum per transaction: $250,000
- Cash dividends are offered.
- Partial dividend reinvestment.
- No discount is available.
- No IRA option is available.
- Optional cash purchases allowed.
- Direct debits are available.

Zeneca Group PLC
United Kingdom: Health care
NYSE: ZEN
c/o Morgan Guaranty Trust Company
PO Box 9073
Boston, MA 02205-9948
www.zeneca.com

Spun off from Imperial Chemical Industries in 1993, London-based Zeneca Group develops primarily cancer and cardiovascular drugs as well as migraine and asthma treatments. The company also makes herbicides and other chemicals.

Phone to enroll:
Morgan Guaranty Trust Company
800-997-8970

EasyStock Investment Plan:
- Initial minimum investment: $250
- Minimum per month (optional): $50
- Maximum annual investment: $100,000
- No cash dividends paid.
- Partial dividend reinvestment.
- No discount is available.
- No IRA option is available.
- Optional cash purchases allowed.
- Direct debits are available.

Zindart Limited
China: Manufacturing
NASDAQ: ZNDTY
c/o Bank of New York
48 Wall Street
New York, NY 10286
www.zindart.com

Working harder than Santa's elves, die-cast and injection-molded products maker Zindart fulfills the wishes of firms that market toys and collectibles. Products include model cars for Ertl, Hot Wheels for Mattel, and holiday ornaments for Hallmark.

Phone to enroll:
Bank of New York
888-BNY-ADRS or 888-269-2377

EasyStock Investment Plan:
- Initial minimum investment: $250
- Minimum per month (optional): $50
- Maximum annual investment: $250,000
- Cash dividends are offered.
- Partial dividend reinvestment.
- No discount is available.
- No IRA option is available.
- Optional cash purchases allowed.
- Direct debits are available.

CANADIAN FEE-FREE EASYSTOCKS

Alberta Energy Company Ltd.
Canada: Oil and Gas
TSE: AOG, NYSE: AEC
421 – 7th Avenue S.W.
Calgary, Alberta T2P 4K9
www.aec.ca
403-266-8111

Alberta Energy Company is one of the largest oil and gas companies in Canada. AEC also holds a major interest in Syncrude, the world's largest synthetic oil producer.

Phone to enroll:
The CIBC Mellon Trust Company
800-387-0825

EasyStock Investment Plan:
- One share is required to enroll.
- Minimum quarterly investment: $50
- Maximum quarterly investment: $5,000
- Partial dividend reinvestment.
- No discount is available.
- Dividends paid at the end of June.
- Optional cash purchases allowed.
- Not available to U.S. residents.

Alcan Aluminum Limited
Canada: Aluminum/Base Metals
TSE/NYSE: AL
1188 Sherbrooke Street West
Montreal, Quebec H3A 3G2
www.alcan.com
514-848-8050

Alcan is one of the largest producers, distributors, and marketers of aluminum products worldwide.

Phone company to enroll:
514-848-8050

EasyStock Investment Plan:
- One share is required to enroll.
- Minimum quarterly investment: $100
- Maximum quarterly investment: $12,000
- Partial dividend reinvestment.
- No discount is available.
- Dividends paid at the end of March, June, Sept. and Dec.
- Optional cash purchases allowed.
- Available to both U.S. and Canadian residents.

Amtelecom Group Inc.
Canada: Telecommunications
TSE: ATM
18 Sydenham Street, PO Box 1800
Aylmer, Ontario N5H 3E7
www.amtelecom.ca
519-773-8441

Amtelecom Group Inc. provides local telephone services and cable television services in rural Ontario.

Phone to enroll:
The CIBC Mellon Trust Company
800-387-0825

EasyStock Investment Plan:
- One share is required to enroll.
- Maximum annual investment: $5,000
- No partial dividend reinvestment.
- No discount is available.
- Optional cash purchases allowed.
- Dividends paid in Feb., May, Aug. and Nov.
- Plan available to Canadians only.

B

Bank of Montreal
Canada: Banking/Financial Services
TSE/NYSE: BMO
129 St. Jacques Street, 3rd Floor
Montreal, Quebec H2Y 1L6
www.bmo.com
514-877-2500

The Bank of Montreal is one of the largest banks and brokerage firms (through Nesbitt Burns) in Canada.

Phone to enroll:
Trust Company of Bank of Montreal
514-877-2500

EasyStock Investment Plan:
- One share is required to enroll.
- Minimum quarterly investment: -
- Maximum annual investment: $40,000
- No partial dividend reinvestment.
- No discount is available.
- Dividends paid on the last day of Feb., May, Aug. and Nov.
- Optional cash purchases allowed.
- Not available to U.S. residents.

Bank of Nova Scotia
Canada: Banking/Financial Services
TSE/NYSE: BNS
Scotia Plaza, 44 King Street West
Toronto, Ontario M5H 1H1
www.scotiabank.ca
416-866-4790

The Bank of Nova Scotia is one of the largest commercial banks in Canada and owns ScotiaMcLeod, a major brokerage firm. BNS is also the most international of all Canadian banks, with operations in Latin America, Europe, and Asia.

Phone to enroll:
The Montreal Trust Company
800-663-9097

EasyStock Investment Plan:
- One share is required to enroll.
- Minimum annual investment: $100
- Maximum annual investment $20,000
- No partial dividend reinvestment.
- No discount is available.
- Dividends paid at the end of Jan., April, July, and Oct.
- Optional cash purchases allowed.
- Not available to U.S. residents.

BCE Inc.
Canada: Telecommunications
TSE/NYSE: BCE
1000 de la Gauchetiere Street West
Montreal, Quebec H3B 4Y7
www.bce.ca
800-339-6353

BCE is the Canadian telecom monopoly, serving over 65% of the population. BCE also has a major interest in Nortel Networks.

Phone to enroll:
The Montreal Trust Company
514-982-7666

EasyStock Investment Plan:
- One share is required to enroll.
- Maximum annual investment: $20,000
- No discount is available.
- Optional cash purchases allowed.
- Dividends paid in Jan., April, July, and Oct.

BC Gas Inc.
Canada: Utilities
TSE: BCG
1111 West Georgia Street
Vancouver, British Columbia
V6E 4M4
www.bcgas.com
800-667-9177

BC Gas is a leading provider of energy and utility services in Western Canada and the U.S. Pacific Northwest.

Phone to enroll:
The CIBC Mellon Trust Company
800-387-0825

EasyStock Investment Plan:
- One share is required to enroll.
- Minimum annual investment: -
- Maximum annual investment: $20,000
- No partial dividend reinvestment.
- No discount is available.
- Dividends paid at the end of Feb., May, Aug. and Nov.
- Optional cash purchases allowed.
- Not available to U.S. residents.

BC Telecom Inc.
Canada: Telecommunications
TSE: BCT
3777 Kingsway, 19th floor
Burnaby, BC V5H 3Z7
www.bctel.com
1-888-228-4636

B.C. Telecom provides services to a majority of British Columbians. BCT is also involved in the research and manufacture of voice, data, text, and imaging products.

Phone to enroll:
The Montreal Trust Company
800-380-7757

EasyStock Investment Plan:
- One share is required to enroll.
- Minimum annual investment: $100
- Maximum annual investment: $20,000
- Partial dividend reinvestment.
- No discount is available.
- Dividends paid at the start of Jan., April, July, and Oct.
- Optional cash purchases allowed.
- Not available to U.S. residents.

Bruncor Inc.
Canada: Telecommunications
TSE: BRR
PO Box 5030
Saint John, NB E2L 4L4
www.bruncor.com
800-561-9030

Bruncor is the parent company of New Brunswick Telephone, the monopoly telecom provider in that province.

Phone company to enroll:
(506) 694-6838

EasyStock Investment Plan:
- One share is required to enroll.
- Minimum quarterly investment: $1
- Maximum quarterly investment: $10,000
- Partial dividend reinvestment.
- No discount is available.
- Dividends paid in Jan., April, July, and Oct.
- Optional cash purchases allowed.
- Not available to U.S. residents.

C

Canadian General Investments Ltd.
Canada: Investment Management
TSE: CGI
110 Yonge Street, Suite 1601
Toronto, Ontario M5C 1T4
800-207-0067

Canadian General Investments is a closed-end investment fund.

Phone to enroll:
The Montreal Trust Company
800-663-9097

EasyStock Investment Plan:
- One share is required to enroll.
- Minimum quarterly investment: $100
- Maximum quarterly investment: $5,000
- No partial dividend reinvestment.
- No discount is available.
- Dividends paid in March, June, Sept. and Dec.
- Optional cash purchases allowed.
- Only available to Canadians.

Canadian Imperial Bank of Commerce
Canada: Banking/Financial Services
TSE: CM; NYSE: BCM
Commerce Court
Toronto, Ontario M5L 1A2
www.cibc.com
416-980-6657

The Canadian Imperial Bank of Commerce is Canada's second largest bank and owns CIBC World Markets, one of Canada's largest brokerage firms.

Phone to enroll:
The CIBC Mellon Trust Company
800-387-0825

EasyStock Investment Plan:
- One share is required to enroll.
- Minimum monthly investment: $100
- Maximum annual investment: $50,000
- No partial dividend reinvestment.
- 5% discount available.
- Dividends paid at the end of Jan., April, July, and Oct.
- Optional cash purchases allowed.
- Available to both U.S. and Canadian residents.

Canadian Pacific Limited
Canada: Oil and Gas/Railroads
TSE/NYSE: CP
Suite 800, Place du Canada
PO Box 6042, Station Centre-Ville
Montreal, Quebec H3C 3E4
www.cp.ca
514-395-6757

CP operates worldwide in energy, hotels, and transportation, through Pancanadian Petroleum, CP Hotels and Resorts, and CP Rail.

Phone to enroll:
Trust Company of Bank of Montreal
800-332-0095

EasyStock Investment Plan:
- One share is required to enroll.
- Minimum monthly investment: -
- Maximum annual investment: $30,000
- Partial dividend reinvestment.
- No discount is available.
- Dividends paid at the end of Jan., April, July, and Oct.
- Optional cash purchases allowed.
- Only available to Canadians.

Dofasco Inc.
Canada: Steel
TSE: DFS
PO Box 2460
Hamilton, Ontario L8N 3J5
www.dofasco.com
800-363-2726

Dofasco is one of Canada's largest steel producers.

Phone to enroll:
The CIBC Mellon Trust Company
800-387-0825

EasyStock Investment Plan:
- One share is required to enroll.
- Minimum annual investment: $50
- Maximum annual investment: $50,000
- No partial dividend reinvestment.
- No discount is available.
- Dividends paid at the start of Jan., April, July, and Oct.
- Optional cash purchases allowed.
- Available to both U.S. and Canadian residents.

Enbridge Inc.
Canada: Natural Gas
TSE: ENB
2900 Canada Trust Tower
421 – 7th Avenue S.W.
Calgary, Alberta T2P 2K9
www.enbridge.com
403-231-3900

Enbridge transports and distributes natural gas to 1.4 million customers over 13,000 square kilometres of pipeline.

Phone to enroll:
The CIBC Mellon Trust Company
800-387-0825

EasyStock Investment Plan:
- One share is required to enroll.
- Minimum quarterly investment: -
- Maximum quarterly investment: $5,000
- No partial dividend reinvestment.
- 5% discount available.
- Optional cash purchases allowed.
- Dividends paid at the start of March, June, Sept. and Dec.
- Available to both U.S. and Canadian residents

EnerMark Income Fund
Canada: Oil and Gas
TSE: EIF.UN
Western Canadian Place
Suite 1900, 700 - 9th Avenue S.W.
Calgary, Alberta T2P 3V4
800-319-6462
www.enerplus.com

EnerMark is an unincorporated closed-end trust that produces approximately 20,000 barrels of oil equivalent per day.

Phone to enroll:
The CIBC Mellon Trust Company
800-387-0825

EasyStock Investment Plan:
- One unit is required to enroll.
- Minimum investment per month: -
- Maximum investment per month: $5,000
- No partial dividend reinvestment.
- 5% discount available.
- Distributions paid monthly.
- Optional cash purchases allowed.
- Only available to Canadians.

EnerPlus Resources Fund
Canada: Oil and Gas
TSE: ERF.G
Western Canadian Place
Suite 1900, 700 – 9th Avenue S.W.
Calgary, Alberta T2P 3V4
800-319-6462
www.enerplus.com

EnerPlus, established in 1986, is Canada's oldest oil and gas royalty trust fund. EnerPlus purchases oil and gas properties and provides monthly income to its unitholders.

Phone to enroll:
The CIBC Mellon Trust Company
800-387-0825

EasyStock Investment Plan:
- One unit is required to enroll.
- Minimum monthly investment: -
- Maximum monthly investment: $5,000
- No partial dividend reinvestment.
- 5% discount available.
- Distributions paid monthly.
- Optional cash purchases allowed.
- Only available to Canadians.

F

Fortis Trust Corporation
Canada: Utilities
TSE: FTS
139 Water Street, PO Box 7067
St. John's, Nfld. A1E 3Y3
www.fortis.ca
709-726-7992

Fortis is a diversified company with holdings in five electric utilities; Fortis Trust, a residential mortgage lender; and Fortis Properties, a hotel owner.

Phone to enroll:
The Montreal Trust Company
800-561-0934

EasyStock Investment Plan:
- One share is required to enroll.
- Minimum annual investment: $50
- Maximum annual investment: $20,000
- No partial dividend reinvestment.
- No discount is available.
- Dividends paid at the beginning of March, June, Sept., and Dec.
- Optional cash purchases allowed.
- Only available to Canadians.

I

Imperial Oil Limited
Canada: Integrated Refiners
TSE: IMO
111 St. Clair Avenue West
Toronto, Ontario M5W 1K3
www.imperialoil.ca
416-968-5076

Imperial Oil is the largest producer of crude oil and the largest refiner/marketer of petroleum products in Canada.

Phone to enroll:
Trust Company of Bank of Montreal
800-332-0095

EasyStock Investment Plan:
- One share is required to enroll.
- Minimum quarterly investment: $50
- Maximum quarterly investment: $5,000
- No partial dividend reinvestment.
- No discount is available.
- Dividends paid at the start of Jan., April, July, and Oct.

- Optional cash purchases allowed.
- Available to both U.S. and Canadian residents.

Inco Limited
Canada: Base Metals/Nickel
TSE/NYSE: N
145 King Street West, Suite 1500
Toronto, Ontario M5H 4B7
www.incoltd.com
800-457-1464

Inco's primary metals division supplies about one-third of free world demand for nickel and is also a major copper and cobalt producer.

Phone company to enroll:
416-361-7511

EasyStock Investment Plan:
- One share is required to enroll.
- Minimum quarterly investment: $30 Can. or $30 U.S.
- Maximum quarterly investment per: $12,000 Can. or $10,000 U.S.
- Partial dividend reinvestment.
- No discount is available.
- Dividends paid in March, June, Sept. and Dec.
- Optional cash purchases allowed.
- Available to both U.S. and Canadian residents.

IPSCO Inc.
Canada: Steel
TSE: IPS
PO Box 1670
Armour Road
Regina, Saskatchewan S4P 3C7
www.ipsco.com
800-667-1616

IPSCO is a major player in steelmaking, pipemaking and coil processing, backwards integrated into gathering and processing ferrous scrap.

Phone to enroll:
The Montreal Trust Company
800-334-3305

EasyStock Investment Plan:
- One share is required to enroll.
- Minimum quarterly investment: -
- Maximum quarterly investment: $5,000
- No partial dividend reinvestment.
- No discount is available.
- Dividends paid in March, June, Sept. and Dec.
- Optional cash purchases allowed.
- Available to both U.S. and Canadian residents.

Island Telephone Company Ltd.
Canada: Telecommunications
TSE: IT
69 Belvedere Avenue, PO Box 820
Charlottetown, PEI C1A 7M1
www.islandtel.pe.ca
800-565-7168

Island Tel is the telecommunications monopoly for Prince Edward Island. The company is planning to merge with the other Maritime provinces' local phone monopolies.

Phone to enroll:
The CIBC Mellon Trust Company
800-565-2188

EasyStock Investment Plan:
- One share is required to enroll.
- Minimum quarterly investment: -
- Maximum quarterly investment: $5,000
- No partial dividend reinvestment.
- No discount is available.

- Dividends paid in March, June, Sept. and Dec.
- Optional cash purchases allowed.
- Available to both U.S. and Canadian residents.

M

MDS Inc.
Canada: Health care
TSE: MHG.A
100 International Boulevard
Etobicoke, Ontario M9W 6J6
www.mdsintl.com
416-675-7661

MDS sells radiopharmaceuticals and analytical instruments. The company also provides drug discovery and clinical trial services.

Phone to enroll:
The CIBC Mellon Trust Company
800-387-0825

EasyStock Investment Plan:
- One share is required to enroll.
- Minimum twice-yearly investment: $50
- Maximum twice-yearly: $3,000
- No partial dividend reinvestment.
- 5% discount available.
- Dividends paid at the start of April and Oct.
- Optional cash purchases allowed.
- Not available to U.S. residents.

MacMillan Bloedel Limited
Canada: Pulp & Paper
TSE: MB
925 West Georgia Street
Vancouver, BC V6C 3L2
www.macmillanbloedel.com
604-661-8302

MacMillan Bloedel is one of Canada's largest pulp and paper companies. MB has the largest tree-cutting rights in Canada.

Phone to enroll:
The Montreal Trust Company
800-380-7757

EasyStock Investment Plan:
- One share is required to enroll.
- Minimum annual investment: $500
- Maximum annual investment: $25,000
- Partial dividend reinvestment.
- No discount is available.
- Dividends paid in March, June, Sept. and Dec.
- Optional cash purchases allowed.
- Available to both U.S. and Canadian residents.

Maritime Telephone &Telegraph
Canada: Telecommunications
TSE: MTT
PO Box 880, Station A
Halifax, Nova Scotia B3J 2W5
www.mtt.ca
800-565-7168

Maritime Telephone & Telegraph is the main telecom provider for the provinces of Nova Scotia and Prince Edward Island. MT&T plans to merge with the other Maritime provinces' phone monopolies.

Phone to enroll:
The CIBC Mellon Trust Company
800-565-2188

EasyStock Investment Plan:
- One share is required to enroll.
- Minimum annual investment: -
- Maximum quarterly investment: $5,000
- No partial dividend reinvestment.
- No discount is available.
- Dividends paid in Jan., April, July, and Oct.
- Optional cash purchases allowed.
- Available to both U.S. and Canadian residents.

Molson Companies Ltd.
Canada: Breweries
TSE: MOL.A
40 King Street West, 36th floor
Toronto, Ontario M5H 3Z5
www.molson.com
416-860-6464

Molson Companies owns Molson Breweries, one of Canada's oldest and leading brewers; the Montreal Canadiens; and an interest in The Home Depot Canada.

Phone to enroll:
The CIBC Mellon Trust Company
800-387-0825

EasyStock Investment Plan:
- One share is required to enroll.
- Minimum quarterly investment: $100
- Maximum quarterly investment: $5,000
- No partial dividend reinvestment.
- No discount is available.
- Dividends paid at the start of Jan., April, July, and Oct.
- Optional cash purchases allowed.
- Only available to Canadians.

Moore Corporation Limited
Canada: Paper Products
TSE: MCL
1 First Canadian Place, Box 78
Toronto, Ontario M5X 1G5
www.moore.com
416-364-2600

Moore is the world's largest business forms company. MCL designs, manufactures, and distributes printed and electronic forms, labels, and billing statements.

Phone to enroll:
The CIBC Mellon Trust Company
800-387-0825

EasyStock Investment Plan:
- One share is required to enroll.
- Minimum quarterly investment: $50
- Maximum quarterly investment: $5,000
- No partial dividend reinvestment.
- No discount is available.
- Dividends paid at the start of Jan., April, July, and Oct.
- Optional cash purchases allowed.
- Available to both U.S. and Canadian residents.

N

National Bank of Canada:
Canada: Banking/Financial Services
TSE: NA
600 de la Gauchetiere Street West
Fourth Floor
Montreal, Quebec H3B 4L2
www.bnc.ca
514-394-6547

The National Bank of Canada is the fifth largest bank in the country, operating from coast to coast.

Phone to enroll:
General Trust of Canada
800-341-1419
EasyStock Investment Plan:
- 100 shares are required to reinvest dividends; one share to enroll.
- Minimum quarterly investment: $500
- Maximum quarterly investment: $5,000
- No partial dividend reinvestment.
- 5% discount available.
- Dividends paid at the start of Feb., May, Aug. and Nov.
- Optional cash purchases allowed.
- Not available to U.S. residents.

NewTel Enterprises Limited
Canada: Telecommunications
TSE: NEL
Fort William Building
PO Box 12110
St. John's, Nfld. A1C 6J7
www.newtel.com
800-563-2473

NewTel Enterprises owns the Newfoundland Telephone Co., that province's telecommunications monopoly. The company plans to merge with the other Maritime provinces' local phone monopolies.

Phone to enroll:
The Montreal Trust Company
800-663-9097

EasyStock Investment Plan:
- One share is required to enroll.
- Minimum quarterly investment: $50
- Maximum quarterly investment: $3,000
- No partial dividend reinvestment.
- No discount is available.
- Dividends paid at the end of March, June, Sept. and Dec.
- Not available to U.S. residents.

Nortel Networks Corp.
Canada: Telecom Equipment
TSE/NYSE: NTL
2920 Matheson Boulevard
Mississauga, Ontario L4W 4M7
www.nortelnetworks.com
905-238-7000

Nortel Networks (formerly Northern Telecom) is a global telecom products company that designs and builds digital networks. Nortel recently acquired Bay Networks to compete with Cisco.

Phone to enroll:
The Montreal Trust Company
800-663-9097

EasyStock Investment Plan:
- One share is required to enroll.
- Minimum quarterly investment: $40 U.S.
- Maximum quarterly investment: $5,000 U.S.
- No partial dividend reinvestment.
- No discount is available.
- Dividends paid at the end of March, June, Sept. and Dec.
- Optional cash purchases allowed.
- Available to both U.S. and Canadian residents.

Nova Corporation
Canada: Natural Gas
TSE/NYSE: NVA
801 Seventh Avenue S.W.
PO Box 2535, Station M
Calgary, Alberta T2P 2N6
www.nova.ca
800-661-8686

Nova is an integrated natural gas services and petrochemical company. Nova owns 25% of Methanex, the world's largest producer of methane. It has announced plans to merge with TransCanada Pipelines.

Phone to enroll:
800-387-0825

EasyStock Investment Plan:
- One share is required to enroll.
- Minimum quarterly investment: $50
- Maximum quarterly investment: $5,000
- No partial dividend reinvestment.
- No discount is available.
- Dividends paid in Feb., May, Aug. and Nov.
- Optional cash purchases allowed.
- Available to both U.S. and Canadian residents.

Nova Scotia Power Inc.
Canada: Electric Utilities
TSE: NSI
Scotia Square, PO Box 910
Halifax, Nova Scotia B3J 2W5
www.nspower.com
800-358-1995

Nova Scotia Power is the electric utility monopoly in that province, generating electricity for 99% of its homes and businesses.

Phone to enroll:
The Montreal Trust Company
800-663-9097

EasyStock Investment Plan:
- One share is required to enroll.
- Minimum quarterly investment: $25
- Maximum quarterly investment: $5,000
- Partial dividend reinvestment.
- No discount is available.
- Dividends paid in Nov., Feb., May, and Aug.
- Optional cash purchases allowed.
- Available to both U.S. and Canadian residents.

P

Pengrowth Energy Trust
Canada: Oil and Gas
TSE: PGF.UN
1050 Bow Valley Square 1
202 Sixth Avenue S.W.
Calgary, Alberta T2P 2R9
www.pengrowth.com
800-223-4122

Pengrowth Energy Trust is an unincorporated closed-end trust that invests directly in producing oil and gas properties.

Phone to enroll:
The Montreal Trust Company
800-663-9097

EasyStock Investment Plan:
- One unit is required to enroll.
- Minimum quarterly investment: $100
- Maximum quarterly investment: $3,000
- No partial dividend reinvestment.

- No discount is available.
- Dividends paid in Feb., May, Aug. and Nov.
- Optional cash purchases allowed.
- Only available to Canadians.

R

RioCan Real Estate Investment Trust
Canada: Real Estate Investment Trust
TSE: REI.UN
130 King Street West
Suite 1305, Box 435
Toronto, Ontario M5X 1E3
www.riocan.com
800-465-2733

RioCan Real Estate Investment Trust is an unincorporated closed-end trust that owns and operates a portfolio of sixty-seven commercial properties in Canada. Once its acquisition of CREIT is completed, it will be Canada's largest REIT.

Phone to enroll:
The CIBC Mellon Trust Company
800-387-0825

EasyStock Investment Plan:
One unit is required to enroll.
- Minimum annual investment: $250
- Maximum annual investment: $13,500
- No partial dividend reinvestment.
- No discount is available.
- Distributions paid at the start of each month.
- Optional cash purchases allowed.
- Only available to Canadians.

S

Suncor Energy Inc.
Canada: Oil Refiners
TSE/NYSE: SU
30th Floor, 10020 – 100th Street
Edmonton, Alberta T5J 0N5
www.suncor.com
800-667-4871

Suncor mines and extracts crude oil from the oil sands deposits of Northern Canada. It markets the oil equivalent under the Sunoco brand.

Phone to enroll:
The Montreal Trust Company
800-663-9097

EasyStock Investment Plan:
- One share is required to enroll.
- Minimum quarterly investment: $100
- Maximum quarterly investment: $5,000
- No partial dividend reinvestment.
- No discount is available.
- Dividends paid at the end of March, June, Sept. and Dec.
- Optional cash purchases allowed.
- Available to both U.S. and Canadian residents.

T

Telus Corp.
Canada: Telecommunications
TSE: AGT
30th Floor, 10020 – 100th Street
Edmonton, Alberta T5J 0N5
www.telus.com
800-667-4871

Telus provides telecommunications, cellular, directory advertising, and

consulting services in Alberta. By the time of publication, the company will have completed its merger with BC Tel. The merged entity will likely continue this stock purchase plan.

Phone to enroll:
The Montreal Trust Company
800-380-7757

EasyStock Investment Plan:
- One share is required to enroll.
- Minimum annual investment: $100
- Maximum annual investment: $20,000
- No partial dividend reinvestment.
- 5% discount available.
- Optional cash purchases allowed.
- Dividends paid in Jan., April, July, and Oct.
- Not available to U.S. residents.

TransAlta Corporation
Canada: Utilities
TSE: TA
110–12th Avenue S.W., Box 1900
Calgary, Alberta T2P 2M1
www.transalta.com
800-387-3598

TransAlta generates, transmits, and distributes over 65% of the consumer energy needs in Alberta. TransAlta also operates in Australia and New Zealand.

Phone to enroll:
The CIBC Mellon Trust Company
800-387-0825

EasyStock Investment Plan:
- One share is required to enroll.
- Minimum quarterly investment: -
- Maximum quarterly investment: $5,000
- No partial dividend reinvestment.
- No discount is available.
- Dividends paid at the start of Jan., April, July, and Oct.
- Optional cash purchases allowed.
- Not available to U.S. residents.

TransCanada Pipelines Ltd.
Canada: Natural Gas
TSE/NYSE: TRP
111 Fifth Avenue S.W.
PO Box 1000, Station M
Calgary, Alberta T2P 4K5
www.transcanada.com
800-361-6522

TRP transmits, markets, and processes energy. Its pipeline system transmits energy from Western Canada to the major energy markets. TRP plans to merge with Nova Corp.

Phone to enroll:
The Montreal Trust Company
800-663-9097

EasyStock Investment Plan:
- One share is required to enroll.
- Minimum quarterly investment: $50 Can. or $35 U.S.
- Maximum quarterly investment: $5,000 Can. or $3,500 U.S.
- No partial dividend reinvestment.
- 5% discount available.
- Dividends paid at the end of Jan., April, July, and Oct.
- Optional cash purchases allowed.
- Available to both U.S. and Canadian residents.

W

Westcoast Energy Inc.
Canada: Natural Gas
TSE/NYSE: W
Park Place, Suite 3400
666 Burrard Street
Vancouver, BC V6C 3M8
www.westcoastenergy.com
604-488-8000

Westcoast Energy is one of the largest North American companies that gathers, processes, transmits, stores, and distributes natural gas.

Phone to enroll:
The Montreal Trust Company
800-380-7757

EasyStock Investment Plan:
- One share is required to enroll.
- Minimum quarterly investment: $50
- Maximum quarterly investment: $5,000
- Partial dividend reinvestment.
- 5% discount is available.
- Dividends paid at the end of March, June, Sept. and Dec.
- Optional cash purchases allowed.
- Available to both U.S. and Canadian residents.

FEE-FREE EASYSTOCKS LISTED BY INDUSTRY GROUP (U.S., CANADIAN, AND INTERNATIONAL STOCKS)

Automobiles/Automotive

AUTOMOTIVE
Chrysler Corp.
Consorcio G Grupo Dina
FIAT S.p.A.
Ford Motor Co.
Lucas Varity PLC
Meritor Automotive, Inc.
Valmet Corporation

EQUIPMENT AND PARTS
Borg-Warner Automotive, Inc.
Consorcio G Grupo Dina
Curtiss-Wright Corp.
Lear Corporation
Lucas Varity plc
Tenneco Inc.

TIRES AND RUBBER
Goodyear Tire & Rubber Co.

Chemicals

CHEMICALS
Air Products and Chemicals
Akzo Nobel N.V.
Beijing Yanhua Petrochemical Co. Ltd.
BOC Group
GenCorp Inc.
Jilin Chemical Industrial Co.
Mycogen Corp.
Nova Corp.

SPECIALIZED CHEMICALS
Air Products and Chemicals
Mallinckrodt, Inc.
Morton International, Inc.
Novo Nordisk A/S
Thorn PLC

Construction

BUILDING MATERIALS
ABT Building Products Corp.
Boral Limited
CSR Limited
Johnson Controls, Inc.
Justin Industries, Inc.
Maderas y Sinteticos, S.A. (Masisa)
Owens-Corning

CONSTRUCTION
Bufete Industrial, S.A.
Chicago Bridge & Iron Co.
Empresas ICA, S.A. de C.V.
Grupo Tribasa, S.A. de C.V.
OLS Asia

SHIPBUILDING
Newport News Shipbuilding

Consumer products

APPLIANCES
Electrolux AB

CAMERAS/FILM
Eastman Kodak Co.

CONSUMER PRODUCTS
Amway Asia Pacific Limited
Amway Japan Limited
De Rigo S.p.A
Gillette Co.
Grupo Casa Autrey
Luxottica Group S.p.A.
Makita
Procter & Gamble Company
Snap-on, Incorporated
Sony Corporation
TAG Heuer International S.A.
TDK Corporation
Unilever
Whitman Corp.

CONTRACEPTIVES
London International Group PLC

EYEWEAR
De Rigo S.p.A.
Luxottica Group S.p.A.

FOOTWEAR
Fila S.p.A.

CLOTHING
Benetton Group S.p.A.
Fila S.p.A.
Kellwood Company

HOUSEKEEPING/HOUSEWARES
Industrie Natuzzi S.p.A.
Libbey Inc.
Procter & Gamble Company
Unilever N.V.
Unilever PLC
Waterford Wedgwood PLC

SUPPLIES
John H. Harland Company
Oce N.V.

TOYS
Mattel, Inc.

Diversified Companies

CONGLOMERATE
AMCOR
Koor Industries Ltd.

MULTI-INDUSTRY
GenCorp Inc.
Koor Industries Ltd.
National Service Industries, Inc.
Norsk Hydro ASA
Pacific Dunlop Limited
VEBA Aktiengesellschaft
Wharf Holdings Limited
Whitman Corp.

Farming

AGRICULTURAL
Cresud S.A.C.I.F. y A.

PEARL FARMING
Atlas Pacific Limited

TOBACCO
Empresas La Moderna
Gallaher Group PLC

Financial Services

BANKS
ABN AMRO Holdings N.V.
ADVANTA Corp.
Allied Irish Banks, PLC
Banco BHIF, S.A.
Banco Bilbao Vizcaya
Banco de Galicia y Buenos Aires
Banco de Santander S.A.
Banco Ganadero
Banco Industrial Colombiano
Banco Rio de la Plata, S.A.
Banco Santiago
Banco Wiese Ltdo.
Bank of Ireland
Bank of Montreal
Bank of New York Co., Inc.
Bank of Nova Scotia
Bank of Tokyo-Mitsubishi
Barclays Bank PLC
Canadian Imperial Bank of Commerce (CIBC)
Community Bank Systems, Inc.
Corporacion Bancaria de Espana, S.A.
First Commercial Corp.
GreenPoint Financial Corp.
ING Groep N.V.
Interchange Financial Services
Istituto Mobiliare Italiano
Mercantile Bancorporation Inc.
MidSouth Bancorp, Inc.
National Bank of Canada
National City Corp.
National Westminister Bank

Norwest Corp.
Old National Bancorp
Regions Financial Corp.
Royal Bank of Scotland PLC
SIS Bancorp Inc.
Sonoma Valley Bank
Synovus Financial Corp.
Westpac Banking Corporation

FINANCE COMPANIES
ADVANTA Corp.
Arrow Financial Corp.
Finova Group, Inc.

FINANCIAL SERVICES
ADVANTA Corp.
American Express Co.
Arrow Financial Corp.
AXA-UAP
Banco de Santander S.A.
Banco Santiago
Banco Wiese Ltdo.
Bank of Montreal
Bank of Nova Scotia
Barclays Bank Plc
Canadian Imperial Bank of Commerce (CIBC)
Dow Jones & Co., Inc.
Equitable Companies, Inc.
FAI Insurances Limited
FIRSTPLUS Financial Group
Istituto Mobiliare Italiano
Investors Financial Services
Morgan Stanley, Dean Witter
National Bank of Canada
Nationwide Financial Services,
New York Broker Deutschland
Providian Financial Corp.
Synovus Financial Corp.

INSURANCE
AEGON N.V.
Allstate Corp.
AXA-UAP
FAI Insurances Limited
Frontier Insurance Group, Inc.
ING Groep N.V.
Meadowbrook Insurance Group
SCOR
Sedgwick Group PLC
Unionamerica Holdings PLC

INSURANCE CARRIERS
AFLAC, Inc.
Istituto Nazionale delle Assicurazioni S.p.A.

INVESTMENT MANAGEMENT
AFP Provida
AMVESCAP PLC
Canadian General Investments
First Israel Fund, Inc.
Indonesia Fund Inc.

MORTGAGE FINANCE
Fannie Mae
Redwood Trust, Inc.

MULTI-LINE INSURER
Aetna Inc.

SAVINGS AND LOAN
First Financial Holdings, Inc.

Food and Beverages

Beverages
Boston Beer Co. Inc.
Brahma
Cadbury Schweppes
Coca-Cola FEMSA
Compañia Cervecerias Unidas S.A.
Diageo PLC
Molson Companies
Whitman Corp.

FOOD PRODUCTS
Bob Evans Farms, Inc.
Cadbury Schweppes
Chock Full O' Nuts Corp.
Coca-Cola FEMSA
Food Lion, Inc.
Industrias Bachoco
Mavesa
McCormick & Co., Inc.

Quaker Oats Co.
Sanderson Farms, Inc.
Tyson Foods, Inc.
Vina Concha y Toro, S.A.
WLR Foods, Inc.

RESTAURANTS
Bob Evans Farms
Darden Restaurants Inc.
McDonald's Corp.
Rank Group PLC

Health Care

BIOLOGICAL RESEARCH
MDS Inc.
XXsys Technologies, Inc.

BIOTECHNOLOGY
Biora AB

HEALTH CARE
Aetna Inc.
Fresenius Medical Care AG
MDS Inc.
Novo Nordisk A/S
Zeneca Group PLC

MEDICAL SUPPLIES AND DEVICES
Becton, Dickinson and Co.
C.R. Bard

NUTRITIONAL PRODUCTS
Reliv International, Inc.

PHARMACEUTICALS
Astra AB
Cantab Pharmaceuticals
Eli Lilly and Co.
Flamel Technologies S.A.
Huntingdon Life Sciences Group plc
Medeva PLC
Merck & Co., Inc.
Novo Nordisk A/S
Pharmacia & Upjohn, Inc.
Senetek PLC
SmithKline Beecham
Warner-Lambert Co.
Xenova Group PLC
Zeneca Group PLC

Industrial

FLUIDS MANAGEMENT
Robbins & Myers, Inc.

HEAVY MACHINERY
Deere & Co.
Rauma Oy

INDUSTRIAL PRODUCTS
Makita
Snap-on, Incorporated
Timken Company

MACHINERY
New Holland N.V.
Pfeiffer Vacuum Technology

MANUFACTURING
ABT Building Products Corp.
C.R. Bard, Inc.
Carpenter Technology Corp.
Eastern Company
Ford Motor Co.
Hillenbrand Industries, Inc.
Justin Industries, Inc.
Lear Corporation
Meritor Automotive, Inc.
Snap-on, Incorporated

Media and Entertainment

ENTERTAINMENT
Ascent Entertainment Group Inc.
Carlton Communications PLC
Rank Group PLC
Walt Disney Company

GAMING OPERATIONS
Harveys Casino Resorts

MAGAZINES
Readers Digest Association

MEDIA
Digitale Telekabel
General Electric Co.
Groupe AB
Reuters Holdings PLC
TV Azteca
Walt Disney Company

NEWSPAPERS
Dow Jones & Co., Inc.
Tribune Company

PUBLISHING
Dow Jones & Co., Inc.
Modern Times Group MTG AB
Readers Digest Association
Reuters Holdings PLC
Tribune Company
Walt Disney Company

Mines, Metals & Minerals

ALUMINUM
Alcan Aluminum

IRON
Carpenter Technology Corp.
Pohang Iron & Steel Co. Ltd.

MINERALS
Compania de Minas Buenaventura
Lihir Gold Limited
Rangold & Exploration Company

MINING
Compania de Minas Buenaventura
Lihir Gold Limited
Rangold & Exploration Company
Rio Tinto
Santos Ltd.
WMC Holdings Limited

NICKEL
Inco Ltd.
WMC Holdings Limited

PRECIOUS METALS
Great Central Mines
Harmony Gold Mining Co. Ltd.
WMC Holdings Limited

STEEL
Carpenter Technology Corp.
Dofasco Inc.
Grupo Imsa, S.A. de C.V.
Ispat International N.V.
Pohang Iron & Steel Co. Ltd.
Schnitzer Steel Industries, Inc.
Tubos de Acero de Mexico

Oil and Gas

INTEGRATED/DOMESTIC REFINERS
Amoco Corporation
Cross Timbers Oil Co.
Imperial Oil
Kerr-McGee Corp.
Suncor Energy Inc.

INTEGRATED INTERNATIONAL REFINERS
British Petroleum Co. PLC
Elf Aquitaine
Exxon Corp.
Mobil Corp.
Phillips Petroleum Co.
Royal Dutch Petroleum Co.
Texaco Inc.

NATURAL GAS
IPL Energy Inc.
Nova Corp.
TransCanada Pipelines

OIL AND GAS
Alberta Energy Co.
Canadian Pacific
Chevron Corp.
Coastal Corp.
EnerMark Income Fund
EnerPlus Resource Fund
Norsk Hydro ASA
Pengrowth Energy Trust

PETSEC Energy Limited
Repsol S.A.
Santos
TOTAL S.A.
YPF Sociedad Anonima

Pulp & Paper

LUMBER
Aracruz Cellulose S.A.
Asia Pulp & Paper Co.
MacMillan Bloedel Ltd.

PAPER
Aracruz Cellulose S.A.
Asia Pulp & Paper Co.
MacMillan Bloedel Ltd.
P.T. Inti Indorayon Utama
Stone Container Corp.

PAPER PRODUCER
Aracruz Cellulose S.A.
Moore Corp.
Stone Container Corp.

PRINTING
John H. Harland Company
Moore Corp.

PACKAGING
Grupo Industrial Durango, S.A. de C.V.
Xeikon N.V.

Real Estate

REAL ESTATE
Carey Diversified LLC
CRIIMI MAE
IRSA Inversiones y Representaciones
Israel Land Development Corp. Ltd.
Security Capital Pacific Trust
Storage Trust Realty Corp.
Taubman Centers, Inc.
Thornburg Mortgage Asset Corp.

REAL ESTATE INVESTMENT TRUSTS (REIT)
Bedford Property Investors, Inc.
BRE Properties, Inc.
Canadian REIT
CRIIMI MAE
Crown American Realty Trust
Duke Realty Investments, Inc.
Equity Residential Properties Trust
General Growth Properties, Inc.
Glenborough Realty Trust, Inc.
Glimcher Realty Trust
Home Properties of New York
Liberty Property Trust
Macerich Co.
RioCan REIT
Security Capital Pacific Trust
Sunstone Hotel Investors, Inc.
Thornburg Mortgage Asset
Urban Shopping Centers, Inc.
Weingarten Realty Investors

Retail

CRAFT STORES
Michaels Stores, Inc.

DEPARTMENT STORES
Dayton Hudson Corp.
J.C. Penney Co., Inc.
Sears, Roebuck and Co.
Wal-Mart Stores Inc.

DRUG STORES
Grupo Casa Autrey
Longs Drug Stores Corp.
Walgreen Co.

ELECTRONICS STORES
Tandy Corp.

GENERAL RETAIL
Amway Asia Pacific Limited
Amway Japan Limited
Dayton Hudson Corp.
Grupo Casa Autrey
Koninklijke Ahold N.V.
Super-Sol Ltd.
Thorn PLC

HARDWARE STORES
Home Depot Inc.
Molson Companies Ltd.

MERCHANDISING
Benetton Group S.p.A.
De Rigo S.p.A.
Grupo Elektra
Signet Group PLC

OFFICE EQUIPMENT
CBT Group PLC
NEC Corporation
Oce N.V.
Ricoh Company Ltd.

SUPERMARKETS
Blue Square-Israel Ltd.
Food Lion, Inc.
Supermercados Unimarc

Services

FACILITY RELATED SERVICES
TNP Enterprises, Inc.

FOOD SERVICES/RESTAURANTS
Bob Evans Farms, Inc.
Darden Restaurants, Inc.
Koninklijke Ahold N.V.
McDonald's Corp.
Rank Group PLC

SERVICES
ADVANTA Corp.
Dassault Systems S.A.
Freepages Group PLC

STAFFING SERVICES
Adecco S.A.
Select Appointments PLC

Technology

AEROSPACE/DEFENSE
Asia Satellite
Kaman Corp.
Timken Company

COMPUTER SOFTWARE
Baan Company N.V.
Dassault Systems S.A.
Dr. Solomons Group
Formula Systems Inc.
OzEMail Limited
Small World PLC

COMPUTER SYSTEMS
Baan Company N.V.
Canon, Inc.
Compaq Computer Corp.
Dassault Systems S.A.
Formula Systems Inc.
International Business Machines Corp. (IBM)
Ricoh Company Ltd.
Tektronix, Inc.

ELECTRONICS
ENDESA, S.A.
Matsushita Electric Works, Ltd.
Newport Corp.
Pioneer Electronic Corporation
Sony Corporation
TDK Corporation

EMPOWERING INFORMATION
Bowne & Co., Inc.

INTEGRATED CIRCUITS
Macronix International Co.

SEMICONDUCTORS
SGS-THOMSON Microelectronics

TECHNOLOGY CONSULTING/SERVICES
ECsoft Group plc
Micro Focus Group PLC
NICE Systems Ltd.
Saville Systems PLC
Select Software Tools PLC

Telecommunications

TELECOMMUNICATIONS
AirTouch Communications, Inc.
Ameritech Corporation
APT Satellite Holdings Co.

BCE Inc.
BC Telecom
Bell Atlantic Corp.
BellSouth Corp.
British Telecommunications
Bruncor
COMSAT Corp.
Emcee Broadcast Products, Inc.
Emerging Markets Telecom Fund
Empresas Telex-Chile
Esprit Telecom PLC
General Cable
Grupo Iusacell, Series
Island Telephone
Magyar Tavozlesi Rt. (MATAV)
Maritime Telephone & Telegraph
Matav-Cable Systems Media
MediaOne Group
Nera ASA
NetCom Systems AB
NewTel Enterprises
Nippon Telephone and Telegraph
Nortel Inversora S.A.
P.T. IndoSat
P.T. Pasifik Satelit Nusantara
P.T. Telkom
Telebras
Telecom Argentina STET-France Telecom S.A.
Telecom Italia S.p.A.
Telefonica del Perú S.A.
Telefonos de Mexico
Telus
Tricom, S.A.
U.S. WEST, Inc.
Vimpel-Communications
Vodafone Group PLC

TELECOMMUNICATIONS EQUIPMENT

Alcatel Alsthom
Lucent Technologies Inc.
MediaOne Group
Nortel Networks Corp.
Nokia Corporation
U.S. WEST, Inc.

Transportation

AIRCRAFT

China Southern Airlines Co.
Rockwell International Corp.

AIRLINES

British Airways PLC

TRANSPORTATION

Consolidated Freightways Corp.
CSX Corporation
NFC PLC
Roadway Express, Inc.

RAILROAD

Canadian Pacific Ltd.
CSX Corporation
Guangshen Railway Company

Utilities

DIVERSIFIED UTILITIES

General Electric Co.
Minnesota Power & Light Co.

ELECTRIC SERVICES

American Electric Power Co.
Atlantic Energy Inc.
BEC Energy
Carolina Power & Light Co.
Central and South West Corp.
Central Hudson Gas & Electric
Central Maine Power Co.
Central Vermont Public Service
CILCORP Inc.
CMS Energy Corp.
Connectiv, Inc.
Dominion Resources, Inc.
DQE, Inc.
DTE Energy Co.
Duke Energy Corp.
ENDESA, S.A.
Entergy Corp.
First Energy Corporation
Fortis Trust
Florida Progress Corp.
General Electric Co.
Green Mountain Power Corp.

Hawaiian Electric Industries
Houston Industries Inc.
Idaho Power Co.
Interstate Energy Corp.
IPALCO Enterprises, Inc.
Korea Electric Power Corp.
Long Island Lighting Co. Ltd.
Madison Gas & Electric Co.
MDU Resources Group, Inc.
MidAmerican Energy Co.
Montana Power Co.
Nevada Power Co.
Northern States Power Co.
Northwestern Corporation
Nova Scotia Power Inc.
OGE Energy Corp.
Otter Tail Power Co.
Pinnacle West Capital Corp.
Public Service Enterprise Group
Puget Sound Energy, Inc.
SCANA Corporation
Sempra Energy
Southern Company
Texas Utilities Co.
TNP Enterprises, Inc.
TransAlta Corp.
UtiliCorp United Inc.
Western Resources, Inc.
Wisconsin Energy Corp.
WPS Resources Corp.

MULTI-SERVICE

Illinova Corp.
MDU Resources Group, Inc.
MidAmerican Energy Co.
Montana Power Co.
Pacific Century Financial Corp.
PacifiCorp
SCANA Corporation
Western Resources, Inc.

NATURAL GAS SERVICES

AGL Resources, Inc.
Atmos Energy Corp.
BC Gas
Cascade Natural Gas Corp.
Central Hudson Gas & Electric
CILCORP Inc.
CMS Energy Corp.
Connecticut Energy Corp.
Delta Natural Gas Co., Inc.
Energen Corp.
Enron Corporation
IPL Energy
MCN Energy Group, Inc.
MDU Resources Group, Inc.
MidAmerican Energy Co.
Montana Power Co.
National Fuel Gas Company
New Jersey Resources Corp.
Nova Corp.
NUI Corporation
ONEOK Inc.
People's Energy Corp.
Piedmont Natural Gas Co., Inc.
Public Service Company of North Carolina, Inc.
Public Service Enterprise Group
Questar Corporation
SCANA Corporation
SEMCO Energy
Sempra Energy
Southern Union Co.
Southwest Gas Corp.
TransCanada Pipelines
Westcoast Energy Inc.
Western Resources, Inc.
WICOR, Inc.
Wisconsin Energy Corp.

WATER SERVICES

American Water Works Co.
California Water Service Co.
Connecticut Water Service, Inc.
Philadelphia Suburban Corp.
United Water Resources Inc.

FEE-FREE EASYSTOCKS LISTED BY HOME COUNTRY

Argentina
Banco de Galicia y Buenos Aires S.A.
Banco Rio de la Plata S.A.
Boral S.A.
Cresud S.A.C.I.F. y A.
ARSA Inversiones y Representaciones S.A.
Nortel Inversora S.A.
Telecom Argentina STET-France Telecom
YPF S.A.

Australia
Amcor
Atlas Pacific
CSR
FAI Insurances
Formulab Neuronectics
Great Central Mines
Lihir Gold
OzEMail
Pacific Dunlop
Rio Tinto
Santos
Wharf Holdings

Belgium
Xeikon

Brazil
Aracruz Celulose S.A.
Brahma S.A.
Companhia Brasiliera de Distribucao S.A.
Copel S.A.
Telebras HOLDR

Canada
Alberta Energy Co.
Alcan Aluminum Ltd.
Bank of Montreal
Bank of Nova Scotia
BCE Inc.
BC Gas Inc.
BC Telecom Inc.
Bruncor Inc.
Canadian General Investments
Canadian Imperial Bank of Commerce (CIBC)
Canadian Pacific Ltd.
Dofasco Inc.
Enbridge Corp.
EnerMark Income Trust
EnerPlus Resource Fund
Fortis Trust Corp.
Imperial Oil Ltd.
Inco Ltd.
IPSCO Inc.
Island Telephone Co.
MacMillan Bloedel Ltd.
Maritime T&T
MDS Inc.
Molson Companies Inc.
Moore Corp.
NewTel Enterprises Ltd.
Nortel Networks Corp.
Nova Corp.
Nova Scotia Power Inc.
Pengrowth Energy Trust
RioCan REIT
Suncor Energy Inc.
Telus Inc.
TransAlta Corp.
TransCanada Pipelines
Westcoast Energy Inc.

Chile
AFP Provida
Banco BHIF
Banco Santiago
Compania Cervecerias Unidas
Expresas Telex-Chile
MASISA (Maderas y Sinteticos)
Supermarcados Unimarc
Vina Concha y Toro

China (Mainland)

Asia Satellite Telecommunications Holdings
Beijing Yanhua Petroleum Co.
China Southern Airlines
Guangshen Railway Co.
Huaneng Power International
Jilin Chemical Industrial Co.
Shandong Huaneng Power
Shanghai Petrochemical Co.
Zindart

Colombia

Banco Ganadero
Banco Industrial Colombiano

Denmark

Novo Nordisk

Finland

Nokia
Rauma Oy
Valmet

France

Alcatel Alsthom
AXA-UAP
Dassault Systems
Elf Aquitaine
Flamel Technologies
Groupe AB
SCOR
SGS-Thomson Microelectronics

Germany

Digitale Telekabel
Fresnius Medical Care
VEBA Aktiengesellschaft
New York Broker Deutschland
Pfeiffer Vacuum Technology

Hong Kong, China

Amway Asia Pacific
APT Satellite Co.
CLP Holdings
OLS Asia
WMC Holdings

Hungary

Matav

Indonesia

Indonesia Fund
PT IndoSat
PT Inti Indorayon Utama
PT Pasifik Satelit Nosantara
PT Telekom
PETSEC Energy

Ireland

Allied Irish Banks
Bank of Ireland
CBT Group
Elan
Ryanair
Saville Systems
Warner Chilcott
Waterford Wedgwood
Westpac Banking

Israel

Blue Square-Israel
First Israel Fund
Formula Systems
Israel Land Development Co.
Koor Industries
Matav-Cable Systems Media
NICE Systems
Super-Sol

Italy

Benetton Group
De Rigo
Fiat
Fila
Luxottica Group
Industrie Natuzzi
Instituto Nazionale della Assicurazione
Telecom Italia

Japan

Amway Japan
Bank of Tokyo-Mitsubishi
Makita

Matsushita Electric Industrial
NEC
Nippon Telephone & Telegraph
Ricoh
Sony
TDK

Mexico
Bufete Industrial
Coca-Cola FEMSA
Consorcio G Groupo Dina
Empresas ICA
Empresas la Moderna
Grupo Casa Autrey
Grupo Elektra
Grupo Imsa
Grupo Industrial Durango
Grupo Iuscell
Grupo Tribasa
Industrias Bachoco
Telefonos de Mexico
Tubos de Acero de Mexico
TV Azteca

Netherlands
ABN Amro Holdings
Aegon
Akzo Nobel
Arcadis
Baan Co.
Chicago Bridge & Iron Co.
ING Groep
Ispat International
Koninklijke Ahold
New Holland
Oce
Royal Dutch Petroleum
Unilever

New Zealand
MAS Technology

Norway
Nera
Norsk Hydro

Peru
Banco Wiese
Compania de Minas Buenaventura
Telefonica del Perú

Portugal
Portugal Telecom

Russia
Vimpel-Communications

Singapore
Asia Pulp & Paper Co.

South Africa
Durbam Roodeport Deep
Harmony Gold Mining Co.
Rangold & Exploration Co.

South Korea
Korea Electric Power
Pohang Iron & Steel Co.

Spain
Banco Bilbao Vizcaya
Banco de Santander
Corporacion Bancaria de Espana
ENDESA
Repsol

Sweden
Aktiebolaget Electrolux
Astra
Biora
Modern Times Group
Net Com Systems

Switzerland
Adecco
Tag Heuer International

Taiwan
Macronix International

United Kingdom
Amvescap
Barclays Bank
British Airways
BP Amoco
British Telecommunications

Cadbury Schweppes
Cantab Pharmaceuticals
Carlton Communications
Diageo
Dr. Solomon's Group
ECSoft Group
Esprit Telecom
Gallaher Group
General Cable
Huntington Life Sciences Group
Imperial Chemical Industries
Lucas Varity
Medeva
Micro Focus Group
National Westminster Bank
NFC
Rank Group
Reuters Holdings
Royal Bank of Scotland
Scoot.com PLC
Scottish Power
Sedgwick Group
Select Appointments
Select Software Tools
Senetek
Signet Group
Small World
SmithKline Beecham
Thorn
Unilever
Unionamerica Holdings
Vodafone Group
Xenova Group
Zeneca Group

United States

ABT Building Products
Aetna
AFLAC
AGL Resources
Air Products & Chemicals
AirTouch Communications
American Express Co.
American Water Works Co.
Ameritech
Amoco
Arrow Financial
Ascent Entertainment Group
Atlantic Energy
Atmos Energy
BanPonce
Bank of New York
Becton, Dickinson and Co.
Bedford Property Investors
Bell Atlantic
Bell South
Bob Evans Farms
BOC Group
Borg-Warner Automotive
Boston Beer Co.
Bowne & Co.
BRE Properties
C.R. Bard
Capstead Mortgage
Carey Diversified
Carolina Power & Light
Carpenter Technology
Cascade Natural Gas
Central & South West
Central Hudson Gas & Electric
Central Maine Power Co.
Central Vermont Public Service
Chevron
Chock Full O' Nuts
Chrysler
CILCORP
CMS Energy
Coastal
Community Bank Systems
Compaq Computer
COMSAT
Connecticut Energy
Connecticut Water Service
Consolidated Freightways
CRIIMI MAE
Cross Timbers Oil Co.
Crown American Realty Trust
CSX Inc.
Curtiss-Wright
Darden Restaurants

Dayton Hudson
Deere & Co.
Delta Natural Gas Co.
Dominion Resources
Dow Jones & Co.
DQE
DTE Energy
Duke Energy
Duke Realty Investments
Eastern Company
Eastman Kodak
Eli Lilly and Co.
Emcee Broadcast Products
Emerging Markets
  Telecommunications Fund
Energen
ENOVA
Enron
Entergy
Equitable Companies
Equity Residential Properties Trust
Exxon
Fannie Mae
Fed One Bancorp
Finova Group
First Commercial Corp.
First Energy
First Financial Holdings
Florida Progress
Food Lion
Ford Motor Co.
Frontier Insurance Group
GenCorp
General Electric
General Growth Properties
Gillette Co.
Glenborough Realty Trust
Glimcher Realty Trust
Goodyear Tire & Rubber Co.
Green Mountain Power
Guidant
Harveys Casino Resorts
Hawaiian Electric Industries
Hillenbrand Industries
Home Depot, The
Home Properties of New York
Houston Industries
Idaho Power
IES Industries
Illinova
Interchange Financial Services
International Business Machines
Interstate Power Co.
Investors Financial Services
IPALCO Enterprises
IWC Resources
J.C. Penney Co.
John H. Harland Co.
Johnson Controls
Justin Industries
Kaman
Kellwood Co.
Kerr-McGee
Kerr Group
KeySpan Energy
Lear
Liberty Property Trust
London International Group
Long Island Lighting Co.
Longs Drug Stores
Lucent Technologies
Macerich Co.
Madison Gas & Electric Co.
Mattel
McCormick & Co.
McDonald's
MCN Energy
Meadowbrook Insurance Group
MediaOne
Mellon Bank
Mercantile Bancorporation
Merck & Co.
Meritor Automotive
Michaels Stores
MidAmerican Energy Co.
MidSouth Bancorp
Minnesota Power & Light
Mobil
Montana Power Co.
Morgan Stanley, Dean Witter & Co.

Morton International
Mycogen
National Fuel Gas Co.
NationsBank
Nationwide Financial Services
Newport
Newport News Shipbuilding
Northern States Power Co.
Northwestern Public Service Co.
Norwest
NUI
OGE Energy
Old National Bancorp
Oneok
Owens-Corning
Pacific Century Financial Group
Peoples Energy Group
Pharmacia & Upjohn
Philadelphia Suburban
Phillips Petroleum Co.
Piedmont Natural Gas Co.
Pinnacle West Capital
Providian Financial
Public Service Co. of New Mexico
Public Service Co. of North Carolina
Public Service Enterprise Group
Puget Sound Energy
Quaker Oats Co.
Questar
Readers Digest Association
Redwood Trust
Regions Financial
Reliv International
Roadway Express
Robbins & Myers
Rockwell International
Sanderson Farms
SBC Communications
Scana
Schnitzer Steel Industries
Sears, Roebuck & Co.
Security Capital Pacific Trust
Semco Energy
Sierra Pacific Resources
SIS Bancorp
Snap-on
Southern Co.
Southern Union
Southwest Gas
Stone Container
Storage Realty Trust
Sunstone Hotel Investors
Synovus Financial
Tandy
Taubman Centers
Tektronix
Tenneco
Texaco
Thornburg Mortgage Asset
Timken Co.
TNP Enterprises
Transocean Offshore Drilling
Tribune Co.
Tyson Foods
U.S. West
United Companies Financial
United National Bancorp
United Water Resources
Urban Shopping Centers
Utilicorp United
Valspar
Wal-Mart Stores
Walgreens Co.
Walt Disney & Company
Warner-Lambert Co.
Weingarten Realty Investors
Western Resources
Westernbank Puerto Rico
Whitman
Wicor
Wisconsin Energy
WLR Foods
WPS Resources
XXsys Technologies
York International

Venezuela

Mavesa S.A.

DIRECTORY OF FEE-FREE EASYBONDS

This directory is useful for locating the Federal Reserve Bank branch that services your area. Fee-Free EasyBonds are all offered from the same issuer, the United States Treasury. Information and downloadable forms can also be found on the Internet at www.publicdebt.treas.gov and will soon be available on the Treasury Direct's homepage at www.treasurydirect.gov. By the time this book is published, the Treasury plans to offer online enrolment and reinvestment capabilities, so check their website or visit www.easyinvesting.com for updates.

Using The Directory

To make it easy to find what you need, this directory is organized into the following sections:

- *Federal Reserve Servicing Branches* which lists all the local branches where you can call to receive enrolment information or to deposit funds into a Treasury Direct account. Foreign and Canadian residents should contact the Federal Reserve Bank branch that is geographically closest to them.
- *Treasury Securities Chart* which lists all the securities that the Treasury offers, and specifies the auction dates.
- *Commonly Used Forms* a list of the most-requested forms.

FEDERAL RESERVE SERVICING BRANCHES

Atlanta
104 Marietta Street N.W.
Atlanta, Georgia, 30303
Tel: 404-521-8653

Baltimore
502 South Sharp Street
PO Box 1378
Baltimore, Maryland, 21203
Tel: 410-576-3300

Birmingham
1801 Fifth Avenue North
PO Box 830447
Birmingham, Alabama, 35283
Tel: 205-731-8708

Boston
600 Atlantic Avenue
PO Box 2076
Boston, Massachusetts, 02160
Tel: 617-973-3810

Buffalo
160 Delaware Avenue
PO Box 961
Buffalo, New York, 14240
Tel: 716-849-5000

Charlotte
530 East Trade Street
PO Box 30248
Charlotte, N. Carolina, 28230
Tel: 704-358-2100

Chicago
230 South LaSalle Street
PO Box 834
Chicago, Illinois, 60690
Tel: 312-322-5369

Cincinnati
150 East Fourth Street
PO Box 999
Cincinnati, Ohio, 45201
Tel: 513-721-4794 Ext. 334

Cleveland
1455 East Sixth Street
PO Box 6387
Cleveland, Ohio, 44101
Tel: 216-579-2000

Dallas
2200 North Pearl Street
PO Box 655906
Dallas, Texas, 75265
Tel: 214-922-6100

Denver
1020 Sixteenth Street
PO Box 5228
Denver, Colorado, 80217
Tel: 303-572-2470

Detroit
160 West Fort Street
PO Box 1059
Detroit, Michigan, 48231
Tel: 313-964-6157

El Paso
301 East Main Street
PO Box 100
El Paso, Texas, 79999
Tel: 915-521-8272

Houston
1701 San Jacinto Street
PO Box 2578
Houston, Texas, 77252
Tel: 713-659-4433

Jacksonville
800 West Water Street
PO Box 2499
Jacksonville, Florida, 32231
Tel: 904-632-1179

Kansas City
925 Grand Avenue
PO Box 419033
Kansas City, Missouri, 64141
Tel: 816-881-883

Little Rock
325 West Capitol Avenue
PO Box 1261
Little Rock, Arkansas, 72203
Tel: 501-324-8272

Los Angeles
950 South Grand Avenue
PO Box 2077
Los Angeles, California, 90051
Tel: 213-624-7389

Louisville
410 South Fifth Street
PO Box 32710
Louisville, Kentucky, 40232
Tel: 502-568-9238

Memphis
200 North Main Street
PO Box 407
Memphis, Tennessee, 38101
Tel: 901-523-7171 Ext. 423

Miami
9100 N.W. Thirty-Six Street
PO Box 520847
Miami, Florida, 33152
Tel: 305-471-6497

Minneapolis
250 Marquette Avenue
Minneapolis, Minnesota, 33152
Tel: 612-340-2075

Nashville
301 Eighth Avenue North
Nashville, Tennessee, 37203
Tel: 615-251-7100

New Orleans
525 St. Charles Avenue
PO Box 52948
New Orleans, Louisiana, 70152
Tel: 504-593-3200

New York
33 Liberty Street
Federal Reserve PO Station
New York, New York, 10045
Tel: 212-720-6619

Oklahoma City
266 Dean McGee Avenue
PO Box 25129
Oklahoma City, Okla., 73125
Tel: 405-270-8652

Omaha
2201 Farnam Street
Omaha, Nebraska, 68102
Tel: 402-221-5636

Philadelphia
Ten Independence Mall
PO Box 90
Philadelphia, Penn., 19105
Tel: 215-574-6680

Pittsburgh
717 Grant Street
PO Box 867
Pittsburgh, Pennsylvania, 15230
Tel: 412-261-7802

Portland
915 S.W. Stark Street
PO Box 3436
Portland, Oregon, 97208
Tel: 503-221-5932

Richmond
701 East Byrd Street
PO Box 27622
Richmond, Virginia, 23261
Tel: 804-697-8372

Salt Lake City
120 South State Street
PO Box 30780
Salt Lake City, Utah, 84130
Tel: 801-322-7882

San Antonio
126 East Nueva Street
PO Box 1471
San Antonio, Texas, 78295
Tel: 210-978-1303

San Francisco
101 Market Street
PO Box 7702
San Francisco, California, 94120
Tel: 415-974-2330

Seattle
1015 Second Avenue
PO Box 3567
Seattle, Washington, 98124
Tel: 206-343-3605

St. Louis
411 Locust Street
PO Box 14915
St. Louis, Missouri, 63178
Tel: 314-444-8703

Bureau of Public Debt*
Capital Area Servicing Center
1300 C Street S.W.
Washington, D.C., 20239
Tel: 202-874-4026

***The Capital Area Servicing Center only serves clients living in the Washington, D.C. area.**

COMMONLY USED FORMS

PD F 5381	Treasury Bill, Note, and Bond Tender
PD F 5175	Completing a Treasury Bill Tender
PD F 5177	Statement of Account
PD F 5178	Transaction Request
PD F 5179	Security Transfer Request
PD F 5180	Treasury Bill Reinvestment Request
PD F 5182	New Account Request
PD F 5186	1099 Interest Income Form
PD F 5187	1099B Payments from Broker/Barter Exchange
PD F 5188	Power of Attorney for Disposition of Securities
PD F 5189	Resolution for Disposition of Securities
PD F 5191	Recognition as Natural Guardian of a Minor
PD F 5192	Stop Payment/Replacement Check Request
PD F 5201	Disposition of Payments and Securities
PD F 5207	Income Subject to Withholding
PD F 5262	Reinvestment Request for Treasury Notes/Bonds
PD F 5330	Treasury Direct Account Number

Auction Dates and Multiples

TERM/TYPE	MIN.	MULTIPLES	AUCTION
30-Year Bond	$1,000	$1,000	Feb. and Aug.
Inflation-Indexed Securities	$1,000	$1,000	Jan., April, July, Oct.
10-Year Note	$1,000	$1,000	Feb., May, Aug., Nov.
5-Year Note	$1,000	$1,000	Late in Each Month
3-Year Note	$1,000	$1,000	Feb., May, Aug., Nov.
2-Year Note	$1,000	$1,000	Late in Each Month
52-Week Bill	$1,000	$1,000	Every Fourth Thursday
26-Week Bill	$1,000	$1,000	Every Monday
13-Week Bill	$1,000	$1,000	Every Monday

GLOSSARY

American Depository Receipt (ADR): Shares of international companies that are traded on U.S. markets in U.S. dollars.

Common shares: Securities that represent an ownership position and voting rights in a company. Common shareholders are entitled to participate in the capital appreciation of the company and to receive dividends, if any are declared. If the company goes bankrupt, common shareholders have a right to the company's assets after debt holders and preferred shareholders have been paid.

Dividends: A payment in cash or shares made to a company's shareholders out of their current or retained earnings. Dividends are taxable but treated more favorably than interest income.

Dollar-cost averaging: The process of investing a regular amount of money to average your cost basis and reduce volatility. Dollar-cost averaging allows you to buy fewer shares when the price per share is high and more shares when the price per share is low.

Fractional shares: Ownership of less than one full share of a stock.

Front-end fee: A sales commission that must be paid to financial planners, brokers, or mutual fund sales representatives when buying a mutual fund with a front-end load.

No-load mutual fund: A mutual fund that does not levy a front- or rear-end sales charge.

Portfolio: A combination of stocks, bonds, and cash owned by an individual or corporation. This diversification helps to reduce the risk of financial loss.

Preferred shares: Securities that represent an ownership position in a company. Preferred shareholders are entitled to receive a dividend before any dividends are paid to common shareholders, and have a claim to the company's assets before common shareholders, if the company goes bankrupt.

Street name: Securities (stock certificates or bonds) held in street name are registered to a brokerage firm, but are being held on behalf of the firm's clients.

Ticker symbol: The group of letters that specifies a stock. On the New York or Toronto stock exchanges, ticker symbols are comprised of three letters, but on the NASDAQ ticker symbols have four letters.

Transfer agent: A bank or trust company that engages in maintaining investors' records on a company's behalf.

USEFUL WEBSITES FOR INVESTORS

http://www.easyinvesting.com
At our site, you will find more information about investing and additional links to useful websites.

http://www.edgar-online.com
http://www.sedar.com
For up-to-date financial filings to securities regulators, point your browser to edgar-online for U.S. filings and sedar.com for Canadian filings.

http://www.ft.com
The Financial Times' website contains news from across Europe and the Far East.

http://www.hoovers.com
Hoovers, which bills itself as the ultimate source for company information, enables investors to look up information about companies by name, ticker symbol, and company executive names.

http://www.multex.com
Multex offers free and pay-per-download analyst reports from major brokerage firms.

http://www.netstockdirect.com
Netstock Direct is a great resource for finding out about Fee-Free EasyStocks from around the world.

http://www.publicdebt.treas.gov
The Bureau of Public Debt's website contains information about the Treasury Direct program (Fee-Free EasyBonds) and offers forms for downloading.

http://www.quicken.com
http://www.quicken.ca
Quicken's U.S. and Canadian websites, respectively, are an excellent personal finance resource.

http://quote.yahoo.com
Yahoo! Finance offers stock quotes, news, company profiles, financial filings, and insider trading information.

http://www.sec.gov/mfcc/mfcc-int.htm
The Securities and Exchange Commission's mutual fund cost calculator informs you how much a mutual fund truly costs, compared to other investments.

http://www.wsj.com
The Wall Street Journal's website is a subscription-based news offering. Parts of the site can be accessed without subscribing.

http://www.zacks.com
Zacks Investment Research tracks analysts' buy-and-sell recommendations to rate stocks from 1 (best) to 5 (worst). Their rankings are also available on Yahoo! Finance.

ABOUT THE AUTHOR

Jeff Baryshnik has won the TD Waterhouse Investment Challenge (formerly TD Bank Green Line Investment Challenge) for two years in a row. He divides his time between Toronto and London, Ontario. You may visit Jeff Baryshnik's website at www.easyinvesting.com.

NOTES

NOTES

NOTES

NOTES

NOTES